# WORLD GEOGRAPHY

**Paromita Roy** is a seasoned geographer, with an MSc in Geography. She also holds a BEd and has taught the subject at the senior secondary level in ICSE schools for ten years. Apart from being a passionate geographer, she is a cricket enthusiast, who loves watching and playing the game.

# WORLD GEOGRAPHY

**Paromita Roy**

hachette INDIA

First published in 2025 by Hachette India
(Registered name: Hachette Book Publishing India Pvt. Ltd)
An Hachette UK company
www.hachetteindia.com

1



ISBN 978-93-5731-873-0

Hachette Book Publishing India Pvt. Ltd
4th & 5th Floors, Corporate Centre,
Plot No. 94, Sector 44, Gurugram 122003, India

Typeset in Garamond Premier Pro 11/14.2
by InoSoft Systems, Noida

MIX
Paper | Supporting responsible forestry
FSC® C010615

Printed and bound in India by
Thomson Press India Ltd.

# CONTENTS

## HYDROLOGY



## CLIMATOLOGY



## OCEANOGRAPHY

## BIOGEOGRAPHY



## PEDOLOGY



## HUMAN GEOGRAPHY

### POPULATION AND SETTLEMENT GEOGRAPHY



## ECONOMIC GEOGRAPHY

## ENVIRONMENTAL GEOGRAPHY



## GEOSPATIAL TECHNIQUES

# PREFACE

Geography is more than just maps and locations – it is the story of our planet, a dynamic interplay of land, water, climate and human civilization. It is the art and science that explains why towering mountains rise where they do, why vast deserts stretch across continents and why cities flourish along rivers and coasts. It is also the discipline that connects us to our world, helping us understand how societies adapt, transform and thrive within their environments.

This book is designed as a compact yet comprehensive guide to world geography, bringing together the physical and human aspects of the subject in one reliable reference. It takes you on a journey across continents, exploring the forces that have shaped the Earth's landscapes and the patterns that define human settlements, cultures and economies. Whether you are a student seeking clarity, a teacher looking for an engaging resource, a traveller eager to deepen your understanding of global regions, or simply a curious mind fascinated by the world around you, this book serves as a starting point to navigate the intricate web of geography.

With concise explanations, insightful facts and a structured approach, *World Geography* ensures that the vast domain of geography becomes accessible and engaging. From the icy expanse of Antarctica to the bustling megacities of Asia, from shifting tectonic plates to the effects of climate change, every chapter aims to provide a clear and thought-provoking perspective on the world we inhabit.

Geography is not just about places – it is about connections. It is about understanding how natural processes shape our lives and how human actions, in turn, reshape the planet. As you turn these pages, may you develop a newfound appreciation for the complexity and beauty of the Earth and its ever-evolving landscapes.

Get ready to embark on this journey of discovery!

Happy Reading!

# 1

## GEOGRAPHY AS A DISCIPLINE

Geography. Is it a science or an art? Have you ever wondered from where the word 'geography' is derived? Or whether it is a science subject or a social science subject?

Well, as a discipline, the origin of geography goes back to the ancient times of Roman and German scholars. It was Eratosthenes, the Greek geographer and mathematician, who coined the word 'geography' from 'geo', meaning Earth, and 'graphein' meaning to write.

German scholars have always defined geography as the description and study of the Earth. Geography interprets the different characters on the Earth's surface, its interrelationship with the cultural and social aspects of nature.

Contributions of Indian scholars in the development of geography: Not many records regarding the study of geography by ancient Indian scholars are available in the ancient scriptures. However, the geographical concepts of ancient India were discussed in detail in the works of Hindu mythology, epics, the Vedas, Puranas and sacred laws. Indian scholars always had clear knowledge and understanding of the topography, flora, fauna and sociocultural activities on their land. Both the Ramayana and the Mahabharata give us rich information about the natural landscape and beauty of

India. The Buddhist *Jataka* tales also were a good source of ancient geography. The Indian scholars of the Vedic and Puranic periods showed immense interest in the study of planets, astronomy and the origin of the universe. They were also familiar with the concepts of eclipses and followed several rituals and customs related to these major astronomical events.

**Did you know?**

The concept of latitude and longitude to determine the location of a place was present during the Rig Veda period. The Rig Veda clearly mentions the thickness of the atmosphere and that birds cannot fly through it. They were also aware of the fact that the local time of a place is determined by the position of the sun or moon and that it differs from place to place.

Geography is considered to be the bridge between natural science and social science. It deals with space, place, time and scale. It studies the world around us – the physical aspects, as well as the relationship between the physical and human aspects and its resultant consequences. It is never considered to be a single subject. It is broad and has its wings on the social, cultural and human elements of the society as well.

**Branches of Geography**

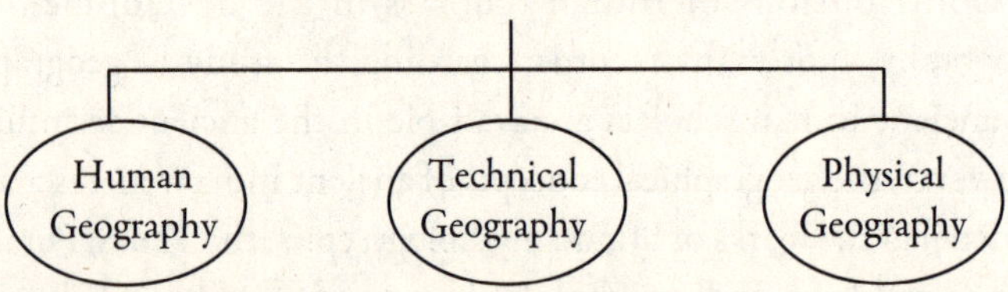

# 2

# THE ORIGIN OF MODERN GEOGRAPHY

The foundation stone of modern geography was laid down long ago in the ancient and medieval periods. However, Alexander von Humboldt and Carl Ritter are considered the founders of modern geography.

The table below shows the contribution of major geographers in the various fields of geography.

| Major Geographers | Contribution to the Discipline |
|---|---|
| Friedrich Ratzel | Coined the term anthropogeography which deals with the study of the relationship between man and Earth. He was highly influenced by Charles Darwin's theory of evolution, which made him develop the Organic Theory of State. He is recognized as the founder of political geography. |
| Paul Vidal de La Blache | He is the founder of human geography. He was considered the father figure of the French school of geographical thought. He believed that nature controls the type of social and human activities on a particular land but the way one responds to the given conditions depends on their traditional way of living. |

| | |
|---|---|
| Ellsworth Huntington | A supporter of environmental determinism, he tried to establish a relationship between human lifestyles and the weather and climatic conditions. He believed weather is the chief factor influencing human habits, energy, attitudes and activities. Civilizations have developed in areas with well-defined seasons, sufficient sunshine and rainfall, permitting the development of agriculture. |
| Immanuel Kant | He developed the concept of astronomical geography and geology. For him, physical geography was anthropocentric, where he believed that man is the most important agent affecting changes on Earth. |
| Alexander von Humboldt | He developed the concept of universal science through his work *Cosmos*.<br>While dealing with the subject matter of geography, Humboldt coined the term 'cosmography' and divided it into uranography and geography. In his opinion, uranography is the descriptive astronomy which deals with celestial bodies. Geography deals with the terrestrial part. He also coined the term 'permafrost' to study Siberian soil. |
| Carl Ritter | Founder of the Berlin Geographical Society. He regarded the Earth as an organism and the continents as organs or individuals. He believed in the influence of the physical environment on human activity and insisted that both history and geography are inseparable parts of each other. |
| Richard Hartshorne | An American geographer, Hartshorne emphasized the influence of people on the natural landscape and the impact of the natural environment on human activities. He called geography a space science and history a time science. |

**What is a paradigm shift?**

The concept of paradigm shift was developed by the American scientist and philosopher Thomas Kuhn. It is the fundamental change or shift in the basic practices and concepts of a discipline.

# PHYSICAL GEOGRAPHY

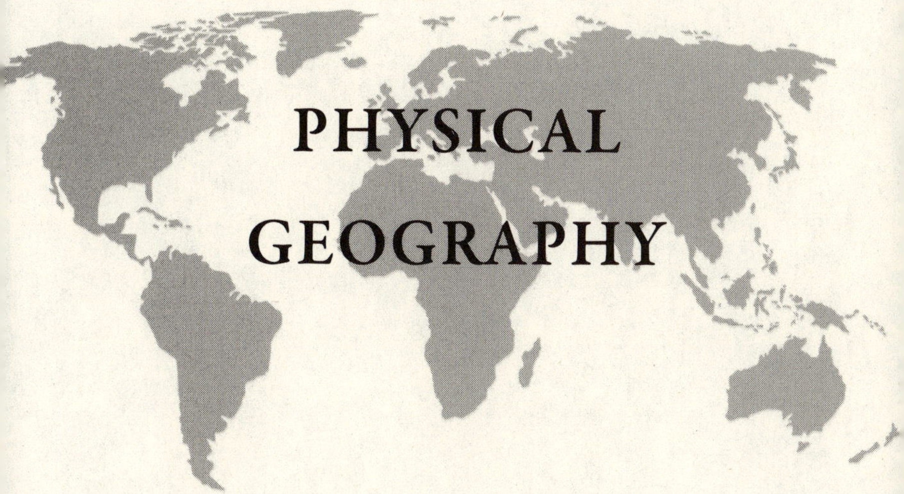

# 3

# THE EVOLUTION AND GEOLOGIC AGE OF THE EARTH

The **EVOLUTION OF THE EARTH** can be divided into three specific stages: i. the period of acquisition of the present shape and size of the Earth. ii. The period of formation of the Earth's interior. iii. The period of formation of mountains, plateaus and plains.

The universe began with the Big Bang, leading to the formation of our solar system and Earth. The early Earth, roughly 4.6 billion years ago, was a molten sphere formed from the accretion of cosmic dust and debris. This molten state allowed heavier elements like iron and nickel to sink, forming the Earth's core. Lighter elements, such as silicates, rose to the surface, eventually solidifying into the early lithosphere, a primitive crust rich in volcanic minerals. Intense volcanic activity released gases like water vapor, carbon dioxide, nitrogen, and sulphur dioxide, creating a reducing atmosphere devoid of free oxygen. As the Earth cooled, the water vapor condensed, forming the hydrosphere, with early oceans likely acidic due to dissolved volcanic gases and rich in dissolved minerals. Land masses, or protocontinents, began to form through tectonic plate movement, driven by the Earth's internal heat. Over billions of years, these land masses coalesced into continents. The emergence of photosynthetic bacteria, roughly 3.5 billion years ago, began to drastically alter the atmosphere, introducing free oxygen. This oxygenation of the atmosphere, known as the Great Oxidation Event, paved the way for the development of more complex life forms, marking the beginning of the biosphere. The interplay between the lithosphere, atmosphere, and hydrosphere created the conditions necessary for life to thrive and evolve, shaping the Earth as we know it today.

**GEOLOGIC AGE OF THE EARTH**: The table below shows the geologic age of the Earth, starting from the oldest to the present. The entire geological history is divided into ERAS. The eras are subdivided into EPOCHS. These epochs are further subdivided into PERIODS.

| ERA | MAJOR INCIDENTS | PERIODS |
|---|---|---|
| Precambrian | No evidence of atmosphere. Granite and gneiss were found. The Laurentian Shield, Gondwana Shield, Siberian Shield and Baltic Shield were formed. | |

| | | |
|---|---|---|
| Palaeozoic | Beginning of early plant and animal life. Invertebrate animals were found. Other rocks like limestone and sandstone were formed. | Cambrian [basic light limestone and sandstone were formed]<br>Ordovician [volcanic eruptions and submergence of large masses of land under water]<br>Silurian [origin of fish and animals that could breathe; vegetation came into existence]<br>Devonian [red sandstone was formed; folding and faulting for mountain building]<br>Carboniferous or Coal Age [coal was formed; amphibians were formed]<br>Permian [Earth's atmospheric temperature began to rise; evolution of mountain building in North America, Central Europe] |
| Mesozoic | Formation and evolution of reptiles. | Triassic [drifting of Gondwanaland towards the north]<br>Jurassic [the growth of reptiles in large numbers, dominating land and water; dense vegetation and flowering plants evolved]<br>Cretaceous [deposition of chalk, formation of thick lava in south India; formation of deciduous trees; initiation of the formation of the Himalayas, Rockies and Alps] |

| | | |
|---|---|---|
| Tertiary | Further evolution of plants and animals. Geosynclinal movements causing the formation of mountains. Period when apemen were formed and major portions of the Earth started getting covered with thick sheets of ice. The Himalayas were formed, and Africa started drifting away from Gondwanaland. | |
| Quaternary or Great Ice Age | Vast ice sheets covered most parts of the Earth. Evolution of several animals and man happened. The alluvial deposits of the world were found. Gradually, the temperature started rising, and this age continues right now. | |

# 4

## GEOGRAPHIC GRID: LATITUDES AND LONGITUDES

Have you ever thought what are those lines on the globe you see? These are the geographic grid – the lines of latitudes and longitudes. These lines help us in determining the exact location of a place.

> **FACT FILE**
>
> The shape of the Earth is an **oblate spheroid.**
> About 71.1% of the Earth's surface is covered with water while 28.9% is covered with land masses.

**Latitudes** are horizontal imaginary lines separating the Earth into unequal parts that run parallel to the most important one, which is the equator at 0°. The equator divides the Earth into two equal hemispheres – the northern and southern hemispheres. The rest of the latitudes parallel to the equator are the angular distance north and south of the equator. The lines of latitude are also called the parallels of latitude as these lines never meet each other. The length of the latitude is longest at the equator, and it gradually decreases towards its north and south as per the circumference of the Earth.

The most important lines of latitude are:

- The Equator: **0**°. It divides the Earth into the northern and southern hemispheres. The equator receives the vertical rays of the sun throughout the year. The speed of rotation is maximum at the equator.
- The Tropic of Cancer: **23.5°N.** It lies to the north of the equator. The sun shines vertically at the Tropic of Cancer on 21 June during the summer solstice. It is the northernmost limit of the apparent movement of the sun.
- The Tropic of Capricorn: **23.5°S.** It lies to the south of the equator. The sun shines vertically at the Tropic of Capricorn on 23 December during the winter solstice. It is the southernmost limit of the apparent movement of the sun.
- The Arctic Circle: **66.5°N.** It is the northernmost latitude of the northern hemisphere and the southern limit of the midnight sun.

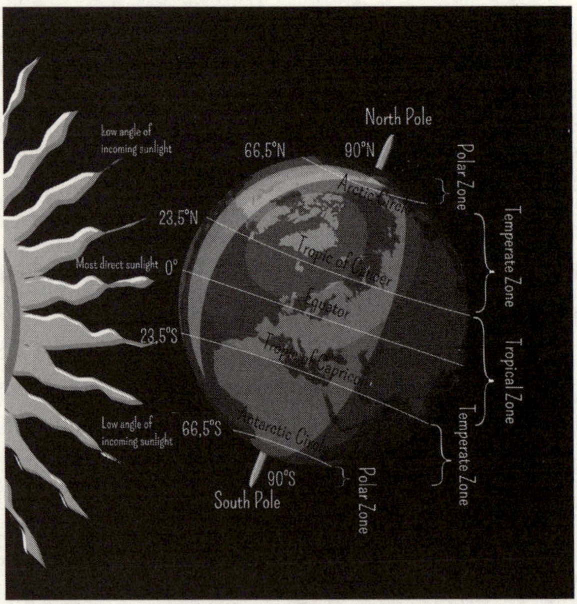


Latitudinal zones of the Earth

- The Antarctic Circle: **66.5°S.** It is the southernmost latitude of the southern hemisphere and the northern limit of the midnight sun.

**Longitudes** are the imaginary vertical lines that converge at the poles 90°. They are the great circles dividing the Earth into equal halves. The most important line of longitude is the prime meridian 0°, which divides the Earth into the eastern and western hemispheres.

The intersection points of latitude and longitude, known as the **coordinates**, give us the exact location of a place. For example, the coordinates or exact location of Delhi is 28.7041°N, 77.1025°E.

Where 28.7041°N stands for the latitude of Delhi in the north and 77.1025°E stands for its longitude in the east.

**What is the International Date Line?**

It is the 180° line of longitude passing through the mid-Pacific Ocean. It is the imaginary boundary between one calendar day and the next. You add a day when you move to the east and lose a day when you move to the west of the line. The line is deviated at some places so that the island groups can come under a single country to avoid confusion.

# 5

# ROTATION AND REVOLUTION OF THE EARTH AND ITS CONSEQUENCES

The Earth rotates on its own inclined axis. At the same time, it also revolves around the sun. The time of rotation is 23 hours 59 minutes and 4 seconds, while the time taken for revolution is 364.25 days.

Since the orbit of the Earth around the sun is elliptical in shape, the period when it is closest to the sun is called the **PERIHELION (in January)**, and the time when it is farthest from the sun is called the **APHELION (in July)**.

The Earth's rotation causes its daily routine of day and night. It also causes tides in the oceans and seas, as well as temperature and humidity changes. The Earth rotates from west to east on its inclined axis of 23.5°, and because of the tilt, the northern and southern hemispheres lean in a direction either away or towards the sun. The part of the Earth facing the sun has day, and the part that is away from the sun has night.

Now let us see what the speed of rotation and revolution of the different planets of our solar system are!

| Planets | Speed of Revolution | Speed of Rotation |
|---|---|---|
| Mercury | 88 days | 59 days |
| Venus | 224.7 days | 243 days |
| Earth | 365.2 days | 23 hours 59 minutes and 4 seconds |
| Mars | 687 days | 24 hours 37 minutes |
| Jupiter | 11.86 years | 9 hours 55 minutes 30 seconds |
| Saturn | 29.46 years | 10 hours 40 minutes 24 seconds |
| Uranus | 84 years | 17 hours 14 minutes 24 seconds |
| Neptune | 165 years | 16 hours 11 minutes |

The seasons happen due to the Earth's revolution, and the length of day and night varies.

On 21 March, the sun's rays fall vertically on the equator and the length of day and night are equal. This is called the **SPRING EQUINOX.**

The apparent movement of the sun northwards till 21 June when the sun's rays fall vertically on the Tropic of Cancer is called the **SUMMER SOLSTICE.** This is the longest day and peak summer in the northern hemisphere and just the reverse in the southern hemisphere.

Then the sun's rays start moving southwards again till it reaches the equator on 22 September, which is called the **AUTUMNAL EQUINOX.** This is again a period of equal day and equal night.

As the sun starts its southward journey, it reaches its southernmost limit, which is the Tropic of Capricorn, on 23 December. This is called the **WINTER SOLSTICE.** It is the shortest day and longest night in the northern hemisphere but peak summer in the southern hemisphere.

> So now you know why you feel cold in December in India, while in Australia it is the reverse. (Hint: Check the location of the two countries in the two different hemispheres.)

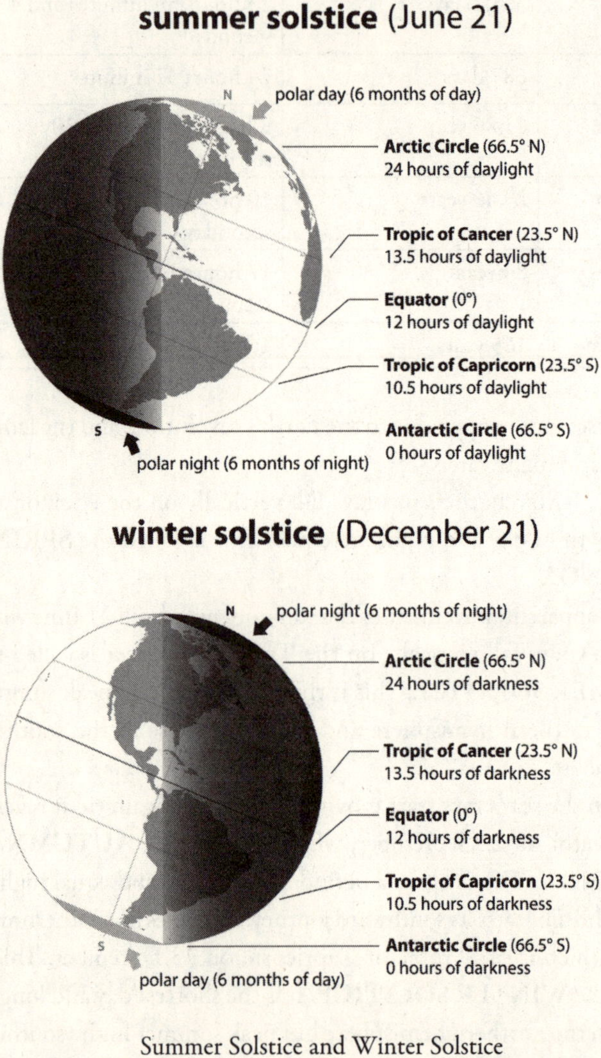


Summer Solstice and Winter Solstice

**Eclipses:**

The Solar Eclipse: The moon, which revolves around the Earth, comes in between the sun and the Earth, as a result of which a part or whole of the sun is invisible from specific places on Earth.

The Lunar Eclipse: Here, the Earth comes in between the sun and the moon, thus, a part or the whole of the moon cannot be seen due to the shadow of the Earth on it.

**FACT FILE**

The complete eclipse of the moon occurs on the day of Amavasya or the new moon!

# GEOMORPHOLOGY

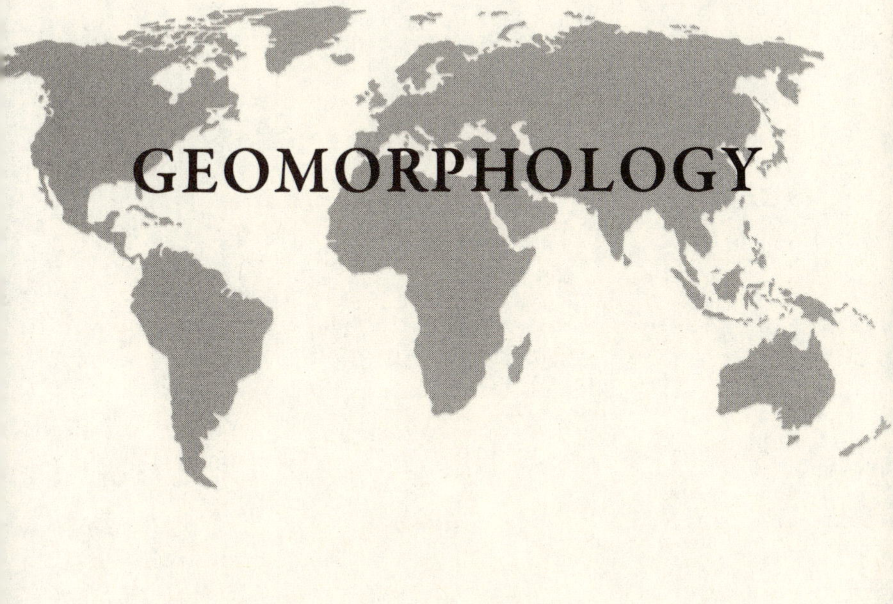

# 6

# THE EARTH'S INTERIOR

The Earth's interior is divided into three concentric layers: crust, mantle and core. The crust or lithosphere is the outermost layer of the Earth. The lighter part is the SIAL or the continental crust, composed of silica and aluminium. The average density of this layer is 2.9, and is dominated by acid and silicates of aluminium, potassium and sodium.

The denser part is the SIMA, or the oceanic part composed of silica and magnesium. This layer is composed of basalt and is the

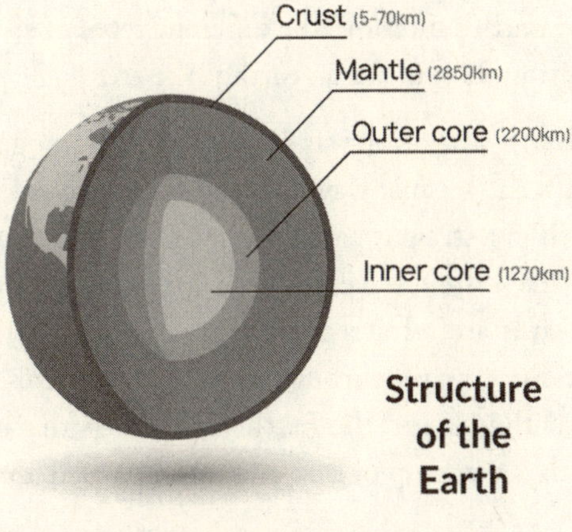


Structure of the Earth

source of magma and lava during volcanic eruptions. The average density is between 2.9 to 4.7. The layer below the crust is the mantle. The boundary between the crust and mantle is called the Mohorovičić discontinuity. The mantle extends up to a depth of 2,900 km. Here, the temperature and density increase with depth.

**ASTHENOSPHERE** is the zone of rocks at the upper part of the mantle. Here, the materials are found in a semi-molten state. The boundary between the mantle and the core is called the Gutenberg discontinuity. In the core, the temperature and density are highest. The outer core is in a liquid state. The inner core is in a solid state due to extreme pressure. The core is composed of NIFE, that is, nickel and ferrous. The presence of iron indicates the magnetic property of the Earth and also its rigidity. It is also known as the barysphere.

> Now it is a known fact that the Earth's interior is a place of extremely high temperature and pressure. Then how are we going to get authentic information about the composition of the Earth's interior?

The study of earthquake waves or seismic waves and the differences in their patterns of wave movement tells us about the nature of the Earth's interior. The different types of seismic waves generated during the time of an earthquake are:

- If the Earth's interior was composed of homogenous solid materials, the seismic waves should have reached the core of the Earth in a straight path, but in reality, this is not the case. In fact, the seismic waves follow a curved and refracted path. These waves are refracted at the place of density changes. S waves cannot travel through liquids, so S waves are totally absent at the core of the Earth. This shows that the core of the Earth is made up of iron and nickel, which are in a liquid state.

| P Waves or Primary Waves | S Waves or Secondary waves | Surface Waves or Long Waves |
|---|---|---|
| These are longitudinal waves and are similar to sound waves, where particles move in the direction of the waves. P waves travel through both solid and liquid mediums. Their average velocity is 8 km per second. | These are transverse waves and are similar to light waves, where the particles move perpendicularly (at right angles) to the waves. S waves cannot travel through liquids. | These waves generally affect only the surface of the Earth and dissipate at a small depth. They cover longer distances. Their speed is lower than P and S waves, but these are the most violent and destructive. |

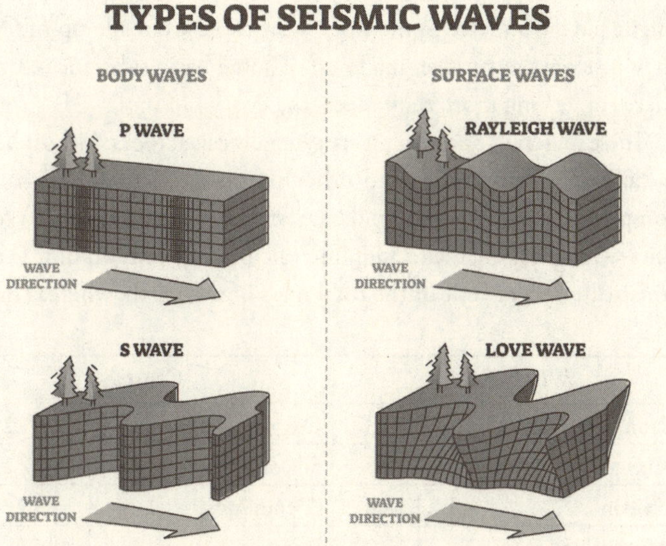


Seismic waves

# 7

# ROCKS OF THE EARTH AND THEIR CHARACTERISTICS

When we see mountains, hills, plains and plateaus around us, we might have wondered sometimes what these are made up of. Are they just on the surface, made up of some basic substances, or is there something more than meets the eye?

These materials on the crust are generally called rocks. Lithosphere means rock sphere as the word 'lithos' means rocks. The whole Earth comprises the eight most abundant elements, which are iron, oxygen, silicon, magnesium, nickel, sulphur, calcium and ammonium. These constitute 99 per cent of the total mass of the Earth, whereas only

| **Whole Earth** | | **Crust** | |
|---|---|---|---|
| Iron | 33.3 | Oxygen | 45.2 |
| Oxygen | 29.8 | Silicon | 27.2 |
| Silicon | 15.6 | Aluminium | 8.2 |
| Magnesium | 13.9 | Iron | 5.8 |
| Nickel | 2.0 | Calcium | 5.1 |
| Calcium | 1.8 | Magnesium | 2.8 |
| Aluminium | 1.5 | Sodium | 2.3 |
| Sodium | 0.2 | Potassium | 1.7 |

four elements – iron, oxygen, silicon and magnesium – account for 90 per cent of the total mass of the Earth. However, 99 per cent of the total mass of the crust comprises the eight most abundant elements, which are oxygen, silicon, aluminium, iron, magnesium, calcium, potassium and sodium.

**Minerals:** When these elements on the Earth's crust are organized to form compounds, they are known as minerals, and minerals are organized to form rocks. Let's talk about the important mineral groups.

**Silicate minerals:** These are rock-making minerals. They include quartz, feldspar and ferromagnesium. Quartz comprises silicon and oxygen and is a hard and resistant mineral. The most important rock-forming silicate mineral is feldspar, which is used in glass and ceramics. It is a very weak mineral and is easily decomposable. Ferromagnesium minerals are a combination of silicon and oxygen with iron and magnesium. They are easy to alter and remove. In fact, if any building, bridge, structure or monument has more ferromagnesium in the rocks used, they are more likely to crumble!

**Carbonate minerals:** Calcite is the most important mineral of this group. These minerals are prone to chemical weathering in humid areas. Limestone and marble have abundant amounts of calcite and are corroded by water. Often, karst landforms (*check chapter 17: Karst Topography)* are made out of them. These mineral-rich rocks are not ideal for the construction of roads, dams, buildings and tunnels since they will form weak structures.

**Sulphide minerals:** These include pyrites and iron sulphides. When they come in contact with water or air, they form acids that cause serious environmental problems.

**Metallic elements:** Iron and aluminium form metal oxides after reacting with atmospheric oxygen. These are commercially very important.

So now we know which mineral-rich rocks to use for construction materials. As nature is all about the painting of landforms on its surface, the famous American geomorphologist W.M. Davis said that the 'landscape is a function of structure, process and time (stages)', where he emphasized the role of rocks in the evolution of landforms.

## Classification of rocks

S.W. Wooldridge and R.S. Morgan said in their book, *The Physical Basis of Geography* (1959), 'Rocks whether igneous or sedimentary, constitute on the one hand the manuscripts of the past Earth history on the other, the basis for contemporary scenery.'

**Igneous rocks:** These are formed due to the solidification of lava/magma either on the Earth's surface or below it. They are called primary rocks.

**Sedimentary rocks:** These are formed due to lithification, compression and cementation of sediments deposited mainly in aquatic areas.

**Metamorphic rocks:** These are formed due to changes in the form and composition of either igneous or sedimentary rocks.

### *How to identify igneous rocks*

They do not have any layers and are quite hard and compact. Igneous rocks do not contain any fossils and are mostly found in volcanic areas. Igneous rocks are impermeable, that is, water cannot enter through these rocks unless it is basalt, which becomes quite soft when it comes in constant contact with water. These rocks are either fine-grained or coarse-grained depending on the rate and place of cooling. It is obvious that if the rate of cooling is slow and below the surface then the magma below leaves behind coarse grains and vice versa.

### Classification of igneous rocks

Based on **mode of occurrence**, igneous rocks are classified into:

**Intrusive igneous rocks:** The cooling and solidification of the magma below the Earth's surface causes these types of rocks. They are of further two subtypes. Plutonic intrusive igneous rocks – when they are formed very deep below the Earth's surface. For example: granite. Hypabyssal intrusive igneous rocks – where the magma is cooled just below the surface. For example: batholiths, laccoliths.

**Extrusive igneous rocks:** The cooling and solidification of lava on the Earth's crust forms extrusive igneous rocks. Extrusive igneous rocks are mostly formed due to fissure volcanic eruptions. They are mainly fine-grained and have a smooth texture because the lava, as soon as it comes to the surface, gets exposed to the comparatively cool atmosphere and thus cools down rapidly. Basalt is a classic example. Extrusive igneous rocks can be either the quiet type or the explosive type.

When the lava comes out slowly through the fissures and openings on the Earth's surface, it forms extensive lava plains or plateaus. These plains are formed of thick deposits of basalt, which ultimately becomes a rich source of black soil. The explosive type of extrusive igneous rocks comprises mixtures of volcanic materials. They may include bombs, lapilli, volcanic dust and ashes.

Based on **chemical composition**, igneous rocks are classified into:

**Acid igneous rocks**, which have silica content between 65 to 85%. They lack iron and magnesium. Granite is an example. These rocks are erosion-resistant.

**Basic igneous rocks** contain silica between 45 to 60%. They are easily eroded, heavy and darker in colour. Basalt is an example.

Based on **size and texture of grains,** igneous rocks are classified into:

- Pegmatitic igneous rocks: the size of the grains is large and very coarse, for example, granite.
- Phaneritic igneous rocks: coarser-grained igneous rocks.
- Aphanitic igneous rocks: these are so fine-grained that they are not visible to the naked eye.
- Glassy igneous rocks: they do not contain any grains.
- Porphyritic igneous rocks: these have a mix of coarse-grained and fine-grained material.

***How to identify sedimentary rocks***

They are formed of sediments derived from plant and animal remains, so they may contain fossils. Sedimentary rocks are the most abundant rocks on Earth. They are called stratified rocks as they contain layers or strata. Most of these rocks are permeable and porous. They can be well consolidated or poorly consolidated depending upon the parent rock material.

**Classification of sedimentary rocks**

| | **Mechanically Formed** | **Chemically Formed** | **Organically Formed** |
|---|---|---|---|
| **Based on the nature of sediments** | Sandstone<br>Conglomerate<br>Shale<br>Loess | Gypsum<br>Salt rock | Limestone<br>Dolomite<br>Coal<br>Peat |
| **Based on transporting agents** | Argillaceous or Aqueous rocks | Aeolian | Glacial |
| | Marine<br>Lacustrine<br>Riverine | Loess | Till<br>Moraines |

### *Agents of metamorphism*

**Heat:** Sometimes, the mineral composition is entirely altered due to intense heat. The source of this heat is the hot and molten magma when it comes out through the cracks. This type of metamorphism is called thermal metamorphism.

**Pressure:** The compressive forces during the process of mountain building release large amounts of pressure, which alter the original form of the rocks. This type of metamorphism is called dynamic or regional metamorphism.

### *Types of metamorphism*

As discussed earlier, metamorphism can be thermal or dynamic. It can also be hydro-metamorphism, which happens when chemically active water brings about chemical changes in the rocks when they come in constant contact with these rocks.

Let us discover more about a few metamorphic rocks that have metamorphosed from igneous or sedimentary rocks!

Limestone [sedimentary rocks] → marble [metamorphic rocks]

Granite [Igneous rocks] → gneiss [metamorphic rocks]

Sandstone [sedimentary rocks] → quartzite [metamorphic rocks]

Shale [sedimentary rocks] → slate [metamorphic rocks]
→ schist [further metamorphism]

### *Rock cycle*

The concept of the rock cycle was first propounded by an eighteenth-century scientist, James Hutton. It is the continuous process of formation, alteration and breaking down of the different types of rocks based on the application of heat, pressure or both over time. We can safely say it is a process where rocks are constantly being recycled and reformed under given circumstances and locations.

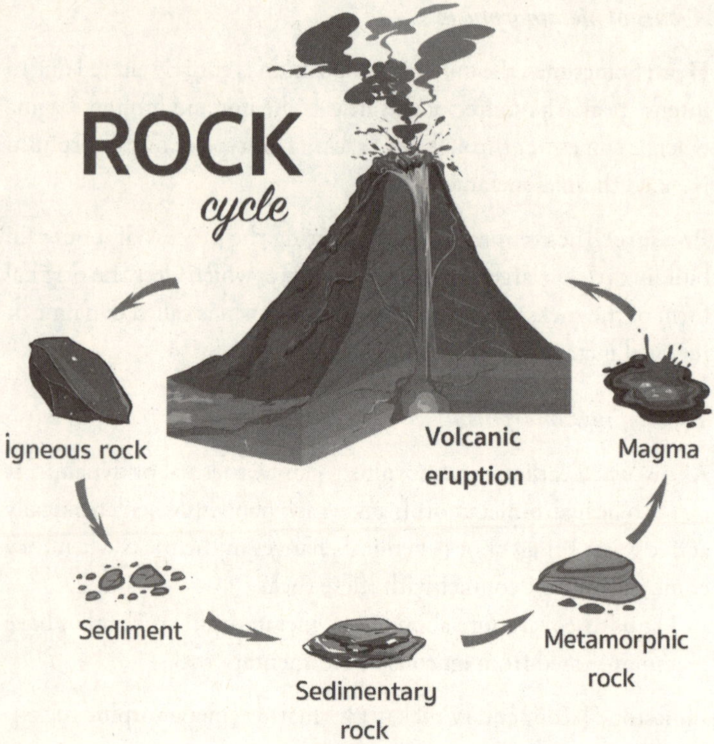


The rock cycle

# 8

# CONTINENTS AND OCEANS

The continents dominate the northern hemisphere, and contrary to this, water bodies dominate the southern hemisphere. But there is a belief that these continents were never in the position that they are now. This theory about the drifting of the continents was propounded by **Alfred Wegener**, a German meteorologist. He believed that there was a single land mass called the Pangaea. The Tethys Sea separated the Pangaea into two land masses – the Gondwanaland to the south of the Tethys Sea and Laurasia to the north.

**Evidence in support of the continental drift theory:** Look closely at the continents of South America and Africa, and they seem to fit with each other as in a jigsaw puzzle as if they were a single land mass.

There is a marked similarity between the fossils and vegetation on the eastern coast of South America and the western coast of Africa.

There is also a similarity between the Caledonian and Hercynian mountain systems of the western and eastern coastal areas of the Atlantic.

Carboniferous glaciations in Brazil, Falkland, South Africa, Australia and parts of India prove that there was a single unified land mass.

**Palaeomagnetism:** This is the study of old magnetic rocks, and it shows the different directions of magnetism that point towards the presence of a unified land mass.

**Interesting fact!**

Lemmings, which are small-sized animals, tend to migrate westwards but are unable to do so due to the absence of any land masses beyond the Norwegian coast. This behaviour of lemmings is testimony to the fact that there were united land masses in the ancient age and the animals would migrate towards the west.

Wegener believed in the three-layer system of the Earth. The outer layer was considered to be the sial, comprising the continental land mass, whereas the oceans were represented by the upper part of the sima. The continents would float on the sima without any force exerted by sima. He believed that all the land masses were unified, named Pangaea, during the Carboniferous age. This Pangea was believed to have been surrounded by a huge water body named Panthalassa by Wegener. As discussed earlier, the northern part of Pangaea represented North America, Europe and Asia, and Gondwanaland consisted of South America, Africa, Madagascar, Peninsular India, Australia and Antarctica, which was the southern part of Pangea.

***Other angles to the theory***

- **What caused the drift?** Wegener believed the drifting of the continents happened in two directions – one towards the equator and the other towards the west. The equatorward movement of the continents was caused due to gravitational force and buoyancy, while the westward movement was caused due to the tidal attraction of the sun and moon.

The sial floated over sima that caused the equatorward movement of the lighter continents on relatively denser sima on the lines of gravity and buoyancy.

- **Formation of the mighty mountains:** Wegener's continental drift theory also tried to solve the mystery of the formation of fold mountains. He believed that the western cordilleras of the two Americas were formed due to the crumbling and flooding of the westward-drifting frontal blocks of north and south Americas against the rocks of the heavier seafloor. Similarly, the Alps of Europe were formed due to the equatorward movement of Europe and Africa along with Peninsular India.
- **What about the island groups?** Wegener associated the formation of the island groups and festoons of eastern Asia and the West Indies with the differential rate of continental drift. The westward movement of the Asian islands could not keep pace with the eastern margin, and they lagged behind, thus resulting in the formation of the island groups of Japan, Kurile, the Philippines, etc. The island group of the West Indies was also formed in this way due to the differential movement of north and south Americas.
- **No idea about the pre-Carboniferous Age?** Wegener's theory had its origin in the Carboniferous age and had no evidence from the pre-Carboniferous era. He believed there were large-scale glaciations during the Carboniferous Age in Brazil, Falkland, Peninsular India, Australia, etc. All the continents unified as Pangea. The South Pole was located in the Pangea. Ice sheets might have spread from the South Pole and covered these continents.

**Plate Tectonic Theory:** Solid lithosphere slabs are called plates. Plate tectonics is the mechanism of the behaviour, movement and evolution of the plates and the resultant reaction. There are six major plates and 20 minor plates. The six major plates are

American, Eurasian, African, Indo-Australian, Pacific and Antarctic. All tectonic activities, be it earthquakes, volcanoes or mountain building, occur along the plate margins.

**Did you know?**

The term 'plate' was first used by John Tujo Wilson, a Canadian geophysicist, in 1965 to describe the gliding of the plates slowly over the surface of the Earth.

### *Types of plate margins*

| Constructive Plate Margins | Destructive Plate Margins | Conservative Plate Margins |
|---|---|---|
| Two plates move away (diverge) from each other, and there is constant upwelling of lava on the surface. Volcanic and seismic activities are common along such edges. | Two plates move towards each other, and there is a collision. There is a lot of crumpling and folding. In the case of the oceanic crust, the lighter plate moves over the heavier one, and trenches are formed at the zone of subduction. This is the zone of orogenesis or mountain building. | Two plates move past each other without any interaction. So there is neither creation nor destruction. |

### *Plate tectonics and the formation of present-day continents*

From the evidence of the continental drift theory and seafloor spreading, it has been validated now that the continents and oceans were never stationary. The Pacific Ocean is constantly shrinking because of the subduction of the American plane along its ridge, while the Atlantic Ocean is constantly expanding.

**Seafloor spreading**

The concept of seafloor spreading was first propounded by Prof. Harry Hess in 1960.

It is the continuous process of magma oozing out of the seabed and solidifying along the Mid-Atlantic Ridge. It is leading to the spreading of the Atlantic Ocean and the diversion of the continental block. Prof. Hess believed that the mid-oceanic ridges lay on the continuously rising thermal convective currents from the mantle. This happened due to the continuous shifting of the oceanic crust away from the continental crust, leading to the upwelling of magma along the ridges. This molten lava cools down and solidifies, leading to the formation of new crust along the oceans.

The continents are coming close to each other wherever the oceans are beginning to shrink, and those lands are drifting from each other where the oceans are expanding.

Let us see the chronological formation of the present-day continents!

About 700 million years ago, all the land masses were a supercontinent called Pangaea.

↓

About 600–500 million years ago, Pangaea broke because of the thermal convective currents, causing seafloor spreading, and the land masses started drifting apart.

↓

This resulted in the formation of two continents, Gondwanaland in the south and Laurasia in the north. Gondwanaland included South America, Africa, Australia, Antarctica, and India; and Laurasia included North America, Europe, and parts of Asia. Again, due to the collision of the land masses due to plate movements, these two continents also started drifting apart.

↓

Gondwanaland began to break again during the early Jurassic period, and Africa broke away from North America.

↓

The European and American plates continued to move eastwards and westwards because of the expansion of the Labrador Sea and the North Atlantic between Europe and Greenland in the middle Miocene period.

↓

The northward drifting of the Indian plate towards the Eurasian plate during the early tertiary period occurred and closed the Tethys Sea.

↓

Antarctica broke away from Australia during the early Eocene period.

**FACT FILE**

The Indian plate is moving north-eastwards towards the Eurasian plate at the speed of 5 cm per year. This is pushing the Himalayas higher and causing further subduction of the Indian plate under the Eurasian plate.

So we can encounter more earthquakes in this zone in the coming years!

***Why is the plate tectonic theory important*?**

On the basis of the knowledge of the crustal plate movements, the future shape of the continents can be guessed, and earthquakes and other seismic activities can be predicted.

The knowledge of plate tectonics helps us get an insight into the new minerals that are thrown up from the core of the Earth at the time of crustal movements. For example, economically valuable minerals like uranium, gold and copper are found in abundance along the plate margins. The study of minerals and ores will help us to get an idea about the past nature of the continents and their movements.

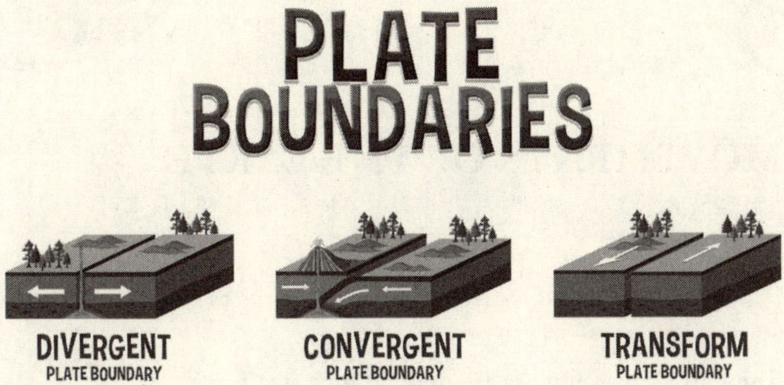


Plate boundaries

# 9

## MOVEMENTS OF THE EARTH

The Earth's movements are divided into two forces:

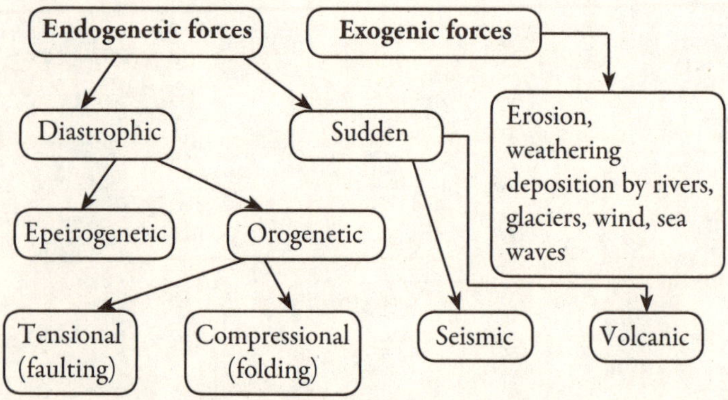


**Endogenetic forces:** These forces come from within the Earth. They cause two types of movements: horizontal and vertical. The various landforms of the Earth, be it mountains, plateaus, plains or lakes, are formed due to these forces.

Endogenetic forces are of two types: sudden and diastrophic.

**Sudden forces:** These sudden forces and movements coming from deep within the Earth cause sudden and rapid events leading to massive destruction. Both earthquakes and volcanoes come under these forces. These forces cause natural disasters when they occur in densely populated regions. Even if these forces are sudden, their preparations take place over a long period under the Earth. Extensive landforms are also formed due to them on the Earth's surface.

**Diastrophic forces:** These forces occur over a long period of time and are caused due to both horizontal and vertical forces deep within the Earth. All the major landforms and continental masses are formed because of these forces.

- **Epeirogenetic:** Epirus means continent and genesis means origin. Vertical movements cause the upliftment and subsidence of continental masses through upward and downward movements. Upliftment of the continents causes the emergence of land masses, while subsidence of continents causes the submergence of land under the sea.
- **Orogenetic:** Oro means mountain and genesis means origin or formation. Horizontal movements cause endogenetic forces either operating towards each other or away from each other. When these forces operate away from each other, they are called tensional forces. When these forces and movements operate towards each other, they cause compressional force. Tensional forces cause the formation of cracks, fissures, ruptures and faults, while compressional forces cause folds or crustal bending.

**Warping and folding:** The process of warping refers to the movement of the crustal rocks leading to bending under the influence of convergent forces. The crustal rocks are either raised upward or downward. Upwarping is the upward rise of the crustal part due to compressional forces operating horizontally, while downwarping is the bending of the crustal part in the form of a basin or depression.

Folds are wave-like bends caused due to compressional forces, leading to the formation of massive mountain ranges. The upfolded part is known as the anticline and the downfolded part is called the syncline. The two sides of a fold are called limbs of a fold. The middle limb is the limb that lies between an anticline and its consequent syncline.

The plane that bisects the angle between the two limbs of the anticline is called the axial plane.

Anticlines may look different depending on the dip angle. They can be either steep anticlines or gentle anticlines. Sometimes, the dip is accentuated so that the anticline looks almost vertical. When the slopes of both limbs are uniform, they are called symmetrical anticlines, and when the slopes are unequal, they are called asymmetrical anticlines.

**Did you know?**

What is anticlinorium and synclinorium?
A series of minor anticlines and synclines within one extensive anticline is called anticlinorium. These are formed when the horizontal compressive forces do not operate regularly. Numerous minor synclines and anticlines in an extensive syncline are called synclinorium.

### *Classification of folds*

**Symmetrical folds:** These are simple folds where the limbs incline uniformly. Symmetrical folds are a rare phenomena.

- **Asymmetrical folds:** They have irregular and unequal limbs. This occurs due to compressive forces acting with different intensities because of which one limb is more inclined than the other.
- **Monocline folds:** Here, one limb inclines with moderate steepness while the other limb inclines steeply, almost at right

angles, and becomes almost vertical. Sometimes, the steepness of one limb becomes so high that there is every possibility that the limb will break through and become a fault.

- **Isoclinal folds:** Here, both limbs become parallel to each other but not horizontal because of intense compressive forces.
- **Recumbent folds:** Both the limbs here become parallel, as well as horizontal.
- **Fan folds:** These are broad folds consisting of a series of small anticlines and synclines and look like a fan. These are the typical anticlinorium or synclinorium.
- **Open folds:** Here, the angle between the two limbs is more than 90° but less than 180°. They are formed due to moderate compressional forces.
- **Closed folds:** Intense compressional forces make an acute angle between the two limbs of a fold.
- **Overturned folds:** One limb of the fold is put on the other limb, and the limbs are not horizontal.

**Nappes:** Intense compressional forces result in the formation of nappes. These are formed on recumbent folds where both the limbs of the fold are parallel and horizontal. Due to intense compressional forces, one limb overthrusts on the other fold. This is called thrust, and the plane along which this occurs is called a thrust plane. Sometimes, the compressive forces become so strong that one limb of the fold, due to intense folding, is thrown several kilometres away from its original place. This broken limb of the fold that overrides distant rock beds is called nappe.

**What are exotic nappes?**

Sometimes, when the limb of a fold overrides the other fold after being broken at a faraway place, the resultant nappe is called an exotic nappe.

Did you know that nappes are a common feature in the Alps? The Alpine nappes look like Earth waves, and sometimes, the overriding nappes have been eroded away, and the lower nappe is exposed to the surface.

**What are periclines?**

It is a type of anticline that forms along the axis in each direction from a central high point. It resembles an elongated dome. Most periclines are vulnerable to breaching along the axis.

**Crustal fractures and faulting:** We have been discussing the intense compressional forces from within the Earth's crust. Now let us know about what happens when the forces are tensional, that is, when the forces operate away from each other. Crustal fractures occur when the tensional forces are moderate, that is, at that time only cracks occur, but when the forces are intense, the rocks are displaced and dislocated, resulting in fault formation.

**Some common terms related to faults**

Fault plane: The plane along which the crustal rocks are displaced due to fracture.
Fault dip: The angle between the fault plane and the horizontal plane.
Fault zone: Numerous small fractures that may be as wide as 100 metres.
Fault block: A displaced unit formed due to intense faulting, either completely or in part.
Upthrown side: The uppermost block of a fault.
Down thrown side: The lowermost block of a fault.
Hanging wall: The upper wall of a fault.
Footwall: The lower wall of a fault.
Fault scarp: Sometimes, faulting of the crustal rocks creates a steep wall-like slope. It becomes so steep that it almost resembles a cliff.

### *Classification of faults*

Faults are classified based on two factors – whether the fault is displaced in the direction of the dip or has displaced in the direction of the strike. Thus, faults can be either dip-slip faults or strike-slip faults or transcurrent faults. Even in the case of strike-slip faults, the displacement of the rock blocks can be either to the left of the strike or to the right of the strike. The former is called left lateral fault and the latter right lateral fault.

- **Normal faults:** When the rock blocks are displaced in opposite directions, normal faults are formed. The fault scarp formed due to normal faults is steep and almost vertical.
- **Reverse faults:** When the displaced rock blocks move towards each other, these types of faults are formed. Here, the vertical stress is minimum and the horizontal stress is maximum. The rock beds on the upper part of the fault are displaced up the fault plane rather than the rock beds below. In fact, reverse faults are also called compressional faults as they are formed due to compressional forces resulting from horizontal movements. When the compressive forces exceed the strength of the rocks an overthrust fault is formed as one block of the fault overrides the other.
- **Strike-slip faults:** The displacement of the rock blocks either to the left or right side of the strike.
- **Step faults:** The series of faults form in such a way that the slope of the fault plane occurs in the same direction. These resemble a flight of stairs.

**Other types of faults**:

Cylindrical faults
Pivotal faults
Oblique/diagonal faults
Radial faults

### Rift valleys

These are long and narrow troughs forming a depression between two crustal blocks. Rift valleys are formed due to the displacement of crustal blocks and subsidence of the middle block between two normal faults. The exact cause behind the formation of a rift valley is still unknown, but it is believed that tensional force may have pulled the two sides apart, leaving the centre to subside. Rift valleys are also termed graben, and the two side blocks that remain upright are called horst or block mountains.

Rift valleys are formed in two ways. Either the middle portion of the crust has subsided, leaving both sides intact in their position, or the middle portion remained stable, but the two side blocks have risen upward.

A classic example of a rift valley is the Rhine Rift Valley, bounded by the Black Forest on one side and Vosges on the other.

**Did you know?**

In India, the Narmada Rift Valley is a good example, wedged between the Satpuras and the Vindhyas.

### Exogenic forces

The different exogenic forces are soil erosion, weathering, etc.

***Types of soil erosion***

| Wind Erosion | Sheet Erosion | Gully Erosion | Rill Erosion |
|---|---|---|---|
| Winds carry away fine soil particles from arid and semi-arid areas and deposit them in other regions, thus decreasing soil fertility. | The removal of thin layers of soil by wind or rain. In the long run, the top fertile soil is removed, and the soil becomes unfit for cultivation. | The formation of large depressions due to the scooping out of topsoil, forming gullies. The land later gets dissected by rivers and is called ravine or badland. | The action of running water results in the formation of finger-shaped rills. It is the second stage of sheet erosion. |

# 10

# WEATHERING AND EROSION

| Types of Weathering | Subtypes | Characteristics |
|---|---|---|
| Physical or mechanical weathering | Block disintegration<br>Granular disintegration<br>Frost action<br>Exfoliation | Common in areas of high diurnal temperature changes, like in hot deserts.<br>Frost action occurs due to alternate freezing and thawing of water during night and day respectively in cold regions. |
| Chemical weathering | Solution<br>Carbonation<br>Hydration | Common in rocks that contain soluble minerals. The main agents are water vapour and water, which mix with the minerals in the rocks, causing chemical decomposition or disintegration.<br>This type is most prevalent in areas of heavy rainfall, like equatorial regions. |

| Biological weathering | Agents: Plants Animals Man | Gradual breaking down of buildings, monuments and structures by plants, burrowing animals, and even man, due to development activities. |
|---|---|---|

**FACT FILE**

Differential weathering helps to develop and modify upstanding topographic firms into columns, pillars, pedestal rocks, Earth pillars and toadstool rocks, which because of their bizarre shapes are sometimes classed as **hoodoo rocks**!

**Biochemical weathering:** It refers to the disintegration and decomposition of rocks due to chemical reactions by flora and fauna. Different kinds of acids, such as humic acids and bacterial acids, are exuded from the roots of the plants, which help in the disintegration and decomposition of the rocks. The different types of acids and their resultant actions are discussed below:

- **Bacteria acids:** They cause the decomposition of rocks having magnesium carbonate, calcium, magnesium silicates, feldspar, etc. They also help in the dissolution of silica when the rocks are submerged under water.
- **Oxalic and citric acids:** These are produced by fungi and lichens. They decompose silicates and clay minerals.
- **Humic acids:** They assist in the decomposition of silicate minerals.

*The significance of weathering*

- Continuous removal and transportation of weathered materials through different agents of weathering and erosion lead to lowering of heights of surfaces.

- Weathering is directly related to the rate of erosion. When there is a rapid rate of weathering due to deforestation or other natural or manmade causes, it also accelerates the rate of erosion. This is because different agents of erosion like wind, running water, rivers and glaciers remove the weathered materials along with them.
- Different types of new landforms are formed due to weathering. Several old landforms are also modified.
- Weathering causes the formation of rock waste. These rock wastes often destroy human habitation when they fall in the form of landslides, avalanches and mass movements.
- Weathering is essential for the formation of new soil. Often, continuous weathering exposes valuable minerals that are otherwise buried deep inside the Earth.

**FACT FILE**

When weathered rock waste settles down on unweathered fresh rock, it is called **regolith**.

**Fact from India**

Did you know that extensive weathering of the lower Himalayas due to indiscriminate felling of trees and deforestation has led to massive siltation of the mighty rivers, such as the Ganga, Yamuna, Koel, Ghagara, etc.? Massive siltation has increased the sediment load because of which any amount of heavy rainfall leads to overflooding of the rivers on their banks.

**Mass movement:**

Definition: Mass movement is the movement of weathered materials or rock wastes down the slope. This falling of rock waste down the slope depends on the gradient of the slope, as well as on the force of gravity. It is also accelerated by the presence of running water, strong winds, glaciers, etc. Mass movement includes both fine particles and huge boulders.

Weathered rock

Mass movements, according to **R.J. Chorley**, include both detachment of rock materials and waste through different agents of weathering, as well as transportation of the weathered rock materials down the slope under the influence of gravity.

***Classification of mass movement***

Based on the speed of movement:

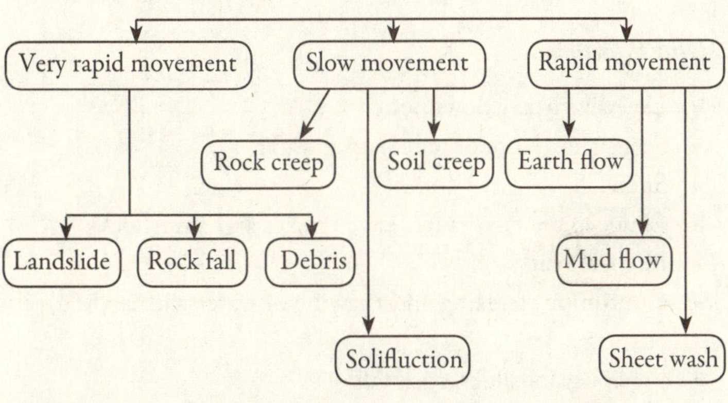

Based on the direction of movement, **R.J. Chorley** has identified the following classification of mass movement:

| Vertical Movement | Lateral Movement | Diagonal Movement |
|---|---|---|
| **Falls:** When rock debris and boulders fall from a steep slope.<br>This includes rock falls, Earth falls and debris falls.<br>**Subsidence or sinking:**<br>This includes collapse and settlements. | **Slides:** The movement of materials along a horizontal plane or between two rocks.<br>**Spreading:** The lateral displacement of series of rocks. | **Creep:** The movement of materials down the slope at low velocity. Includes soil creep, rock creep, talus creep.<br>**Slide:** Based on the materials. Includes rock slide, debris slide and slump.<br>**Flows:** Earth flow, mudflow, debris flow. |

**What are the factors controlling mass movement?**

Needless to say, man is the most dominant factor controlling mass movement and mass wasting. Different anthropogenic activities – such as deforestation, construction of buildings, reservoirs on hill slopes and rapid tourism on hill stations – destabilize the fragile hills and mountains and thus trigger mass wasting. However, the factors controlling mass movement can be classified into:

***Natural factors***

- Excessive heavy downpour
- Seepage pressure of percolating water
- Snowfall
- Endogenetic factors like earthquakes and aftershocks
- High-velocity winds
- Continuous freezing and thawing of water within the cracks of rocks
- Previous landslides, rock fall

- Glacial erosion, fluvial erosion, marine erosion
- Work of burrowing animals

***Anthropogenic factors***

- Construction of pits, quarries
- Mining, blasting of mining sites
- Construction of reservoirs and dams in fragile areas
- Large-scale felling of trees for construction of buildings and hotels on weak hill slopes

**Let us learn some new terms!**

**Lahar:** The debris flow of volcanic materials with water, especially on volcanic cones. Lahars are commonly seen when there is a heavy downpour and the rainwater mixes with the volcanic materials, which causes enormous mud flow.
**Colluvial:** Materials or processes associated with transportation or deposition by mass movement and localized run-off at the base of the slopes.
**Pedoturbation:** The mixing of soil particles by natural processes.
**Talus:** Coarse and angular rock fragments found at the base of a cliff. These fragments accumulate as a result of falling, rolling or sliding.

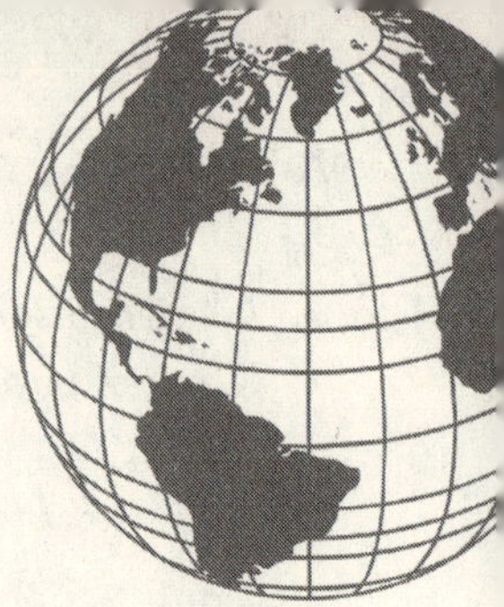

# 11

# THE CONCEPT OF GEOSYNCLINES

According to the ***Oxford Dictionary***, 'geosyncline may be defined as a thick, rapidly accumulating body or sediment formed within a long, narrow, subsiding belt of the sea which is usually parallel to a plate margin'.

It was **James Hall** in 1859 who studied the structure of the northern Appalachians and found out that the folded Palaeozoic sediments were of marine origin, having a thickness of 12 km. He also discovered that the thickness was ten to twenty times greater as compared to the unfolded rock strata in the lowlands towards the west. This suggested that the underlying floor of older rocks had subsided.

**Dustar** classified geosynclines into three types:

- **Intercontinental geosynclines:** located between the continents.
- **Circum-continental geosynclines:** located at the borders of the continents.
- **Circum-oceanic geosynclines:** found along the littoral areas of oceans.

American palaeontologist **Charles Schuchert** classified geosynclines into three types:

| Monogeosynclines | Polygeosynclines | Mesogeosynclines |
|---|---|---|
| They are called mono as they pass through a single cycle of sedimentation and mountain building. These are long and narrow depressions located either within a continent or any littoral tract. *Example:* Appalachian geosynclines. | These are broader than monogeosynclines. They have passed through several stages of orogenesis and sedimentation. *Example:* The Rockies and Urals geosynclines. | These are surrounded by continents on all sides. They have more depth. *Example:* Tethys geosyncline. Mediterranean Sea is its remnant. |

Geophysicists and geologists have always established a relationship between geosynclines and the formation of fold mountains. **Haug** postulated that there are five major land masses belonging to the Mesozoic era that had their origin from geosynclines of the past. They were:

- North Atlantic mass
- Sino Siberian mass
- Africa Brazil mass
- Pacific Ocean mass
- Africa India Madagascar mass

There were four geosynclines present within these rigid masses:

- Rockies geosynclines
- Ural geosynclines
- Circum-Pacific geosynclines
- Tethys geosynclines

***How were the geosynclines formed?***

According to **Arthur Holmes**, there were probably four ways by which geosynclines were formed.

- Geosynclines were formed due to the movement of the hot molten magma from the mantle to the surrounding areas, causing subsidence of the upper layers.
- Converging convective currents caused compressional forces, resulting in subsidence. For example, the formation of the Indo-Gangetic Trough.
- The metamorphosis of rocks is due to the intense pressure generated by convective currents. Subsidence is caused due to greater density of rocks. For example, the Caribbean Sea or the western part of the Mediterranean Sea has been formed in this way.
- The divergence of convective currents at the bottom layer of the crust leads to the thinning of sialic layers, causing the formation of geosynclines.

**Relevance of the theory of geosynclines in today's times**

The theory of geosynclines slowly lost its relevance with the introduction of the plate tectonic theory. According to the plate tectonic theory, a continental margin is considered an active margin when it undergoes the process of subduction and collision. Whereas a continental margin is considered to be a passive one when it shifts away from the axis. The gradual movement of the continents away from the axis makes the lithosphere cooler and denser. While the ocean floor becomes deeper off the passive margin, the sediments continue to get deposited on the ocean floor along the passive margin, thus termed geosynclines. The age-old theory of geosynclines lying parallel to the continents or on a trough bordered by continents has become obsolete. The deposition can take place anywhere on the continental shelf or slope or in a trench.

# 12

## THEORIES OF THE CYCLE OF EROSION

The concept of the cycle of erosion was first presented by **William Morris Davis** in 1899 following the lines of Darwin's theory of evolution. According to Davis, landforms undergo changes as they pass through time from youth through maturity to old age. Landforms are created by endogenetic forces and are destroyed by various exogenic forces in the cycle of erosion.

According to Davis, three factors play an important role in the development or formation of landforms: **time, structure and process**. Here, structure means the lithological characteristics of the landforms. Time means the period taken for the evolution or the stage whether it is youthful, maturity or old age, and process means the agents of weathering and erosion.

Now let us get to know about the stages of the cycle of erosion as presented by Davis.

Reference diagram:

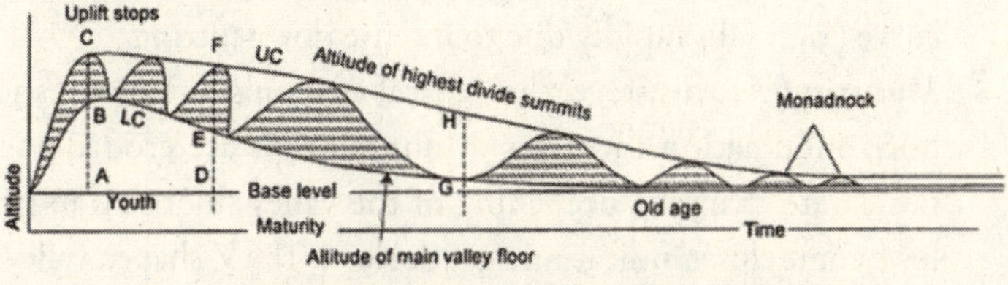


*Graphical presentation of geographical cycle presented by W.M. Davis.*

UC: upper curve or hilltops or crests
LC: lower curve or valley floors
Horizontal line: time
Vertical line: altitude from sea level
AC: maximum absolute relief
BC: initial relief (difference between the upper crest and the valley floor)
ADG: baseline or base level beyond which no erosion can take place. It is the sea level.

**FACT FILE**

When you travel to Haridwar or to the Sundarbans in West Bengal, you are going to encounter the same river – the Ganga.

But have you ever thought that the River Ganga is at the youthful stage in Haridwar and at the old stage in the Sundarbans?

Next time you visit these two places, notice the difference in the characteristics of the same river!

- **Youth:** According to Davis, erosion starts only when the upliftment is complete. Erosion of the uplifted block starts. Small rivers and their streams are involved in downcutting and headward erosion due to which the streams are lengthened. Vertical erosion by rivers is active, which deepens the valleys. As the gradient is steep and the velocity of the river is high, it increases the erosive and transportation capacity of the rivers. V-shaped valleys are formed, while the summits or upper curves (UC) remain unaffected. The river is marked by the presence of waterfalls and rapids. Gorges or canyons are seen. The lower curve (LC) falls rapidly due to intense downcutting.
- **Maturity:** At this stage, the vertical erosion slows down and horizontal action increases. Mountaintops are eroded at a faster rate than the deepening of the valley floors. A and B have come closer indicating a gentle slope. The V-shaped valleys

have started becoming wider. The gradient of the slope has decreased and so has the erosive capacity and velocity of the river.

- **Old age:** Valley deepening is totally stopped, but lateral cutting and valley widening continue. The upper curve falls more rapidly while there is a decrease in the absolute height. The kinetic energy of the river goes down, and the channel gradient is low. Valleys become almost flat. The relief is marked by the presence of broad, flat floodplains, river meanders, broad river channels, monadnocks and low, featureless plains called peneplains.

***Positive aspects of the theory***

- Davis's theory of the cycle of erosion was simple and lucid.
- The concept of change in the base level indicated an initiation of a new cycle. The base level changes indicated a unit of time.
- His model also predicted a historical interpretation of landform development and evolution.

***Negative aspects of the theory***

- Davis believed in the complete suspension of upliftment after erosion, which is considered obsolete.
- An ideal Davisian cycle of erosion would take millions of years. Then what about the Earth's movements during this period?
- There is little evidence that the landforms will ultimately evolve into a peneplain.
- The Davisian theory did not give any validation of the importance of plate movements during his cycle. The plates are constantly in motion and affect the crust. But his theory rejected the plate tectonics.
- He believed that flat slopes are old and steep slopes are young, but there are also other factors, such as the nature of the slope,

bedrock, parent material, climate and vegetation, that are significant.

**Penck's theory of the cycle of erosion**

Walther Penck's theory deviated a little from the Davisian theory. He did not believe in the idea that erosion would start only when upliftment is completed. In fact, he believed that the interaction between upliftment and degradation would be a continuous process. The rate of uplifting, however, continues to change. Penck remarked that there were three types of valley slopes based on the erosional capacity of the river:

a. Straight slope: Uniform erosion intensity and uniform development of landforms. Termed as 'Gleichförmige Entwickelung' in German.
b. Convex slope: Waxing erosion intensity and waxing development of landforms. Termed as 'Aufsteigende Entwickelung'.
c. Concave slope: Waning erosion intensity and waning development of landforms. Termed as 'Absteigende Entwickelung'.

- Stage 1: Penck used the term 'primarumpf' to represent the relief before upliftment. It is the initial surface or primary peneplain that has just emerged from below sea level.
- Stage 2: The rate of downcutting becomes less than the rate of uplifting. There is no significant change in relief.
- Stage 3: The rate of downcutting becomes equal to the rate of uplifting. Not much change in relief.
- Stage 4: No more uplifting; now, downcutting becomes more active. A convex slope develops due to valley deepening. It is the stage of waxing erosion.
- Stage 5: The downcutting and deepening of valleys slow down.

The interfluves are rounded. A concave slope develops. It is the stage of waning erosion.
- Stage 6: Uniform erosion – the formation of end plain or endrumpf.

Penck used the term inselbergs, which are steep-sided conical residuals. Eventually, the inselbergs are eroded, and a series of concave wash slopes or haldenhang are formed.

***Positive aspects of the theory***

1. Penck did not restrict his theory to a particular condition.
2. His approach was forward-looking and more detailed.
3. He established the mutual relationship between upliftment and deepening of valleys.

***Negative aspects of the theory***

- He overemphasized the role of endogenetic forces.
- The sequence of landform development did not match with real life.
- Because of his untimely death, Penck's theory could not be completed.
- The use of German in this model and not using the term 'cycle' in his theory worked against him.

### The normal fluvial cycle of erosion

Since fluvial processes are most widespread, the normal cycle of erosion by Davis has been developed in humid areas where the river is the most important geomorphic agent.

According to Davis, the land passes through successive stages of development. It starts from the upliftment of the land mass and then ends in the formation of peneplains. The whole duration of this cycle has been divided into three stages: youth, maturity and old age. River valleys also pass through these three stages.

*Youthful stage*

- A few short streams are formed. These streams have high erosive capacity because of the steep gradient of the slope.
- The slopes are marked by numerous gullies and rills.
- These gullies and rills lengthen their longitudinal profiles through downcutting and headward erosion.
- The transportation capacity of the river is maximum, thus leading to valley incision.
- V-shaped valleys are formed due to intense downcutting. The valley walls are narrow and almost vertical.
- The valley floors are marked by **potholes.**
- The river valleys are characterized by numerous **rapids** and **waterfalls.**
- **River capture** occurs, where the main river having more volume of water and a steep gradient captures the smaller streams through headward erosion.

*Maturity stage*

- The velocity of the river declines due to a decrease in the gradient.
- There is a decrease in the transportation capacity of the river.
- The main work of the river becomes valley widening through lateral cutting, which replaces downcutting.
- The deep and narrow valleys become broad and flat.
- Sudden decrease in the channel gradient and transportation capacity of the river leads to the dropping of the load carried by the river at the foothills.
- These materials form **alluvial cones** and **alluvial fans.**
- Other marked relief features are the formation of **meanders** and **oxbow lakes.**

- There is an equilibrium achieved between the transportation capacity of the river and the load to be transported.
- The river starts its work of deposition of sediments in a gentle and flat terrain, thus forming floodplains and **natural levees**.

***Old stage***

- Now the river has become very broad and is joined by several tributaries and distributaries.
- The gradient is low, and there is almost a total absence of valley incision.
- The volume of water along with sediment load is maximum.
- The transportation capacity of the river is reduced to a minimum as the river becomes overloaded.
- The river flows sluggishly. The main river is divided into several distributaries so the river forms braided channels.
- Extensive **floodplains** or flat plains called **peneplains** are formed.
- The river, while joining the sea, deposits its sediments in the form of deltas.

**FACT FILE**

When you travel to Haridwar or to the Sundarbans in West Bengal, you are going to encounter the same river – the Ganga.

But have you thought that the River Ganga is at the youthful stage in Haridwar and at the old stage in the Sundarbans?

Next time you visit these two places, notice the difference in the characteristics of the same river!

**Interruptions in the cycle of erosion**

Here, interruption refers to any obstacle in the normal cycle of erosion. The reason behind the interruption can be either natural or anthropogenic. It is important to note that if there is a positive movement at the base level due to a rise in sea level or related factors, it would shorten the cycle as the stages will be advanced forward. So, if it is in the mature stage, it will advance to the old stage. If there is a negative change in the base level due to a fall in sea level or land mass upliftment, then the cycle will be pushed backwards. So, if the cycle is in the mature stage and suddenly there is a fall in sea level or base level, the cycle will be pushed back to the youthful stage. This process is called **rejuvenation.**

When a normal cycle of erosion is marked by several interruptions in its cycle, it is called a polycycle.

The interruptions can be of two types:

| Climatic Causes | Tectonic Causes |
|---|---|
| Major changes in the climate of a region can cause interruptions in the cycle of erosion. Suppose the river is in a humid tropical region and suddenly the region faces extreme climate change and there is drought and aridity setting in, then the cycle of erosion will be definitely interrupted. | Volcanic eruptions or seismic activities can disturb a normal cycle of erosion. Often, volcanic eruptions cause an outpouring of lava through fissures and cracks that spread over large areas. This basaltic lava clogs the river flow and the relief, and when it cools down and solidifies, a new base level is created.<br>Similarly, major earthquakes also change the course of the river, and a new relief is formed. |

### The concept of rejuvenation

Rejuvenation simply means lengthening the cycle of erosion. Rejuvenation occurs when the river is passing through the mature stage when the channel gradient is lowered and valley incision is decreased but sudden upliftment or a change in the sea level makes the river youthful again.

***Causes***

Rejuvenation is caused due to the following reasons:

- Dynamic rejuvenation: Upliftment of the land mass or tilting of the land mass.
- Static rejuvenation: Increase in the volume of the river or decrease in the sediment load of the river.
- Eustatic rejuvenation: Glaciations causing a fall in sea level or subsidence of sea level.

**FACT FILE**

**What is a knickpoint?**

It is the break in a slope in the longitudinal profile of a river caused by rejuvenation. The elevation in the long profile of the river drops suddenly, and the water descends vertically in the form of waterfalls. Example: the Dhuandhar Falls of the Narmada River.

# 13

# MAJOR LANDFORMS OF THE EARTH

**Mountains**: A high landform that rises significantly than its surrounding area. A mountain can be either coastal (the Appalachians, Rockies, Alps), inland (the Himalayas, Urals, Kunlun, Tien Shan) or oceanic (Mauna Kea of Hawaii).

***Classification of mountains***

Based on the **mode of origin**, mountains are classified as the following:

- **Fold mountains:** They are formed due to the folding of sedimentary rocks by the compressional forces coming from inside the Earth. These are the most extensive and highest mountain ranges of the world. They are of two types: young fold and old fold mountains. Young fold mountains are characterized by steep slopes and pointed peaks. They are higher in height. For example: the Himalayas, Alps and Rockies. Old fold mountains have gentle slopes and round peaks. They are mostly affected by weathering and denudation. For example: the Aravallis, Vindhyas.

*Characteristics of fold mountains*

- These are the youngest in the mountain group.
- Fold mountains are either young fold or old fold mountains.
- They are formed due to the compression of layered sedimentary rocks. The presence of marine sedimentary rocks in fold mountains indicates that these ranges are formed due to the deposition and consolidation of sediments on the ocean floor.
- The fossil remains in these mountains indicate that they must have lived in shallow seas. The gradual subsidence of the seafloor due to sedimentation led to the consolidation and cementation of sediments over millions of years.
- Fold mountains are always found in long chains of parallel ranges.
- It is interesting to note that almost all the fold mountain ranges are found along the margins of the continents and face the oceans. Except for the Himalayas, the Rockies and Andes lie on the western margins of North and South America and face the Pacific Ocean.

**Block mountains:** Also called as fault block mountains, they are formed due to tensional forces operated by endogenetic forces from deep within the Earth's crust. They are formed when the two side blocks on either side of the two faults move downwards while the middle block remains in its position. Or they can form when the middle block moves down, forming a rift valley while either of the side blocks remains intact forming a horst. For example: Vosges and Black Forest mountains bordering the Rhine Rift Valley, the Sierra Nevada Mountains of California.

*Characteristics of block mountains*

- Block mountains are formed due to the upliftment of the middle block between two normal faults. The upthrown block is termed a horst.

- Block mountains are generally steep sloped with almost flat summits.
- They can also form when the middle block subsides, forming rift valleys. The side blocks remain upright as horsts.
- Block mountains, because of their steep slopes, often look youthful and are rugged.
- They are mainly formed due to tensional forces, unlike fold mountains.
- They often take a rectangular shape, and their composition might vary. Often, block mountains consist of sedimentary layers.

**Volcanic mountains:** These are formed due to the accumulation of volcanic materials.

**Dome mountains:** They are formed by the upwarping of the surface due to the emergence and cooling of magma.

**Relict mountains:** They are formed due to denudation and erosion of higher mountains. Constant weathering of the mountains has lowered these mountains. For example: the Aravallis, Satpuras.

Based on **height**, mountains are classified as:

- Low mountains: having an altitude between 700 to 1,000 m
- High mountains: having an altitude between 1,000 to 1,500 m
- Rugged mountains: having an altitude between 1,500 to 2,000 m
- Very high mountains: having an altitude above 2,000 m

Based on the **period of formation**, mountains are classified as:

- Precambrian mountain ranges: Mountains formed during the Precambrian era, such as the Laurentian Mountains.

- Caledonian mountain ranges: Mountains formed between the Silurian and Devonian periods. Example: the Appalachians, and the Satpuras and Vindhyas of India.
- Hercynian mountains: Mountains formed during the Carboniferous era. This period marked the formation of the Black Forest and Vosges, the plateau region of central France, Tarim Basin, Tien Shan, etc.
- Alpine mountains: Almost all the present-day major mountains of the world were formed in this period. For example, the Rockies, the Andes, the Alps, the Himalayas, as well as the mountain chains coming out of the Pamir Knot.

**Formation of mountains**

There have been several theories about the formation of mountains. The theory of geosynclines has already been discussed in the previous chapter. The most concrete and comprehensive theory about mountain building is the **plate tectonic theory**.

***The crux of the theory of plate tectonics***

Plates are rigid lithospheric slabs that float on the asthenosphere. These plates are constantly in motion, either towards each other or away from each other. We have already studied the theory of plate tectonics in the previous chapter on continents and oceans.

Now let us learn about the crux of the theory.

We know that mountains are formed due to the collision of two plates with each other. This collision generates compressional or tensional forces resulting in the formation of folded or block mountains respectively. So, mountains are formed along the destructive plate boundaries. The denser plate subducts below the lighter plate. This subduction creates lateral compressional forces that cause squeezing or folding of sedimentary rock layers.

Mountains can form due to the collision of two oceanic plates or continental plates or the collision of oceanic and continental plates. Let us go through the examples of mountains formed due to each of the above processes:

| The Convergence of Two Oceanic Plates | The Convergence of Two Continental Plates | The Convergence of Oceanic and Continental Plates |
|---|---|---|
| The formation of the Japanese island arcs. | The alpine mountains of Europe. The Himalayan mountain system. | The Western Cordilleras of North America and South America (the Rockies and the Andes). |

The Himalayas originated in the subduction of the Tethys Sea geosynclines. The Tethys Sea began to contract in size due to the northward movement of the Indian plate below the Asiatic plate. The collision of the Indian plate and Asiatic plate caused compressional force, which squeezed the sediments of the Tethys Sea, and the fold mountains of the Himalayas were formed ultimately!

Types of mountains

**Plateaus:** This is a tableland feature with steep slopes higher than the surrounding areas with the upper part almost flat.

Based on its **location**, plateaus can be:

- Intermontane plateaus: These are surrounded by mountains on all sides. For example: the Tibetan Plateau.
- Piedmont plateaus: These are located at the foot of mountains. For example: the Patagonian Plateau.
- Continental plateau: These are away from mountains and are mostly surrounded by coastal plains. For example: the Arabian Plateau, Australian Plateau.
- Volcanic plateau: These are formed due to the accumulation of thick basaltic lava. For example: the Columbia Plateau (USA).

> The Deccan Plateau, one of the oldest plateaus of the world, is highly dissected and is bordered by the Western Ghats in the west and the Eastern Ghats in the east.

Based on **shape**, plateaus are classified as:

- Dome-shaped plateau: Ranchi Plateau (India)
- Dissected plateau: Deccan Plateau (India)
- Flat-topped plateau: Tibetan Plateau (China)
- Step plateau: Rewa Plateau (India)
- Rejuvenated plateau: Missouri Plateau (USA)

Based on **age**, plateaus are classified into:

- Young plateau: Colorado Plateau (USA)
- Mature plateau: Ranchi Plateau (India)
- Old plateau: Deccan Plateau (India)
- Rejuvenated plateau: Missouri Plateau (USA)

On the basis of **climatic location**, plateaus are classified as:

- Arid plateau: Arabian Plateau (Southwest Asia)
- Humid plateau: Shillong Plateau (India)
- Cold plateau: Greenland Plateau (Greenland)

**The formation of plateaus**

As we have seen, there are different criteria on the basis of which plateaus can be classified, so each of the plateaus have unique characteristics depending on their mode of origin or their process of formation.

- **Fluvial plateaus:** The continuous deposition of alluvium brought down by rivers causes the formation of fluvial plateaus. These sediments are gradually consolidated and stratified to form layers of sedimentary rocks. These sediments are further uplifted due to tectonic movements as compared to their surrounding regions, thus taking the shape of a tableland feature. Rewa Plateau and Bhander Plateau are classic examples of fluvial plateaus.
- **Aeolian plateau:** The deposition of fine sediments by wind in arid and semi-arid regions causes the formation of Aeolian plateaus. The Loess Plateau in China was formed due to the continuous deposition of fine sand over the years.
- **Glacial plateaus:** These types of plateaus, as the name suggests, are not formed from glaciers. Rather, these plateaus are modified by glaciers. As we know that all plateaus are formed due to tectonic forces from within the Earth's crust, glacial plateaus derive the shape of a plateau due to glacial erosion or movements. The deposition of glacial moraines leads to the shape of a plateau.

**Fact to note!**

Although we are discussing glacial plateaus, aeolian plateaus or fluvial ones, it is always important to remember that plateaus are formed by tectonic activities only. They are formed due to horizontal and vertical movements caused by endogenetic forces. Thus, all plateaus are diastrophic in nature, and so they are truly called tectonic plateaus.

- **Intermontane plateaus:** As already mentioned, intermontane plateaus are surrounded by mountains on all sides. These are formed at the time of the formation of fold mountains. The upwarping of the geosynclines in the middle portion led to the formation of a plateau-like feature.
- **Piedmont plateaus:** Plateaus formed at the foot of a mountain range are called piedmont plateaus. They are surrounded by mountains on one side and plains on the other side. The sides facing the plains have steeper slopes, forming escarpments.
- **Continental plateaus:** These are large and extensive plateaus located away from mountains and near coasts. These plateaus are considered to be the oldest of all plateaus and are dissected by many rivers and their tributaries. The Deccan Plateau is a good example of a continental plateau. It is bordered by the Western and Eastern Ghats on its two sides. It is highly dissected and is composed of rich basaltic lava soil.
- **Dome-shaped plateau:** This type of plateau is formed when the land mass is uplifted in such a way that the middle portion takes the shape of a dome. The slopes are almost gentle and rounded. These plateaus are formed due to volcanic actions. The lava coming out gets solidified and cools down, taking the shape of domes on the surface. Continuous deposition of basaltic lava increases the height of the dome as compared to the surrounding area.

- **Volcanic plateau:** The accumulation of thick layers of basaltic lava spread over large areas leads to the formation of this type of plateau.

**Plains:** They are flat areas with low, undulating surfaces and very gentle slopes. They can be either higher or lower than sea level.

Based on **mode of origin**, plains can be:

- **Diastrophic plains:** Formed due to upliftment or subsidence of land due to diastrophic movements. For example: the Great Plains of USA.
- **Erosional plains:** Lateral erosion by rivers causes the formation of these plains. For example: the Lorraine Plains, France.
- **Depositional plains:** Gradual deposition of sediments by rivers, wind and glaciers cause such extensive plains.

**The Great Plains of India,** also known as the **Indo-Gangetic Plains,** are formed due to the deposition of sediments brought down by the rivers flowing in that region.

The Great Ganga Brahmaputra Plains are either Bhangar or Khadar types. Khadar plains are more fertile; they get renewed every year with fresh alluvium. Bhangar plains are older alluvium and are filled with lime nodules and kankar.

Based on **location**, plains can be classified as:

- Inland plains
- Coastal plains

### *Characteristics of plains*

- Plains are generally flat or undulating with a low height.
- Most plains are formed due to upliftment or subsidence of submerged land masses due to diastrophism.
- The height of the plains can never be determined on the basis of sea level because there are plains that lie even below sea level.

- Plains are the most densely populated regions of the world because of their flat surfaces, suitable climatic conditions and often rich, fertile soil that helps in agriculture.

Now let's discuss the major types of plains based on their process of formation:

1. **Diastrophic plains**: These plains are formed due to the upliftment or subsidence of submerged land masses due to diastrophism, for example, the Great Plains in the USA. The Great Plains were formed due to the emergence of a submerged land mass under sea. This is also an example of a continental plain. It is believed that the Great Plains remained underwater during the Cretaceous period. Thick deposits of marine sediments were accumulated and consolidated layer after layer. Diastrophic movements caused the upheaval of the plain. By the end of the Cretaceous period, the land mass rose above sea level and was further modified by exogenic forces.
2. **Erosional plains**:

| Formed by River Erosion | Formed by Glaciers | Formed by Wind | Karst Plains |
|---|---|---|---|
| Peneplains are the classic examples of this type of plain. These are formed due to lateral erosion by rivers and weathering. The weathered materials get deposited on the plains, forming rounded monadnocks. | Rounded peaks and broad and flat valleys interspersed with small lakes are the characteristic features of these plains. | Winds blows away fine sand particles and deposits them over years in another region. This results in the transformation of a land mass into a sandy plain. | Chemical weathering and erosion of limestone areas by ground water make way for the formation of low-relief undulating karst plains. |

3. **Depositional plains**: The gradual deposition of sediments by rivers, wind and glaciers causes such extensive plains.

   - **River-deposited plains:** They can be either piedmont alluvial plains or floodplains or delta plains.

     **Piedmont alluvial plains** are formed at the foothills of the mountains. The river, while leaving the mountains, starts dropping its sediments at the foot of the mountain due to the sudden fall in the channel gradient. These cobbles, pebbles and gravel are deposited in the foothills in the form of alluvial fans and cones.

     **Floodplains** are flat extensive plains formed due to the deposition of fine sand, silt, clay, pebbles, etc., brought down by the river. Floodplains are the most densely populated regions as they contain rich alluvial soil. So floodplains are also rightly called the granaries of the world. Floodplains in India are either of bhangar type (old alluvium) or khadar type (new alluvium).

     **Deltaic plains** are formed when the river almost completes its journey and is about to enter the sea. The gradual deposition of sediments brought down by the river in its long journey at its mouth leads to the formation of deltaic plains.

4. **Lacustrine plains:** Sometimes, plains are also formed by the filling up of lakes by sediments brought down by the rivers.
5. **Lava plains:** These form due to the deposition of thin layers of lava coming out through fissures. Lava plains are rich in black lava soil, which is good for cotton cultivation.
6. **Wind plains or loess:** These are undulating and irregular plains marked by sand dunes and barchans. They are formed over years due to the gradual deposition of sand particles by the wind.

7. **Glacial plains:** The deposition of glacial moraines and deposits results in the formation of extensive glacial plains. They are either outwash plains or till plains. Outwash plains are formed due to the dropping of materials after glacial ablation. Outwash plains comprise clay, silt, gravel, etc. Till plains comprise finer materials brought by the glaciers. They have an undulating wave-like surface comprising small, rounded peaks. Examples are drumlins and eskers.

# 14

## FLUVIAL LANDFORMS: LANDFORMS FORMED BY RIVERS

Before we start discussing landforms formed by rivers, we need to understand that a river passes through three cycles in its lifetime – youth, maturity and old age. This is exactly in line with the Davisian cycle of erosion. Let us take a quick glance at the three cycles of erosion of a river:

- **Youthful stage**: Starting from the source of the river, the velocity of the running water is maximum. Down cutting is most active, and gradients are steep. Landforms formed are V-shaped valleys, waterfalls and rapids. Erosion is the most dominant activity.
- **Mature stage**: The transportation of load is most active, and the gradient becomes gentler, causing lateral cutting. The volume of water increases. Landforms formed are meanders and oxbow lakes.
- **Old stage**: The deposition of sediments starts, and the gradient is gentlest as the river approaches its mouth. The river is unable to carry load any longer, so there is sluggish flow. Landforms formed are deltas, braided streams and vast alluvial plains.

Now let's know in detail what each stage of a river produces in its journey!

**The erosional work of the river**: The erosional capacity of the river depends on several factors, such as:

a. The velocity of the river
b. The steepness of the channel gradient
c. The volume of water
d. The amount of sediment load

The amount and size of the river load are driving factors in determining the erosive capacity of the river. The amount of load should be optimum, that is, neither overloaded nor underloaded. This is because if the river is overloaded, it will not be able to transport, and hence, will start depositing, and if the river is underloaded, it will lose its erosive power.

The erosive power of the river also depends on the channel gradient and velocity of the river. Steep channel gradient with high velocity will always empower the erosional capacity of the river.

**Types of Fluvial Erosion**

| **Corrosion** | **Abrasion** | **Attrition** | **Hydraulic action** |
|---|---|---|---|
| It involves the dissolution of soluble materials through disintegration and decomposition of carbonate-rich rocks. The carbonate materials are mixed with the running water. | The boulders, pebbles and gravel that are brought down by the river pass through the steep channel gradient along with the water. These erosional agents remove the loosened materials of the valley walls and valley floor. Abrasion can be of two types: vertical erosion and lateral erosion. | These erosional agents (boulders, pebbles, gravel) also collide against each other and undergo wear and tear. They break down into smaller particles. | The sole action of water in the removal and breaking away of rock materials. |

***Landforms from the erosional work of a river***

**River valley:** We know the upper course of the river starts from hilly or mountainous regions. At this stage, the river flows down a steep gradient, and as a result, its velocity and erosive power are maximum.

So valley deepening due to vertical erosion is at its peak. The weathered rock materials are carried by running water through the action of gravity or sometimes due to heavy rainfall. Weathering leads to valley incision, giving it a typical V-shaped cross section. These valleys are called **V-shaped valleys.**

Sometimes, the bedrock is hard and resistant, so widening of the valley cannot take place at its top, and severe downcutting of the river leads to the formation of a **gorge**. A gorge is a deep or narrow valley with wall-like steep valley sides. The extended form of a gorge is called a canyon. A very deep gorge or a canyon with vertical walls is also called an **I-shaped valley**.

The Grand Canyon in the Colorado River, USA is a very deep gorge running for hundreds of kilometres.

**Waterfalls:** When water falls from a certain height, they are called waterfalls. Waterfalls are mainly formed when there is a difference in the resistance power of the rocks. The soft rocks get eroded away, leaving only the hard rocks. This happens when there are alternate layers of hard rocks and soft rocks. These types of waterfalls formed due to the difference in the lithological characteristics of the rocks in the course of rivers are very large, and are termed **cataracts**. A series of small step-like faults are called **cascades**.

Let's discuss the different possibilities in the formation of waterfalls.

- The arrangement of alternate layers of hard rocks and soft rocks in the course of a river produces step-like falls. These waterfalls are called **rapids**. They are smaller in size and formed due to the difference in erosion between the hard and soft rocks.

- Fault scarps across river valleys due to faulting may also create waterfalls.
- When a river meets a steep escarpment of a plateau, it drops down to a significantly low height, thus forming a waterfall.
- When there are alternate bands of hard rocks and soft rocks in a vertical manner, soft rocks get eroded away, leaving behind the hard rocks. These hard rocks remain upright, forming a scarp in the course of a river. So a steep waterfall is formed.
- When there are alternate bands of hard rocks and soft rocks in a horizontal manner, the caprock or hard rock remains resistant while the underlying soft rocks get eroded away from the resistant caprock. This forms wall-like scarps in the course of the river, also termed **cataracts**.

**Good to know!**

**What are these hard rocks and soft rocks that we are discussing?**

Here, hard rocks refer to dolomitic limestone, quartzite, granite gneiss and basalt, while the soft rocks referred to here are shale, carbonate rocks, volcanic ash and other unconsolidated materials.

- Caprock rapids are formed when there is a sudden dip in the course of the river. The hard rocks form rapids while the softer ones get eroded and washed away.
- Rivers descending a sea cliff form waterfalls. Such waterfalls are also called coastal waterfalls as the river, after falling, meets the sea.
- The rejuvenation of a river causes breaks in the channel gradient, called knickpoints. These knickpoints are formed due to sudden drops in elevation in the long profile of the river. The water falls vertically, giving rise to waterfalls or knickpoint falls.

**Point to note!**

Waterfalls can also form if there is any obstruction in the long profile of the river. These obstructions can be caused by the formation of lava barriers or deposition of debris across the river valley from nearby hilly areas or by damming of the river flow due to morainic deposits.

**Potholes and terraces:** These are small kettle-like depressions that are almost cylindrical, formed in the beds of the river valleys. The erosive tools of the rivers, such as pebbles, gravel, boulders, are caught in a whirlpool, and they start moving in a circular fashion and grind and drill the river valleys. This repeated action forms small holes due to drilling, and the holes get enlarged with time. These are called potholes. The potholes are deepened and enlarged both in depth and diameter.

When the potholes become very large, they are called **plunge pools**. Plunge pools are mostly seen at the base of a waterfall due to the falling of rocks with great force along with the gushing water.

**Terraces:** These are flat, narrow surfaces on either side of the valley floor. They are found in step-like formations. River terraces are formed when there is a dissection of the riverine sediments of the floodplains deposited along the valley floor.

Terraces are formed on extensive floodplains mainly when it is at its late maturity stage. These floodplains comprise thick deposits of alluvium. A sudden rejuvenation of the river due to a fall in the sea level causes the river to move back to its youthful stage. As a result, the erosive power of the river is rejuvenated. The river starts its work of valley incision and vertical erosion again. Now the river forms new vertical valleys within the already existing flat valleys. In this way, a new pair of terrace-like features are formed.

There are either paired terraces or unpaired terraces.

- **Paired terraces:** The rapid rate of vertical erosion results in the formation of sets of terraces on either side of the river valley almost at an equal level.
- **Unpaired terraces:** This occurs due to the twin processes of vertical and lateral movements of the river channel.

**Transportational work of the river:** The transportational work of the river starts in its middle course. Here, the vertical erosion is replaced by lateral erosion. Lateral erosion of the river widens the V-shaped river valley. At this stage, the river leaves the hilly areas and is on its journey towards the plains. Now the gradient becomes gentle, and the volume of water increases due to the joining of several tributaries. The sediment load of the river increases, which decreases its velocity.

Landforms formed by the transportational work of a river.

**Meanders:** At this stage, even a minor obstacle faced by the river forces it to swing in loops or go around. These loops are called **meanders.** The term 'meanders' is derived from the Büyük Menderes River in Türkiye because of the curvy course of its lower reaches.

**Formation of meanders:** Meanders are the result of both the erosional and depositional work of the river. The formation of a meander depends on the following factors:

- The general slope of the land
- The lithological characteristics
- The annual precipitation
- The type of vegetation cover
- The stage of the river in its cycle of erosion

It is important to note that meanders are more developed when the land is even and has a gentle slope. A river will never follow a straight path as in theory, when the speed of the river goes down, it starts the work of both erosion and deposition. Sometimes, it becomes so weak that any obstacle in its path makes it change its course. This goes on and on with time. When the bends become more pronounced, the river performs its erosional work on its concave bank and depositional work on its convex bank.

Here, we must know that the meander of a river has two limbs – the concave bank that is steep and the convex bank that is gentle.

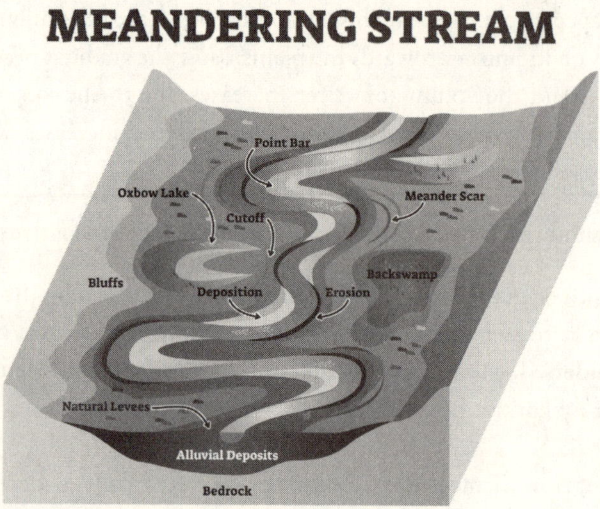


Meandering stream

### *Types of meanders*

**Simple meanders:** The meanders that are formed at the first stage of the erosion cycle are formed by lateral erosion. They can be of **three subtypes** based on the shape:

a. Wavy meanders
b. Oxbow-shaped meanders
c. Horseshoe meanders

Now, there are certain **prerequisite conditions** for the formation of simple meanders. They are:

- Only mature streams can form meanders. That's because young streams are more engaged in erosional activity and valley incision than deposition. Older streams have so much sediment load that they are busy with only depositional activity.
- A vast alluvial plain, gentle slope, sufficient rainfall and the absence of vegetation cover are necessary.
- There should be an obstacle in the course of the river because it will force the river to bend and change its course.
- The concave side becomes steeper as the channel strikes against it. The loops become sharper due to a high degree of curvature.

**Incised meanders:** These are special types of meanders that reform not when the river is performing lateral erosion but when it is deepening the valley through vertical erosion. That means the river is rejuvenated and goes back to its youthful stage. These are deep and narrow meanders formed due to valley incisions within large and simple meanders. In other words, we can say that incised meanders are meanders of deep and narrow valleys within older broad meanders. They can either have equal slopes on both sides of the valley of the meandering loops or can have ununiform slopes.

**Misfit meanders:** Sometimes, the volume of water in the river, due to any reason, becomes very low, which makes the channel narrow. These narrow channels are unable to fit themselves within the broad flat valley, so they create their own meandering course of narrow valleys within the older broad valleys. Such meanders that are formed within the wider meanders due to a substantial decrease in the volume of water in the concerned river are called misfit meanders.

**River cliff and slip-off slope:** As mentioned, the river performs erosional work on its concave bank and depositional work on its convex bank. The speed of the river is more on the concave bank, which results in the formation of steep slopes called river cliffs while the gentler convex slopes form slip-off slopes.

**Oxbow lake:** When the curvature of the meandering loops becomes so strong due to lateral erosion that they become almost circular, the loop ends come closer to each other and take the shape of a separate water body, called an oxbow lake. Often, oxbow lakes are filled with sediment deposition and are completely plugged in due course of time.

**Alluvial fans and alluvial cones:** In the middle course of the river, vertical erosion of the river is replaced by lateral erosion. This lateral erosion widens the V-shaped river valley. The volume of water in the river increases significantly due to the addition of many tributaries and distributaries. This increases the sediment load of the river. A sudden drop in the channel gradient makes the river weak in its transportation capacity as it enters plain land. So it starts dropping all the sediments it was carrying all this while at the point of break in the slope or at the foothill zone. This takes the shape of a fan called **alluvial fan**.

**FACT FILE**

**Point bar:** The term was applied to those bars that develop on the inside of a meander bed. They are formed by the slow additions of individual accretions that accompany the migration of the meander. As the point bar extends itself into a meandering curve, a series of alternating arcuate ridges and troughs make the accretions.

An alluvial fan is semicircular and points upstream. There is always a gradual growth in the extent of the alluvial fan because of regular debris supplied from upstream. It also increases in height due to the deposition of debris upon debris.

Alluvial cones are made up of coarser materials. They have steeper slopes as the formation of alluvial cones requires less water and more debris.

**Depositional work of the river:** In the lower course of the river, the main work of the river is the deposition of its sediment load. It starts building up its bed and creates an extensive floodplain. At this stage the river is passing through plain land. The channel gradient has become gentle, and its velocity has also decreased. The river is joined by several tributaries and distributaries. These tributary streams provide additional sediment load. Sediment load is also provided by gully and rill erosion. The reduction in the stream velocity reduces the transportation capacity of the river due to which the river starts leaving its additional load to settle down.

***Landforms formed due to the depositional work of a river***

**Braided stream:** The excessive deposition of sediments on the floor of the river channel divides the stream into a network of channels forming bars of sand and islands called braided streams. Braided streams are formed when the river moves slowly and there is a reduction in its carrying capacity.

**Natural levees:** Natural levees are raised banks or embankments. We know that the speed of the river is slowest at its sides and the bottom because of friction. In the lower course of the river, a little drop in speed results in instant deposition of the sediments at the bottom and sides of the river. With the passage of time, the riverbed gets raised and the river flows between the raised banks along the bed, which are at a higher level than the surrounding plains.

Levees can also be artificial ones built on the embankment of a river as protection from floods.

**Did you know?**

The natural levees of the Mississippi River in the USA are as high as seven metres. The levees of Hwang He in China are higher than the roofs of the houses built in that area. This makes Hwang He the sorrow of China.

**The relevance of natural levees:** Natural levees often protect the people living in the surrounding regions from the wrath of floods. But that does not happen when the levees give in to the excessive pressure of the river water. At that time, it floods the entire region. The sediments get deposited all over the riverbanks. In this way, a broad, extensive plain is formed, called a floodplain. Floodplains are regarded as the granaries of the world as they consist of fresh alluvium, that is renewed every year after floods. The soil here is very fertile and supports agriculture.

**Delta:** When the river is almost at the stage of meeting the sea, it starts depositing its entire load at the mouth, giving rise to the formation of a delta. A delta is a triangular relief feature with its apex pointing upstream and looks like a fan-shaped region of fine alluvium. The word 'delta' was first used by Greek historian Herodotus, for the triangular depositional feature seen at the mouth of the River Nile.

All rivers cannot form deltas. Let us see **the prerequisite conditions needed for the formation of a delta**.

- A tide-less sheltered coast.
- A relatively calm and sheltered sea at the mouth of the river, that is, no strong current at the mouth that might wash away the sediments.
- Shallow sea adjoining the delta.

- Long course of the river. The river must have a long journey from its origin to its mouth. This will help in bringing large amounts of sediments.
- Medium size of the sediments. Large sediments will settle down on the sea bottom and will not form a delta. Very fine particles will remain suspended in seawater.
- Large and continuous supply of sediment.
- Active vertical and lateral erosion in the upper course of the river that will facilitate the sediment supply.

**Good to know!**

Deltas may also undergo subsidence. This happens under three conditions:

1. Gradual sedimentation and compaction of the sediments, leading to increased weight of the load of the delta.
2. Increased thickness of the sediments.
3. Isostatic reasons.

***Are deltas stationary?***

The answer is *no*. However, the rate of growth of deltas may vary depending on several factors.

- The supply of sediments
- The nature of the sea
- The presence of ocean currents
- The velocity of the river channel
- The slope and height of the delta

The growth of deltas is always sluggish as the river velocity is extremely low, and so, the river starts depositing its load at its mouth. If the velocity of the river is high, then it can transport its load for great distances into the sea. That accelerates the growth of a delta. However, these deltas are generally narrow and long.

***Types of delta: (based on shape)***

| Arcuate Delta | Estuarine Delta | Bird-Foot Delta | Truncated Delta |
|---|---|---|---|
| These types of deltas take the shape of an arc of a circle where the middle portion has a maximum extent towards the sea. They are formed in shallow seas where the river is dense, and the sediments are mainly coarse gravel, silt and sand. The main river is divided into several distributaries. Examples: the Nile Delta, the Ganga-Brahmaputra Delta. | The deltas formed due to the filling up of estuaries are called estuarine deltas. These are long and narrow. They are found in areas where the mouth of the river is submerged under the sea. The sea waves and currents are constantly removing the deposited sediments, while the river is constantly depositing its sediments. When the river succeeds in depositing its load, this type of delta is formed. Examples: Narmada and Tapi Delta. | It looks like the foot of a bird. These are formed of lightweight sediments brought down by the river. These sediments float on the river. When they come in contact with seawater, which is denser, they settle down on either side of the main delta. This deposition of sediments in a linear way on either side of the distributaries of the main river channel resembles a bird's foot or human finger. Example: the Mississippi Delta. | These are eroded deltas that are destroyed by sea waves and currents. |

*Based on growth*

**Abandoned delta:** Sometimes, due to tectonic movements, the river shifts its mouth and forms new deltas. The old deltas remain abandoned and unnourished.

The growth of the delta can also get blocked by sea waves and currents due to their erosional activities, at which time blocked deltas occur.

**You must know!**

The Ganga-Brahmaputra Delta is the world's most extensive delta, covering a huge area from the eastern part of India in the state of West Bengal to coastal Bangladesh. The land is also home to the world's largest mangrove forest with rich wildlife like the Royal Bengal tiger and Gangetic crocodiles.

**IMPORTANT TERMS**

- **Source of the river:** The point of origin of a river, which can be a mountain glacier or a lake.
- **Mouth:** When the river meets the sea or ends its journey, typically when it is unable to carry its load.
- **Confluence:** When the river meets its tributary.
- **Tributary:** A river is divided into several small streams in its journey towards the sea.
- **Distributary:** Several smaller streams come out of the main river.
- **Estuary:** Sometimes, a river may not form a delta, but it takes the shape of a gradually widening mouth cutting inland.

# 15

# AEOLIAN LANDFORMS: LANDFORMS FORMED BY WIND

These are most active in arid and semi-arid regions. The velocity of the wind is more as there is no obstruction in the form of trees or vegetation. Arid and semi-arid areas are the **hot deserts** of the world. These places receive less than 25 cm per annum rainfall and experience very high temperatures throughout the year. The rate of evaporation is also very high, and humidity is low. Under such climatic conditions, the land is exposed to wind, which carries away the loose sand particles from the surface.

***Which are the hot deserts of the world***

- **Africa:** The Sahara Desert is the largest in the world. South of the equator are the Kalahari Desert and the Namib Desert.
- **Asia:** The Arabian Desert in the Middle East and the Thar Desert in Pakistan and India. Gobi and Turkistan deserts (central Asia) are cold deserts.
- **North America:** The Sonoran Desert and the Arizona Desert.
- **South America:** The Peruvian Desert and the Atacama Desert in Chile.
- **Australia:** The Great Victoria Desert and the Great Sandy Desert.

### *The erosional work of wind*

The wind acts as an erosion tool. It only carries away the loose rock or sand materials that are close to growth. It is unable to carry bigger particles high up from the surface. The erosional capacity of the wind depends on the size of the materials being carried, the velocity of the wind and the duration of wind blow.

There are three ways by which wind erosion takes place:

1. **Deflation:** The weathered particles that are blown away by wind. The **Qattara Depression** in Egypt is a deflation hollow.
2. **Abrasion:** The air already consists of loose, light sand and dust particles. These particles are floating in the air. When high-velocity wind blows, these particles act as erosive tools, and they wear and tear down the rocks by rubbing, undercutting, etc. Loess are extensive sand plains and are common in China.
3. **Attrition:** The dust and sand particles also rub against each other in the air.

### *Landforms from the erosional work of wind*

**Deflation hollows:** These are depressions formed due to the blowing away of sand particles by wind. The size of deflation hollows may vary from small ones to very large ones. The depth of these depressions depends on the underground water table.

**Blowout:** It is a shallow depression that is formed by deflation.

**Oasis:** Continuous deflation results in the gradual lowering of the ground. The depth of the deflation depends on the presence of the underground water table. When the depth of the depression hits the water table below, the wind is incapable of removing sand particles any more. Although the moist particles cannot be blown away by the wind, it continues its activity by removing the pebbles from its way. When such activity moves downward and cuts the water table, an oasis is formed.

**Mushroom rock:** These rocks resemble mushrooms as they have a broad upper part and a narrow base. These types of rocks get their typical shape due to the abrasive action of wind. The base of the rock is eroded rapidly from all sides, but the upper part is left untouched. This happens because the erosional capacity of wind is limited to a certain height from the surface, as already mentioned before.

**Inselbergs:** These are residual hills and mounds of relatively hard rocks that could not be eroded by wind. The word 'inselberg' is a German term meaning 'island mountain'. They look like islands situated in the sea. They are dome-shaped or are shaped like a pyramid standing out in a desert.

**Demoiselles:** They are also called Earth pillars. They consist of relatively hard and resistant rock at the top and soft rock below. These are formed due to differential rates of erosion of the hard and soft rocks. The protected rock acts as a pillar below the hard rock. Demoiselles remain intact as long as the soft rocks are protected.

**Zeugen:** Sometimes, the hard and soft rocks are arranged in horizontal layers parallel to each other. The hard rocks remain intact, while the soft rocks get eroded fast. The upper hard rocks look like rock masses of tabular form, called zeugen. Zeugen are common in areas where the diurnal range of temperature is high. During the night, the temperature falls, so the water in the joints and crevices freezes, while in the day, the moisture thaws. This alternate freezing and thawing of moisture within the joints and crevices causes the breaking down of rocks along the fractures. The disintegrated materials are then blown away by the wind.

**Yardangs:** These are found in areas where the wind blows steadily from one direction. These are sharp, steep-sided overhanging rock crests separated from one another by long corridors or grooves. They are formed when alternate layers of hard and soft rocks are arranged in a slightly vertical manner. The soft rocks are eroded and form long corridors between the deeply undercut ridges of overhanging hard rocks.

**Dreikanter:** These are typical rock pieces that are subjected to wind abrasion. These rock blocks or ventifacts may have as many as eight facets. The rock pieces having three abraded facets are called dreikanter. They develop sharp edges when they roll away from their position. Their surface becomes smooth with the passage of time due to abrasion.

**Stone lattice:** When rocks of different resistance are abraded by high-velocity wind, the weaker sections of the rock are abraded more, while the hard and resistant portions are least affected. These weaker parts are removed from the rock. Such fluted surfaced rocks are called stone lattices.

**Wadi:** Wadis are steep-sided narrow dry valleys found in desert areas. These deep and narrow valleys often resemble a gorge or a canyon. They are formed when any river passing through the desert causes vertical erosion. These features are also termed fluvial arid features.

**Wind bridges:** Continuous abrasion of stone lattices cause holes. These holes gradually widen, and ultimately, reach the opposite side of the rocks. Such holes formed across rocks are called **wind windows**. The wind windows are further abraded and deepened, forming arc-like roofs called wind bridges.

*Transportation work of wind*

The transportation work of wind occurs in three ways:

- **Suspension:** When very fine particles less than 0.2 mm are kept in suspension by the wind, they are carried for long distances by the wind. These particles are generally dust and fine particulate matter.
- **Saltation:** The materials that are larger than 0.2 mm in diameter are carried by the wind in a hopping, bouncing fashion. This mechanism is called saltation.
- **Soil creep:** When large materials are carried by the wind by rolling them down a surface, it is called soil creep.

*Depositional work of wind*

The depositional work of the wind starts when the wind faces any obstacle in its path and starts dropping its load. This also happens when the velocity of the wind is reduced.

Landforms formed due to the depositional work of wind:

**Sand dunes:** Sand dunes are the most common depositional landforms found in deserts. These are heaps or mounds of sand that vary in height and length. Their height ranges from a few metres to about 20 metres and around 5 to 6 km in length. The windward slope is gentle, while the leeward slope is steep.

It is interesting to note that you may also notice sand dunes in coastal areas or along riverbanks. That means dunes are formed wherever sand is available in plenty and wind has the capacity to transport and deposit the sand constantly.

*How are sand dunes formed?*

Sand dunes are formed when the wind carrying the sand faces an obstacle in its path. This obstacle can be trees, bushes, rocks or hills. The accumulated low sand mounds, with the passage of time, become large in height and length and become typical sand dunes. At that time, they become an obstacle in themselves. Dunes are always formed in groups or colonies.

Now, let us go through the conditions needed for the formation of sand dunes:

- Abundant supply of sand
- High-velocity wind
- Presence of an obstacle in the path of the wind
- Suitable place for the accumulation of sand

***Are sand dunes mobile or stationary?***

Sand dunes are mobile. Most sand dunes migrate from their place of formation downwind. The sand grains are moved up the windward slope by the wind, and they fall on the leeward slope. This makes the windward slope gentler and the leeward slope steeper. When this action is repeated, the sand dunes shift constantly from their

Sand dunes

place, leading to a desert spread. However, the speed of migration may vary from place to place.

*Types of sand dunes*

Based on **location**, sand dunes are classified as:

- Coastal sand dunes
- Desert sand dunes
- Riverine sand dunes

Based on **shape**, sand dunes are classified as:

**Longitudinal sand dunes or seif dunes:** These are sand dunes formed parallel to the wind direction. The windward slope is gentle while the leeward slope is steeper. The conditions needed for the formation of longitudinal dunes are:

1. They are formed in the interiors of the big deserts.
2. They are formed when there are high-velocity winds blowing in a constant direction.
3. There must be no vegetation in their place of formation.

Longitudinal dunes are formed parallel to each other and separated from each other by sand-free surfaces called **reg.**

**Transverse sand dunes:** These are sand dunes formed transverse to the direction of prevailing wind. They appear in a wave-like pattern.

**Barchans:** These are crescent-shaped or moon-shaped sand dunes having two horns projecting downwind. The gentler windward slope is convex while the steeper leeward slope is concave. These are special types of transverse dunes that become barchans when the supply of sand becomes less downwind. The barchans are found in groups when there is an abundant supply of sand. The horns of the barchans are sharpened with the passage of time and are extended downwind by the wind. Sand is removed from the middle portion and deposited on its two sides.

It is interesting to note that barchans also migrate like regular sand dunes. Regular migration of barchan dunes leads to desertification. However, the rate of migration increases when there is a constant supply of sand. The height of barchans continues to rise when the supply of sand increases, but the speed of movement falls.

**Parabolic dunes:** These are U-shaped sand dunes with a convex side downwind. They are formed when the lateral edges of transverse dunes are obstructed by vegetation cover, the wind removes sand from the middle portion and deposits it on the leeward side. Thus, the middle portion advances more than the sides.

**Star dunes:** Sand dunes having a high central portion and two or three arms radially extending outward are called star dunes. These dunes resemble a star. They are formed by variable winds and grow vertically.

**Whaleback dunes:** The migration of longitudinal dunes leaves behind mounds of coarser sand particles. These are called whaleback dunes. Very large whale back dunes are called **draas.**

**Reverse dunes:** Dunes having intermediate characteristics between transverse dunes and star dunes are called reverse dunes. Here, winds blowing from opposite directions are balanced in strength, and they have two faces opposite each other.

> In India, most sand dunes and seif dunes are common in the western part of the Thar Desert, adjoining Pakistan.

**Loess:** These are deposits of fine-grained, porous, yellowish dust deposited by wind. These are found in low-relief areas where the sand particles are bound together by grass. The loess has a distinct look as it is not removed by wind any further. Loess is formed from sediments accumulated in desert areas, floodplains, coastal areas or glacial regions. It does not have layers like sedimentary rocks. Loess is also found in humid areas, where they are eroded by rainfall, forming gullies and rills.

China is famous for its desert loess. The deposits have been formed from the accumulation of impervious fine particles from the deserts of Central Asia. Hwang He is known as the sorrow of China due to its menacing floods. The erosion of loess results in the deposition of sediments on either bank of the River Hwang He, forming natural levees. The riverbeds are constantly uplifted due to the deposition of silt from the nearby loess. As a result, the riverbeds become higher than the surrounding areas, leading to the breaching of natural levees and floods.

**Sand shadow:** Sometimes, the blowing wind faces obstacles in the form of a tree, shrub or rock. At that time, the velocity of the wind is reduced, and the wind drops the sand behind the obstacle. These are called sand shadows. The height of the sand shadows is not more than the obstacle because the wind blows faster outside the obstacle. The sand continues to get deposited at the obstacle, forming a slope.

**A few more important terms**

1. **Pediments:** Broad extensive gentle sloping areas spread across the mountain bases.
2. **Bolsons:** These are intermontane basins in arid or semi-arid regions.
3. **Playa:** They are temporary lakes formed due to the filling up of water from several ephemeral streams flowing from surrounding mountains in the centre of the bolsons. These bolsons form playas. The water in the playas often totally evaporates leaving behind salt pans known as **salinas**.
4. **Bajada:** Several alluvial fans coalesce to form a bajada. Bajada are gently sloping depositional plains between pediments and playa.

# 16

# GLACIAL LANDFORMS: LANDFORMS FORMED BY GLACIERS

Glaciers are nothing but moving ice. They are formed due to the accumulation of ice beyond the snow line in extreme cold climatic conditions. The glaciers are generated in extensive snowfields. The snow gets gradually transformed into granular snow and then finally into glacial ice.

> **What is a snow line?**
>
> It is the height beyond which there is permanent snow cover, or in other words, it is the boundary between permanent and seasonal snow.

***Classification of glaciers***

- **Continental glaciers:** These are extensive ice sheets that cover most parts of the continent. The biggest continental glaciers are seen in Greenland and Antarctica. These glaciers have an average thickness of about 4,000 m.
- **Mountain glaciers or valley glaciers:** The body of ice moving downslope under the impact of gravity along the steep rock valley walls is called a valley glacier or mountain glacier. Notable

mountain glaciers found in the Himalayas are the Kedarnath Glacier, Siachen Glacier, Punmah Glacier and Kosa Glacier.

- **Piedmont glacier:** These glaciers are formed at the foothills of the mountains only in cold frigid regions and not in tropical or temperate areas.
- **Cirque glacier:** The armchair-shaped features occupied by ice found in high-altitude regions are cirque glaciers.
- **Ice field:** Flat and extensive sheets of ice.
- **Ice shelf:** Floating mass of ice found close to the shore.

**What do you mean by the movement of a glacier?**

Glaciers move under the impact of gravity. When they advance forward, it is called the **advancement of** the **glacier**, and when they move backward, it is called the **retreat of the glacier**. Glaciers move at an average velocity of 3 to 300 m per year. However, there may be an increase in the velocity of glaciers suddenly, known as glacial surge. At that time, glaciers move at a speed of 4 to 8 km per year.

### *Erosional work of glaciers*

The erosional work of glaciers includes the mechanisms of abrasion, plucking and polishing.

A glacier erodes its valley along with erosive tools, such as gravel, pebbles and unconsolidated materials. This mechanism is called abrasion. Plucking involves the detachment of large rock particles by the moving glacier.

### *Landforms formed due to erosional work of glaciers*

**U-shaped valley:** These are the typical valleys formed by mountain glaciers. They have a flat valley floor and steep valley walls with concave slopes. It is believed these were formerly valleys formed by rivers, which were later modified by glaciers through abrasion and plucking.

**Hanging valley:** Sometimes, the tributary glaciers also join a main glacier, like that of a river, and thus, the tributary glacial valley joins the main glacial valleys of greater depth, called hanging valleys. This difference in overdeepening between the main and the tributary glacier causes the tributary glacier to hang over the main valley. This happens as the main glacier is much broader and wider, so it erodes its valley more extensively. Hence, the valley of the main glacier becomes deeper than the tributary valley.

**Cirques:** These are bowl-shaped features almost resembling an armchair, where the snow collects. Cirques can be simple cirques, compound cirques, hanging cirques or nivation cirques. The base of the cirque is devoid of any deposition, which indicates that it is purely a work of erosion. The floor of the cirque forms a basin, which is often filled with water, forming lakes after deglaciation. The head of the cirque resembling an armchair is a steep, vertical wall.

**Arêtes:** This is a sharp tooth that divides two cirque basins. Sometimes, arêtes appear in converging patterns, looking like a starfish known as **starfish arêtes**.

**Nunatak:** These are glacial islands as they look like islands in a vast extensive ice mass from a distance. They are higher peaks and mounds that are surrounded by ice from all sides.

**Col:** This is a saddle-like narrow depression formed by two headward eroding cirques. These cirques reduce an arête.

**Bergschrund:** This is mostly found in summer when there is no snow cover when a crevasse opens up along the headwall of a glacier.

**Horn:** A sharp, pointed peak that forms when several cirques gorge a mountain peak from all sides.

**Fjord:** A glacial trough found along a sea coast. They have several hanging valleys and steep-sided walls. They are shallow towards the sea but very deep towards the coast. Fjords are considered to be formed due to glacial erosion below sea level.

**Tarns:** A small mountain lake formed at the base of the cirque basin behind rivers of rock materials.

**Tills:** They are a mixture of soil that is unsorted and unstratified, made up of coarse materials.

**Paternoster lakes:** A series of small circular step-like lakes formed in individual rock basins along the course of a glaciated valley.

**Crag and tail:** These are peculiar in shape as they contain vertically eroded steep-sided walls on the up glacial side and tail-like low-height features on the down glacial side.

**Glacial grooves:** These are small depressions on extensive ice sheets.

**Erratic:** A unique rock carried by a glacial formation that is different in size and type.

**Truncated spurs:** When glaciers carve their way through rocks, cutting off the edges of interlocking spurs.

***Transportation work of glaciers***

Glaciers or moving ice carry with them large boulders of rock fragments along their journey. The debris or materials that are transported by the glaciers are called moraines. The debris collected by the glaciers are also called glacial drifts. Glacial drifts are of three types:

- **Englacial debris:** that is transported within a glacier
- **Supraglacial debris:** that is found on the surface of the glacier
- **Subglacial debris:** found at the base of a glacier

### *Depositional work of glaciers*

When a glacier starts melting or retreats, the load it is carrying starts getting deposited. These are called **moraines.** Moraines look like ridges of deposition of glacial tills. They are long and narrow.

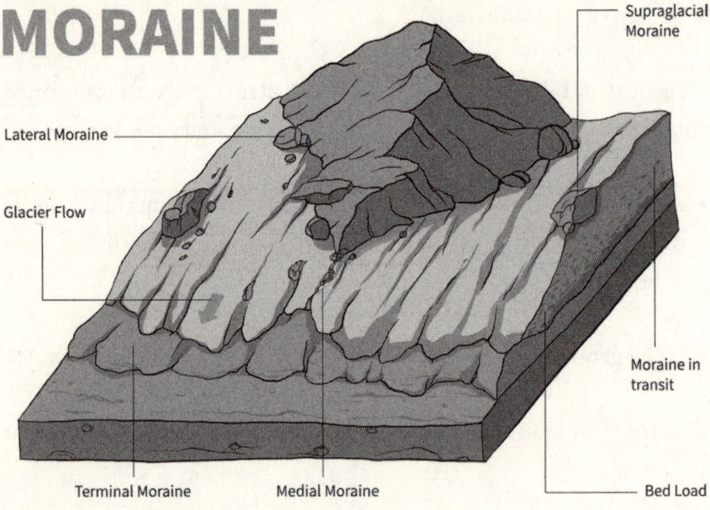


Moraine

The different **types of moraines** are:

- **Terminal moraines:** the debris gets deposited at the end of the glacier in the form of a ridge
- **Lateral moraines:** deposition of moraines on either side of a glacier
- **Medial moraines:** formed at the confluence of two glaciers
- **Ground moraine:** deposits left behind after the glaciers melt in an area

- **Interlobate moraines:** moraines deposited between two adjacent active ice lobes

**What is knob and basin topography?**

It is the topography marked by the presence of several mounds, irregular ridges separated by basins. These are formed due to recession of glaciers.

**Drumlins:** They are rounded hummocks from the deposition of glacial till. They look like spoons. They have steep slopes on one end and gentler slopes on the other end.

***Depositional landforms made by continental glaciers***

- **Till plain:** These are formed behind an end moraine. They have a low, rolling relief and unstratified coarser till.
- **Eskers:** A curving narrow deposit of coarse gravel that forms along a stream channel, developing a tunnel beneath a glacier. The sides of eskers are very steep. They are formed in regions of varying relief, covering extensive areas of valleys, swamps or lakes.
- **Kames:** A depositional feature of glaciers. These are small hills of poorly sorted unconsolidated materials of sand and gravel that are deposited at the edge of retreating ice sheets. Kames form **kames terraces** when they make narrow flat terraced ridges between the glacier and valley sides along the trough.
- **Kettles:** Isolated blocks of ice may be present on a ground moraine or on an outwash plain or valley floor. When the ice block melts after the glacier retreats, it leaves behind a depression on the outwash plain. These depressions or holes are frequently filled with water.

- **Outwash plains:** They consist of well-sorted sediments formed due to the ablation of a glacier. Glacial ablation leads to water descending through the terminal moraine. This water spreads like thin sheets and erodes the terminal moraines while moving down. The sediments eroded from terminal moraines are spread like a plain, called an outwash plain.

# 17

# KARST TOPOGRAPHY

The landforms that are formed due to the chemical weathering of calcium carbonate and magnesium carbonate rocks by surface and subsurface water are called karst topography. These are the typical landform features that are common in the limestone areas of erstwhile Yugoslavia along the eastern margins of the Adriatic Sea. Karst topography, anywhere in the world, has features similar to the karst region of erstwhile Yugoslavia.

***Conditions required for the formation of karst landforms***

1. The presence of thick, massive well-jointed and well-cemented limestone.
2. The limestones must be located above the groundwater table so that the water can disappear through sinks, crevices and joints.
3. The presence of non-porous limestone because if the limestones are porous, then the water will pass through the rocks, and the entire rock mass will become weak and collapse.
4. There should be a wide distribution of limestone.
5. The limestone should be layered, folded or fractured.
6. There should be an abundant supply of rainfall so that the required amount of water is present to dissolve the rocks.

***Distribution of karst regions:***

- Western Cuba, Jamaica
- Erstwhile Yugoslavia
- Southern France
- Northern Puerto Rico
- Central Florida, USA

In **India**, major karst regions are found in the caves of the Himalayas, Pachmarhi, Bastar District of Chhattisgarh and coastal areas of Vishakhapatnam.

**Erosional landforms**

**Lapies:** A fluted topography marked by the presence of small rills, gullies, minor ridges and pinnacles. They are formed due to limestone corrosion along the surface where the limestone is exposed. Red residual soil, called **terra rosa** is left behind as residue after weathering at the surface.

**Sinkholes and dolines:** Sinkholes are small holes that are formed due to continuous chemical weathering of the limestone rocks. The rainwater dissolves the limestone rocks along the surface, and numerous small holes called sinkholes are formed. These sinkholes can be either funnel-shaped or cylindrical.

Very large sinkholes formed due to the coalition of two or more sinkholes are called **dolines**.

In some instances, the surface of the doline is plugged due to clay deposition, as a result of which water cannot pass through. So the doline is filled with water, called **karst lakes**.

**Karst windows** are formed due to the collapse of the roof of the sinkholes because of the dissolution or collapse of bedrock.

**Uvalas:** The coalescence of several dolines due to their continuous enlargement leads to the formation of uvalas. Uvalas are elongated and large dolines. Uvalas are also referred to as compound sinkholes as they are formed due to the coalescence of several sinkholes. They are depressions with steep sides.

**Poljes:** These are more extensive depressions – bigger than dolines. They are characterized by flat alluvial floors, vertical steep side walls, irregular borders, independent drainage systems, and sometimes, a central lake. Poljes are extensively found in Yugoslavia, where they are believed to have been formed due to the tectonic movement of limestone areas.

**Karst valley:** These are U-shaped valleys developed on limestone. They are temporary in nature as they become dry when the stream disappears through sinkholes.

**Sinking creek:** Often, the sinkholes and dolines act as funnels through which the water seeps underground. When the water disappears by seeping through these sinkholes, the resultant feature formed is a sinking creek.

**Limestone caves:** These are the most extensive erosional features formed in limestone areas. Limestone caves are generally extensive. They are formed due to the corrosion of limestone by the groundwater above the underground water table. A classic example of a limestone cave in India is the Borra Caves near Vishakhapatnam. It is considered to be the deepest cavern in India.

**Ponors:** The vertical pipe-like feature that connects caves and swallow holes are ponors. The continuous extension of swallow holes downwards due to the dissolution of carbonate rocks leads to the formation of ponors.

**Natural bridge:** The collapse of roofs of limestone caves results in the formation of natural bridges. Often, they are also formed due to the disappearance of surface streams or the formation of valleys below the ground surface due to the reappearance of disappeared streams on the surface.

### Depositional landforms

**Stalactites:** These are conical pillars growing downward from the roof of a cavern. They are needle-shaped and they grow downward and end up hanging. Gradually, there is an increase in the thickness of stalactites. They look almost perpendicular to the cave roof. If the cave ceiling is slightly inclined, then elongated and somewhat inclined stalactites are formed.

**Stalagmites:** These are conical pillars growing upward from the cavern floor. Sometimes, a group of stalagmites is formed due to the crystallization of solution at different places, known as **compound stalagmites**.

> **Good to know!**
>
> Sometimes, dripstones develop sideways from stalactites and stalagmites. They are then called **helictites** and **heligmites**.

**Cave pillars:** Often, stalactites and stalagmites meet, and they form cave pillars.

**Dripstones:** These are drops of calcareous deposits along with water in dry caves.

**Curtains:** These are several needle-shaped dripstones hanging from the cave roof.

**What is a cockpit?**

The collapse of the ground surface leads to the formation of steep-sided depressions called cockpits.

**Flowstones:** When water flows out of stalagmites and floor deposits form due to the seepage of water, they are called flowstones.

# 18

# MARINE LANDFORMS: LANDFORMS MADE BY SEA WAVES

As an agent of gradation, the work of sea waves includes erosion, transportation and deposition. Sea waves dashing against the coast have a great erosive force. The four activities performed by sea waves are:

- **Abrasion:** Sea waves loaded with rock fragments and other unconsolidated materials strike against the coastal rocks.
- **Attrition:** The rock particles present in water hit against each other and break down into smaller particles.
- **Solution:** Rocks made up of limestone or calcium carbonates are subjected to dissolvement by sea waves.
- **Hydraulic action:** This is the broadening of cracks, fissures and crevices in the coastal cliff due to the attack of sea waves.

### *Erosional landforms*

**Sea cliffs:** These are hollows under the rock formed due to the rapid erosion of the lower part of the rock. The impact of the sea waves is maximum at the lower part of the rock while the upper part remains intact. Excavation in the lower part of the rock becomes larger with the passage of time. Thus, the upper part that is uneroded projects towards the sea. With time, this projected part falls into the sea, forming a vertical rocky wall-like structure called a sea cliff.

**Sea caves:** When there are both hard rocks at the top and soft rocks at the bottom of the coast, the rate of erosion is not uniform. The hard rocks remain intact, while the soft rocks get eroded fast. Due to this differential erosion, a hollow is created in the lower soft rock. When the waves dash against this hollow, the air in it gets compressed. When the waves come through the hollow, the pressure on the air expands. Due to this continuous compression of the air in the hollow, the rocks come under pressure, and they collapse. The rocks in the lower part of the hollow keep enlarging. With the passage of time, sea caves are formed.

**Sea arches:** These are broad door-like features. Sometimes, a part of the coast extends to the sea. Sea waves dash against the coast from opposite sides, which cuts a passage through the soft rocks. Over time, this passage becomes narrow and enlarged into a broad arc.

**Sea stacks:** Sometimes the roof of a sea arch is broken by erosion or due to its own weight, and a part of the rock remains standing intact. It may be the rock forming the side of an arch. These are called sea stacks. Sea stacks are of different shapes and sizes depending on the nature of the rock. Sometimes, they are in the shape of an island, but those are temporary in nature. Underwater sea stacks that are smaller in size are called **stumps**.

***Transportation by sea waves***

The work of transportation is done in two ways:

1. Removal of eroded materials and their transportation towards the sea.
2. Transportation of materials like seashells, corals and sea conches from the sea to the coast.

### *Depositional landforms*

The deposition of materials eroded from coastal areas is done by sea waves. Ocean currents also help in the deposition of these transported materials. The larger materials are deposited near the coast while the finer particles are deposited away from the coast.

**Sea beach:** A flat or undulating plain formed of gravel and sand picked up and deposited by the sea, causing the coastal area to rise above the adjoining sea, which becomes shallow.

**FACT FILE**

The Marina Beach in Chennai is the longest beach in India.
Chilika Lake and Pulicat Lake are examples of lagoons.

**Sandbars:** They form a barrier between the sea and the shore. They are caused by deposits of gravel, rocks and sand brought by waves and currents.

**Spit:** This is when one end of the sandbar extends to the sea and the other end is attached to the coast. Spits are formed due to the accumulation of sand and gravel brought by waves.

**Lagoon:** A saline shallow water lake separated from the sea or a larger water body by a sandbar or coral reef. These are an enclosed part of the sea, forming a saline water body.

**Sabkha:** Flat and barren coastal lands found in dry tropical regions formed by deposition in coastal areas.

**Coastal wetlands:** These are flat and undulating marshy lands found in the humid tropics. They are formed behind spits and bars. The seawater is shallow and remains stagnant in these wetlands. Generally, mangrove vegetation is dominant here. The water is saline, and the coast is formed of fine sediments.

# 19

# PERIGLACIAL LANDFORMS

What do you mean by **permafrost?**

Alexander von Humboldt coined the term permafrost to explain the Siberian soils. It refers to the permanently frozen subsoil. It happens when the temperature remains below zero degrees Celsius for at least two years. Permafrost can be continuous, discontinuous or sporadic.

### *Periglacial landforms*

These are mainly composed of ice found in frigid zones. The different types of ice found here are:

- **Ground ice:** These are thick sheets of ice formed due to the freezing of subsurface water.
- **Pore ice:** Subsurface water frozen in the soil pores.
- **Segregated ice:** Buried ice layers that increase in mass by water intrusion as the ground freezes.
- **Wedge ice:** Surface water entering a crack and then freezing.

### Landforms

**Pingo:** These are circular ice-made mounds formed from large areas of frozen ground. It is an Eskimo term used for isolated mounds found in the Arctic areas.

**Palsa:** These are round or elliptical mounds of peat containing thick ice lenses. They are common in swampy areas.

**Hummocks:** These are small upstanding wrinkles on the surface of permafrost. They occur due to the squeezing of the ground caused due to lateral compression exerted by the freezing of the surface. This squeezing of the surface forms small knots. They are formed either on vegetative areas or barren lands.

**Patterned ground:** An area comprising sorted and unsorted accumulations of rocks that takes the shape of polygons formed due to a system of ground ice and frost action.

**Involutions:** These are deposits of unconsolidated materials found just below the ground of permafrost regions. They are similar to hummocks and are formed due to the squeezing of unconsolidated stratified materials. The gentle squeezing of the materials with the passage of time makes the deposits lose their original shape.

**Some new terms to know!**

- **Solifluction:** The flow of soil from high elevation to low elevation during a thaw cycle.
- **Gelifluction:** The flow of soil from high elevation to low elevation during a thaw cycle with the presence of permafrost, resulting in flattening of the land.
- **Thermokarst:** Similar to the term karst, thermokarst means the thawing of frozen ground in permafrost areas due to heating or rise in temperature. It involves the collapse of the relief features due to the melting of ice.

# 20

# VOLCANOES

**Volcanoes:** A vent or an opening from which heated materials, gases, smoke, liquid lava and fragments of rocks come out of the interior of the Earth to the surface. Hot molten materials called magma are thrown out to the surface with great force from the magma chamber below. These materials, when they reach the surface, are called lava.

### *Components of a volcano*

An important component of a volcano is the presence of a volcanic cone. The volcanic materials are accumulated in the form of a cone or volcanic mountain. There is a vent or opening, which is either circular or nearly circular, almost in the centre of the cone. This is called a volcanic vent. It connects the interior of the Earth with the vent by a narrow pipe, called a volcanic pipe. All the hot molten materials are ejected through this pipe and the vent situated at the top of the pipe. When repeated explosions and weathering cause the vent to enlarge, then it is called a volcanic crater or caldera.

### *Classification of volcanoes*

Based on the **periodicity of eruptions**, volcanoes can be:

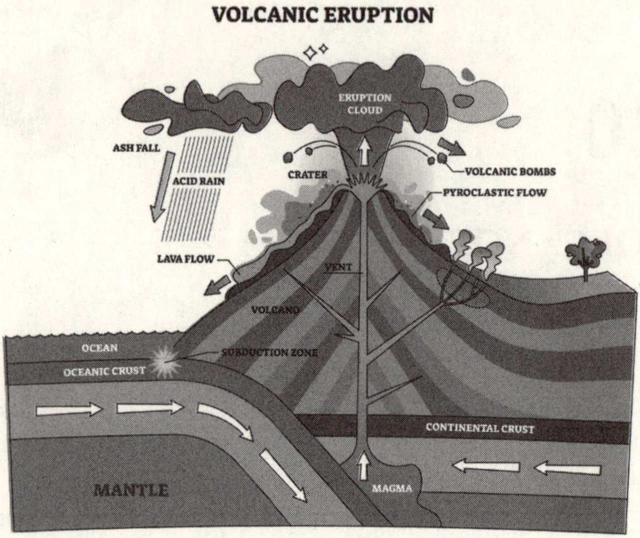


Components of a volcano

**Active volcanoes:** These are constantly erupting and ejecting volcanic lava, gases, smoke, ash and fragmented materials. Etna and Stromboli volcanoes of the Mediterranean Sea are classic examples. Stromboli is known as the lighthouse of the Mediterranean as it constantly ejects luminous and burning gases.

**Dormant volcanoes:** These have not erupted in the recent past but can erupt any time in the future. These volcanoes are most dangerous as they can erupt suddenly and violently, causing huge damage to life and property. Vesuvius is one such example, which erupted in 79 CE and then stayed dormant for a long time before erupting once again in 1631 CE.

**Extinct volcanoes:** These have not erupted in the recent geologic past. The craters of such volcanoes are filled with rainwater, forming lakes. These are dead volcanoes.

Based on the **mode of eruption.**

**Central eruption type:** These are explosive volcanoes where the materials come out through the central pipe and small opening. The crustal surface is broken because of the violent and explosive gases, which try to come out through the opening due to the accumulated pressure deep inside the Earth. These volcanoes are most destructive and very violent. The eruption becomes so rapid and violent that large quantities of fragmented rock particles, lava, dust and ashes are thrown up to several thousand meters in the sky.

***The subtypes of these volcanoes are***

**Hawaiian type:** These volcanoes are most common in the Hawaiian islands. They are generally silent, where less viscous lava and gases come out quietly. The red molten lava that comes out looks like long threads of hair as it waves due to the strong glides of wind in the air. Hawaiian people call this lava Pele [goddess of fire in Hawaii].

**Strombolian type:** These volcanoes erupt with moderate intensity. The eruptions are mostly continuous. They eject lava and fragmented materials thousands of metres into the sky, and when the lava descends, it accumulates in and around the volcanic craters.

**Vulcanian type:** These volcanoes erupt with great force and intensity. The lava here is so viscous that it immediately solidifies between two eruptions and plugs the volcanic vents. As a result, it creates an obstacle in the next eruption. Consequently, the accumulated pressure causes the materials to erupt violently, shattering the lava crusts into angular fragments, which appear as dark ash-laden clouds in the sky taking a convoluted or cauliflower shape.

**Pelean type:** This is the most violent and explosive type. They make a roaring noise when the materials come out with explosive intensity. These volcanoes are often associated with avalanches on hill slopes.

**Vesuvius type:** They are similar to the strombolian or vulcanian type. The only difference is that there is an enormous volume of gases that erupts with a massive expulsion of magma.

**Fissure type:** A slow expulsion of magma occurs along the fissure's faults and cracks. The magma spreads over the ground as lava and forms extrusive landform features. The speed of the lava depends on the nature and volume of the magma, the gradient of the slope and temperature conditions.

***Volcanic materials***

- Vapour and gases → Volcanic gases include carbon dioxide, nitrogen dioxide, hydrogen, carbon monoxides, etc.
- Magma and lava → Based on silica percentage, magma and lava can be acidic or basic. Acidic magma and lava have a greater percentage of silica.
- Magma and lava can also be classified based on their colour into felsic and mafic lava. Mafic lava has maximum fluidity and is also the hottest lava.
- Fragmented materials → Volcanic dust (very fine particles), ash (2 mm in size) and lapilli pea-size) and volcanic bombs (6 cm in size).

**FACT FILE**

In the Hawaiian language, aa lava is more viscous, while pahoehoe lava has more fluidity. It spreads like thin sheets on the surface and is thus also called ropy lava.

### *Causes of volcanic eruptions*

Just like earthquakes, volcanoes are also associated with lines of weakness. These lines of weaknesses are found along the destructive plate margins.

- Destructive plate boundaries are associated with the most violent form of volcanoes. When two plates collide against each other, the heavier plate gets subducted below the lighter plate. This subducted plate, when it reaches a certain depth inside the Earth, melts and forms magma. This magma is expelled forcefully along with explosive gases because of tremendous pressure underneath. These types of volcanic eruptions are most prevalent in the Pacific Ring of Fire. The volcanoes of the islands of the Pacific are mainly due to the collision and subsequent subduction of the Pacific Plate below the lighter Asian Plate.
- Constructive plate boundaries are associated with quiet fissure-type eruptions. This is because, here, the pressure release of magma is slow and gradual.

> **FACT FILE**
>
> The mid-oceanic ridges are always known for their supply of basaltic lava. Hence, most active volcanoes are found near these ridges. As the distance from the ridges increases, the volcanoes become more inactive and extinct.

## Terms to remember

### *Extrusive landforms*

- **Cinder cones:** The accumulation of finer particles around the volcanic vent. Cinder cones are of low height and are made up of volcanic dust, ash and pyroclastic matter.

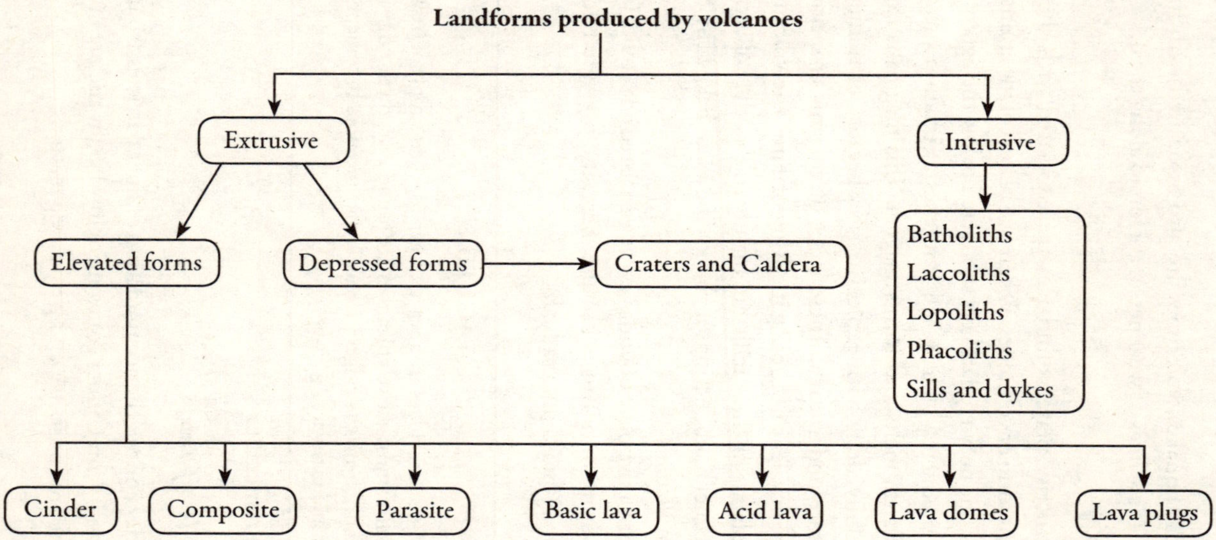

Landforms produced by volcanoes
Extrusive
Intrusive
Elevated forms
Depressed forms
Craters and Caldera
Batholiths
Laccoliths
Lopoliths
Phacoliths
Sills and dykes
Cinder
Composite
Parasite
Basic lava
Acid lava
Lava domes
Lava plugs

- **Composite cones:** The highest of all cones. They are composed of alternate layers of lava and pyroclastic materials, where the lava acts as the cementing factor for the compaction of fragmental materials.
- **Parasite cones:** Many branches of pipes come out from the main central pipe. The lava comes out through these small pipes, and these materials are found around newly formed vents located on the outer surface of the main cone.
- **Basic lava cone:** Lighter magma consisting of less silica. It cools and solidifies after spreading on a larger area.
- **Acid lava cone:** The lava is highly viscous and rich in silica. It gets immediately cooled and solidified as it has less mobility.
- **Lava domes:** They are formed due to the accumulation of solid lava around the volcanic vents.
- **Lava plugs:** Formed due to the plugging of volcanic pipes and vents when they become extinct.
- **Volcanic neck:** The lava-filled volcanic pipe.
- **Craters and caldera:** Craters are depressions found at the top of the volcanic vent. These are usually funnel-shaped. Enlarged forms of craters are called **caldera.**

> Sometimes, the crater of a volcano becomes so large that there are a few eruptions of small intensity. After a long time, several smaller cones are found within the larger one. When these formations of several small-sized craters are found within one crater, they are called craters within craters or **nested craters.**

*Intrusive landforms*

- **Batholiths:** These are dome-shaped forms of solidified magma. The side walls are very steep and almost vertical. Sometimes, the upper part of the batholiths can be seen protruding over the surface due to continuous denudation. However, their bases can never be seen as they are buried deep inside the Earth.

These batholithic domes are common in the Ranchi Plateau.

- **Laccoliths:** They are found along the bedding planes of horizontally bedded sedimentary rocks. These are mostly mushroom-shaped.
- **Phacoliths:** They are found due to magma intrusions along the anticlines and synclines of fold mountains.
- **Lopoliths:** Magma gets solidified in a shallow basin, where the central part is bent downward. These are mostly coarse-grained magma because of the slow rate of cooling.
- **Sills and dykes:** Sills are found parallel to the beds of sedimentary rocks. Thin beds of magma are called sheets. Dykes are perpendicular to the beds of sedimentary rocks.

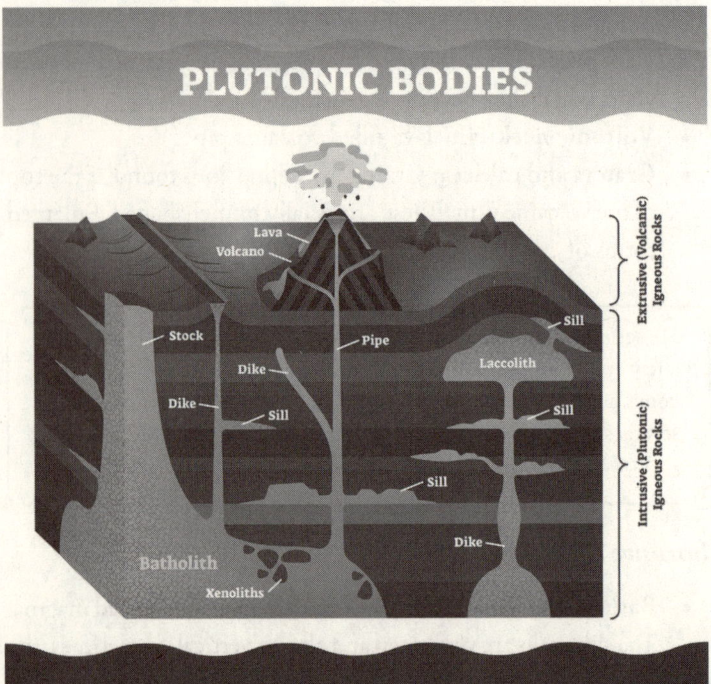


Landforms formed by volcanoes

### *Destructive effects of volcanoes*

- They may bury human structures, killing people and animals.
- They destroy crops, vegetation and forests due to expulsion of huge quantities of molten lava and pyroclastic materials that spread on the surface.
- They may trigger landslides and acid rain.
- Volcanic eruptions may generate huge seismic waves on the seafloor, leading to tsunamis.
- The radiation balance of the Earth and atmosphere may change. Greater concentrations of smoke and harmful gases in the atmosphere will affect the incoming solar radiation and the outgoing terrestrial radiation, leading to climate change. The temperature will rise, contributing to global warming.

Volcanic eruptions and the consequent solidification and cooling of lava on the surface give birth to black lava soil, which is good for cotton and sugarcane cultivation.

### *Good effects of volcanoes!*

**A few more new terms!**

**Mesas and buttes:** Mesas is a Spanish term meaning table. It is a hill characterized by an almost flat top with very steep slopes on all sides. Mesas become butts when they are subjected to continuous erosion. Both mesas and butts consist of lava-capped tops. Sometimes, the magma is injected into the sedimentary rocks through a vertical column. The upper part of the vertical column appears as a butte when the overlying rocks get eroded. These are called **volcanic buttes**.

### *World distribution of volcanoes*

Volcanoes are associated with earthquakes as both are found along the lines of weakness, like fault zones or the meeting of continent and ocean plate boundaries.

***The three major zones are***

**The Circum-Pacific Belt:** This is also called the Pacific Ring of Fire. Most of the volcanoes here are found in chains. Cotopaxi is the highest volcanic mountain in the world and is located in this belt. This zone includes the mountain belts of both the eastern and western coastal areas of the Pacific Ocean, the western coastal margins of Asia and the islands on the east coast of Asia.

**The Mid-Continental Belt:** This belt includes the Alpine mountain chain and the Mediterranean Sea. Here, volcanic eruptions occur due to the convergence of the Asiatic, Indian and African plates. The famous volcanoes of Stromboli, Etna and Vesuvius fall under this belt.

**The Mid-Atlantic Belt:** This has mainly fissure eruption-type volcanoes along the divergent plate boundaries.

**What are geysers and hot springs?**

Geysers and hot springs are features that constantly spout hot water and vapour. These features are mainly found in regions that are typically associated with vulcanicity. The hot water and steam are rich in sulphur and good for patients with arthritis.

The main difference between geysers and hot springs is that in hot springs, there is continuous sprouting of water, while in geysers, the water sprouts periodically along with hot steam. The geyser takes out water and steam from a narrow vent that is connected to an underground aquifer by a pipe. This pipe is called a geyser pipe.

# 21

## EARTHQUAKES AND SEISMIC WAVES

Earthquakes are sudden vibrations felt on the surface of the Earth ranging from a mild tremor to a destructive motion. They are caused due to the transmission of energy waves through the surface layer of the Earth.

### *Important terms to remember*

- **Focus:** the place of origin of an earthquake
- **Epicentre:** the place on the ground that is perpendicular to the focus
- **Seismic waves:** the waves generated during an earthquake
- **Seismology:** the science dealing with the study of seismic waves
- **Seismograph:** an instrument to measure the seismic waves

> The **Richter scale** is used to measure the intensity of an earthquake. The scale ranges between 0 and 9.

### *Causes of an earthquake*

Earthquakes are mainly caused due to two reasons:

Tectonic activities like folding or faulting and volcanic activity.

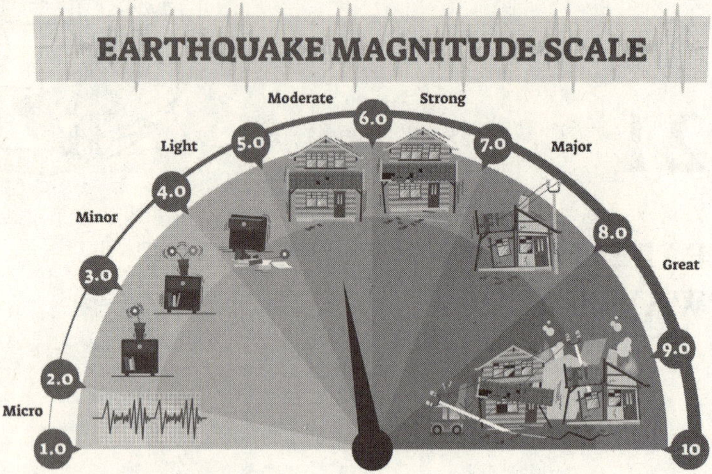


As we know, the Richter scale measures the intensity or magnitude of an earthquake. The diagram above illustrates what each unit means.

But the most plausible answer to the cause of an earthquake is related to the plate tectonic theory. We know that the Earth's crust is made up of several lithosphere slabs, which float over the asthenosphere. These plates are either oceanic or continental. They are constantly moving, either towards or away from each other. All tectonic activities take place along the plate margins.

- High-magnitude earthquakes are formed along the margins of destructive plate boundaries. When two plates move towards each other and collide, the heavier plate is subducted below the lighter plate. This zone of subduction becomes the focal point of tectonic activities.
- Moderate earthquakes are found along the constructive plate boundaries as the movement of the plates away from each other allows the rate of rupture to be low.

Earthquakes are all about the release of energy waves. Let us know about the type of seismic waves generated at the time of an earthquake:

- **P waves:** These are longitudinal waves. They can travel through both solid and liquid mediums.
- **S waves:** These are transverse waves. They can travel through solids but not through liquid mediums.
- **Surface waves:** These are long waves mainly found on the surface of the Earth. They are the most violent and destructive waves as they travel the longest distance. However, their speed is lesser than P and S waves.

**Classification of earthquakes:**

| Based on | Types | Characteristics |
|---|---|---|
| Causes | A. Natural earthquakes | Formed due to endogenetic forces. |
| | Volcanic earthquakes | Due to volcanic eruptions. The intensity of such earthquakes depends on the intensity of the volcanic eruption. |
| | Tectonic earthquakes | Due to the movement of tectonic plates or faulting activity. |
| | Isostatic earthquakes | Sudden disturbance in the isostatic balance, triggering an earthquake. |
| | Plutonic earthquakes | Deep-focus earthquakes at a depth of 240–660 km. |

| | | |
|---|---|---|
| | B. Artificial earthquakes | Due to human activities like underground drilling of oil, mining, blasting of rocks for constructional purposes, etc. |
| Focus (according to Gutenberg) | Moderate earthquakes | Foci at a depth of 0–50 km. |
| | Intermediate earthquakes | Foci at a depth of 50–250 km. |
| | Deep-focus earthquakes | Foci at a depth of 250–700 km. |
| Human casualties | Moderately hazardous earthquakes | Human casualty is less than 50,000. |
| | Highly hazardous earthquakes | Human casualty is between 50,000 to 1,00,000. |
| | Most hazardous earthquakes | Human casualty is above 1,00,000. |

**World distribution of earthquakes**

1. **The Circum-Pacific Belt:** This includes the coastal margins of North and South America and eastern Asia. More than 65% of the earthquakes occur here. It is a zone of high tectonic movements, active volcanoes, as well as the subduction zones of destructive plate boundaries. This zone is famously called the Pacific Ring of Fire.
2. **Mid-Continental Belt or the Alpine-Himalayan Belt:** This is the zone of subduction of continental plates.

The earthquakes occurring in the Indian Himalayas are due to the northward movement of the Indian plate, as it is getting subducted below the Asiatic plate. The Himalayan Belt is an extensive area of some complex faults along the zone of collision.

***India is divided into five damage risk zones for earthquakes.***

| Zone I: Of least damage | Zone II: Of low damage | Zone III: Of moderate damage | Zone IV: Of high damage | Zone V: Of very high damage |
|---|---|---|---|---|
| Parts of Bihar, Punjab, Haryana, Uttar Pradesh, some portions of the plains of West Bengal, delta areas of the Godavari | Southern Punjab, Haryana, Uttar Pradesh, coastal districts of Tamil Nadu, Odisha | Most of Madhya Pradesh, Karnataka, Maharashtra | Jammu and Kashmir, Himachal Pradesh, hilly areas of Sikkim, Bihar and Uttarakhand | Entire north-eastern part, Kutch region of Gujarat, western north Bihar, parts of Jammu and Kashmir |

**Did you know?**

Although the plains of West Bengal fall under the least damage zone, a devastating earthquake struck the then Calcutta on 11 October 1737, killing almost 3,00,000 people!

***Destructive effects of earthquakes***

- Damage to human structures
- Loss of life and property
- Landslides and debris falls
- Deformation of ground surface
- Flash floods
- Fires breaking out

**What are tsunamis?**

Series of ocean waves are triggered by earthquakes on the seafloor, which causes an upwelling of sea waves as high as 100 ft onto land. These waves cause massive destruction when they crash ashore. Since the Pacific Ocean is notorious for its Ring of Fire, tsunamis are most common here. When tsunamis appear in mid-ocean, they are only a foot high, but as they approach the shore, they slow down by entering the shallow water and start collecting energy and pace. The tops of the waves move faster than the bottom.

The retreating of sea waves is often seen as a warning sign of a tsunami because the trough of the tsunami often reaches the shore first. It creates a vacuum that sucks the coastal water seaward and exposes the seafloor.

A tsunami usually comprises a series of waves called **wave trains**, so its destructive force increases with each successive wave.

# HYDROLOGY

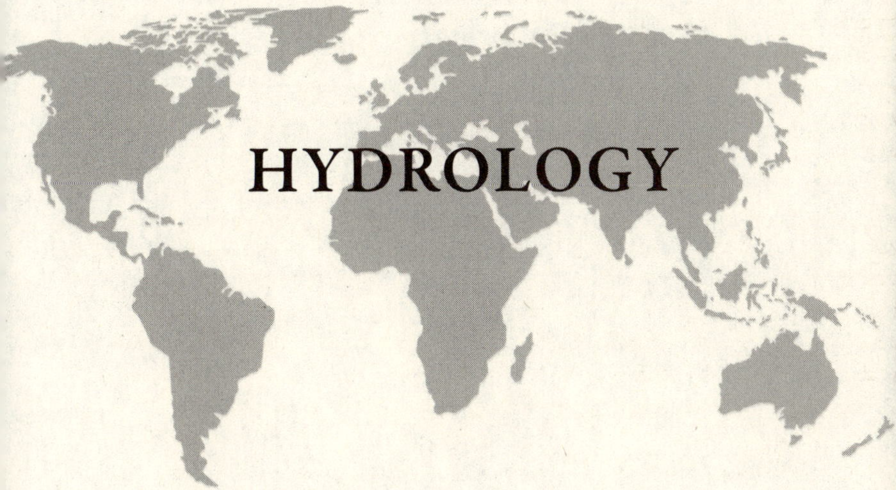

# 22

# MAJOR DRAINAGE SYSTEMS AND DRAINAGE PATTERNS

*Drainage systems of the world*

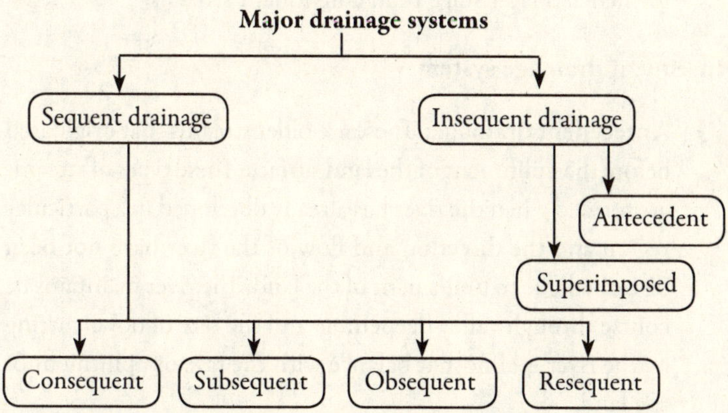


- **Sequent drainage:** The drainage that follows the regional slope and the normal geologic structure.
- **Insequent drainage:** The drainage that does not follow the regional slope and normal geologic structure.

**Sequent drainage system**

- **Consequent streams:** These are the first streams to be formed in a particular region. These streams follow the regional slope. Consequent streams developed in folded regions flow through the synclinal troughs.
- **Subsequent streams:** The streams that are formed after the master consequent streams. Subsequent streams, according to some geologists, are formed either parallel to the master consequent streams or have joined the master consequent streams at right angles.
- **Obsequent streams:** These are streams that flow in the opposite direction to the master consequent stream.
- **Resequent streams:** These are tributary streams that flow in the direction of the master consequent streams. They are formed at a later stage than consequent streams.

**Insequent drainage system**

- **Antecedent drainage:** These are older streams that originated before the upliftment of the land surface. These types of streams are formed when the river has already developed in a particular region and the direction and flow of the river have not been disturbed due to upliftment of the land. The river maintains its course through valley deepening, and the rate of downcutting by the river is almost at balance with the rate of upliftment of the land.
- **Superimposed drainage:** These are anti-consequent drainage systems. These types of streams develop when there is a marked contrast between the upper geologic formation and the lower geologic formation. The nature and characteristics of the consequent river valley of the upper geologic structure is superimposed on the completely different lower geologic structure. The upper geologic structure may comprise

horizontally bedded sedimentary rocks while the lower geologic structure may be either bedded sedimentary rock or igneous intrusions. The streams continue their action of downcutting and develop valleys. With time, the lower structure is exposed to the river and extends to the lower geologic structure. The valley developed on the upper structure is superimposed on the lower part.

Let us have a quick look at the examples of different drainage systems from India.

| Type of Drainage System | Examples from India |
|---|---|
| Consequent drainage | River Godavari in the Deccan Plateau |
| Subsequent drainage | The Song River in the Dehradun Valley is the subsequent stream to the River Ganga |
| Obsequent drainage | Suru River, a tributary of the River Indus |
| Resequent drainage | Asan River, a tributary of the Yamuna River |
| Antecedent drainage | Indus, Sutlej and other Himalayan rivers |
| Superimposed drainage | The Damodar and Subarnarekha rivers |

**Drainage patterns**

- **Dendritic drainage pattern:** It is the most common of all the drainage patterns. The word 'dendritic' is derived from the Greek word 'dendron' meaning 'a tree'. Dendritic patterns look like the branches of a tree. The main river is the trunk of the tree, and the tributaries are its branches. A dendritic drainage pattern is developed on homogenous rock structure. Both the Ganga and Godavari have dendritic drainage patterns.
- **Trellis drainage pattern:** These are developed on folded

structures where the rock strata are not homogenous. These are long, straight rivers joined by the tributaries at right angles. They develop on a terrain consisting of anticline ridges separated by synclinal valleys. Example: Seine River in the Paris Basin.

- **Parallel drainage pattern:** These are developed on steep slopes with the master stream and its tributaries flowing almost parallel to each other for a particular distance till they meet. These types of drainage patterns are commonly seen in the great plains of India.
- **Radial drainage pattern:** These are formed on a dome shape or conical hill. The streams flow down in different directions, like the spokes of a wheel. Radial drainage is found in Sri Lanka.
- **Centripetal drainage pattern:** It is just the opposite of the radial drainage pattern. Because, unlike in radial drainage where the streams come out or radiate outward from a dome or a highland, in centripetal drainage, the streams meet at a depression or a basin.
- **Annular drainage pattern:** Here, the tributaries of the master river are developed in the form of a circle around a dome. They are found in areas having alternate bands of hard rock and soft rock.
- **Barbed drainage pattern:** Here, the tributaries flow in an opposite direction to the master river. The tributaries join the master river in a hook shape.
- **Pinnate drainage pattern:** These are found in steep, narrow valleys. The tributaries from the steep slopes of the parallel ridges join the main stream at an acute angle.
- **Herringbone drainage pattern:** These are a series of streams that flow in a V-shape pattern. They resemble the rib bones of herring fish. The master consequent stream develops on parallel longitudinal valleys while the tributaries, after originating from the hill slopes of the bordered parallel ridges, join the master consequent almost at right angles.

# CLIMATOLOGY

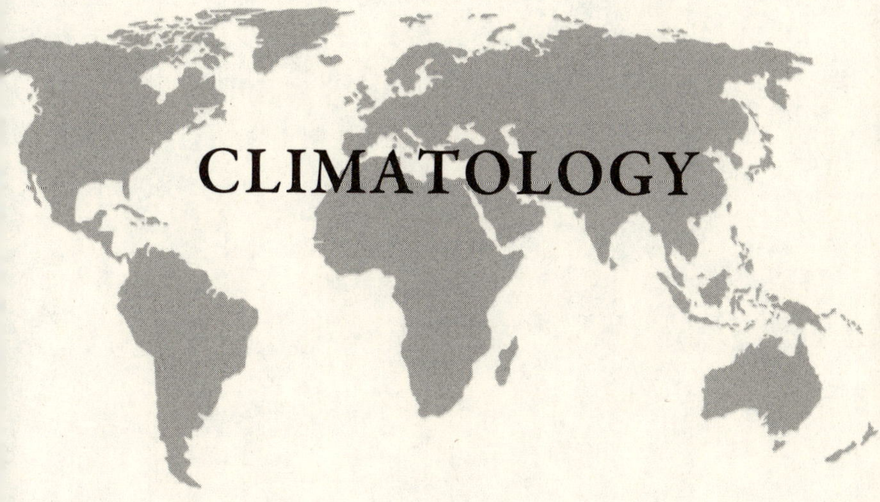

# 23

# ATMOSPHERE: IMPORTANCE, COMPOSITION AND LAYERS

The atmosphere is the mixture of gases that envelopes the Earth from the surface to at least 1,000 km. More than 99% of the atmospheric mass is found within 32 km due to the gravitational pull of the Earth.

The importance of atmosphere:

- The atmosphere acts as a protective layer of the Earth, safeguarding us from the ultraviolet rays of the sun.
- It provides us with oxygen, nitrogen, carbon dioxide, water vapour and all the necessary gases and components needed for the survival of life. For plants to make food through the process of photosynthesis, plants use $CO_2$ and release $0_2$, which are used by humans and animals for respiration. Nitrogen is needed for soil fertility and for the production of amino acids and protein.
- It maintains a steady temperature and does not make the Earth too hot or too cold for survival.
- It prevents the solar rays from escaping the Earth during daytime and helps in outgoing terrestrial radiation, thus maintaining a perfect heat balance.
- The atmosphere protects us from meteor attacks.

- It promotes the water cycle and even allows sound waves to travel so we can hear.
- Without atmosphere, there would have been no weather, no clouds, no rainfall.
- Without atmosphere, the weathering of rocks would not have occurred. Consequently, there would not have been soil formation. The entire Earth would have remained unaltered and pristine without any soil formation, denudation or erosion.

***Composition of the atmosphere***

| Main gases | Amount in % | Secondary gases | Amount in % |
|---|---|---|---|
| Nitrogen | 78.1 | Argon | 0.9 |
| | | Carbon dioxide | 0.03 |
| Oxygen | 20.9 | Hydrogen | 0.01 |
| | | Neon | 0.0018 |
| | | Helium | 0.0005 |
| | | Ozone | 0.00006 |

**Water vapour:** It is the source of all clouds and precipitation. It regulates the hydrological cycle. However, the composition of the atmosphere varies from one place to another, like in desert areas, the composition of water vapour is less.

**Dust particles:** These contribute to the vibrant colours of the sky at dawn and dusk. Dust particles act as the condensation nuclei. These particles absorb terrestrial radiation.

*Layers of the atmosphere*

**Troposphere**

1. The lowest layer of the atmosphere. Its average height is 16 km over the equator and 6 km over the poles.
2. All the weather phenomena occur in this layer.
3. Temperature decreases with an increase in height at the rate of about 6.5°C per 1,000 m. Called a normal lapse rate.
4. The word 'troposphere' means 'zone of mixing' while the word 'tropopause' means 'where mixing stops'.

**Stratosphere**

1. The layer just above the troposphere. This layer is particularly devoid of any weather phenomena.
2. It is suitable for flying aircraft.
3. The lower portion of the stratosphere has the maximum concentration of ozone and is called the ozonosphere.
4. Ozone is found between the limits of 15 km to 35 km from sea level.
5. The temperature rises with increasing height in the stratosphere, which stops again at the stratopause.
6. There is the presence of feeble air and cirrus clouds in the lower stratosphere.
7. The lower layer of the stratosphere has the maximum concentration of ozone, so it is also called the ozonosphere.

**Mesosphere**

1. The coldest layer of the atmosphere.
2. The uppermost layer of the mesosphere where the temperature goes down to –80°C.
3. In mesopause, which is the uppermost limit of the mesosphere, the temperature again starts increasing with increasing height.

**Ionosphere**

1 It extends from 80 km to 640 km.
2. This layer reflects the radio waves back to Earth.
3. In this layer, the temperature increases with an increase in height as much as 1700°C in its upper limit.

**Exosphere**

1. The uppermost layer of the atmosphere.
2. The density is very low, and the air is almost rarefied.

**What is ozone?**

Ozone, consisting of three oxygen atoms, is a blue irritating gas with a pungent odour. It absorbs most of the harmful UV rays of the sun. The ozone molecules are unstable as they are constantly formed and destroyed in the stratosphere. The gradual depletion of ozone is known as ozone depletion. The breaking down of ozone into $O_2$ and O results in the depletion of ozone. The main reasons behind ozone depletion are the use of chlorofluorocarbons in refrigerators, air conditioners, nitrogen oxides and halons.

# 24

## INSOLATION AND HEAT BUDGET

### *Factors affecting the distribution of insolation*

**Insolation** (also known as incoming solar radiation) received at the Earth's surface decreases from the equator towards the poles due to various factors.

**The angle of the rays of the sun:** The angle of the sun's rays decreases from the equator towards the poles. The sun's rays are more or less vertical at the equator, but they slant at the poles. This causes the amount of insolation received at the equator to be more than at the poles. The simple reason being the vertical rays concentrate on a smaller area where the intensity of heat is higher, while in the poles, the oblique rays spread over a large area, so the intensity of the heat is less.

**Length of day:** The amount of insolation will be greater when the length of the day is longer and vice versa. The length of day and night is almost the same at the equator throughout the year, while it increases as one marches towards the North Pole due to the northward apparent movement of the sun at the time of summer solstice. During the winter solstice, it is just the reverse when the length of the night is maximum at the North Pole.

**FACT FILE**

Even if the length of the day is more at the poles, the amount of insolation will be less at the poles due to two reasons:

- The ice cover reflects back most of the rays.
- The sun's rays have to travel a long distance, so they remain parallel to the ground surface.

**Distance between the Earth and the sun:** Since the orbit of the Earth around the sun is elliptical, the period when it is closest to the sun is called the **PERIHELION (in January)** and the time when it is farthest from the sun is called the **APHELION (in July)**. When it is supposed to be receiving maximum insolation in January (as we are closest to the sun), we don't feel the heat as it is winter at that time in the northern hemisphere due to the inclination of the Earth's axis.

**Effects of the atmosphere:** All of the sun's rays are not absorbed by the atmosphere. They are partly absorbed, partly reflected and partly scattered by the atmosphere.

- **Absorption:** If we take the total units of incoming solar radiation to be 100 units, then out of this, about 14% is absorbed by the Earth's atmospheric gases and water vapour (mostly ozone).
- **Scattering:** Some portions of insolation, around 23%, are scattered by dust particles and haze. 6% of it is sent back to space while 17% reaches the Earth's surface. Scattering is possible when the diameter of the suspended dust particles and molecules of the gases present are shorter than the wavelength of solar radiation.
- **Reflection:** When the diameters of the dust particles are longer than the wavelength of the incoming solar radiation,

some portions are sent back to space while some linger in the lower layers of the atmosphere. This is called diffuse reflection.

**What is an albedo?**

The portion of energy that is reflected back is called **albedo**. The albedo of ice-covered areas is always more than that of forest areas.

**Why does the sky look blue?**

The blue light of the incoming shortwave length is more scattered than red light. The brilliant and vibrant hues of sunrise and sunset are due to the scattering of all colours except red and orange.

### *Heat zones of the Earth*

- **Torrid zone/Tropical zone:** Extends between the Tropic of Cancer (23.5°N) and Tropic of Capricorn (23.5°S). Here, the sun's rays are almost vertical throughout the year. The equator is the zone of no seasons. The temperature remains hot and humid throughout the year in the equator.
- **Temperate zone:** Extends between 23.5° and 66.5° N and S in both hemispheres. There are marked seasonal contrasts with the northward and southward apparent movement of the sun during the solstices. The range of temperature is high between summer and winter.
- **Frigid zone:** extending between 66.5° latitudes and the poles in both hemispheres. The sun's rays slant throughout the year. Days and nights are of six months duration at the poles. The ground remains almost covered with snow at the poles throughout the year.

### *How is the balance achieved?*

It is important to remember that although the Earth maintains its balance between the incoming solar radiation and outgoing terrestrial radiation, the amount of insolation always depends on the latitude. In the tropics, the amount of insolation is higher than the outgoing radiation. So it is a region of heat surplus while the poles are regions of heat deficit.

| **Incoming solar radiation** | **Units in %** |
|---|---|
| Let us take the total heat received | 100 |
| Reflected back to space<br>Back to space from the top of the atmosphere<br>Reflected by clouds<br>Reflected by snow and ice cover | **35**<br>6<br>27<br>2 |
| Reaches the Earth's surface | **51** |
| Absorption by gases, water vapour and dust particles | **14** |
| | **100** |
| **Outgoing terrestrial radiation** | |
| Terrestrial radiation<br>Absorption by the atmosphere<br>Directly goes to space | 51<br>34<br>17 |
| The atmosphere radiates back to space | 48 |
| Solar unit reflected back to space by atmosphere | 17 + 48 = 65 |

**What is a thermal anomaly?**

It is the difference between the mean temperature of latitude and the actual temperature of a place located at that latitude.

For example, if the mean temperature of latitude 30°N is 20°C and the actual temperature of place A located at that latitude is 30°C, then the thermal anomaly is 10°C.

The imaginary lines joining places with the same thermal anomaly are called **isanomals.**

**Heat budget of the Earth**

The heat budget of the Earth is the balance between the incoming solar radiation absorbed by the Earth and outgoing terrestrial radiation. If this balance is not achieved, then the Earth will become too hot or too cold to survive.

***Horizontal distribution of temperature***

- **Latitude:** The angle of incidence decreases from the equator to the poles. The higher the angle of incidence, the greater is the temperature. So, as the latitude increases, the temperature starts falling.
- **Land and sea differences:** The land gets heated and cools down more rapidly than water bodies. So the land temperature is always higher than water in the daytime, and it is higher in water at night-time. Similarly, there is a seasonal contrast between land and water temperature. During summer, the land is heated more than the oceans. This contrast between land and sea temperatures causes differences in the rate of heating.
- **Relief and altitude:** We have already learnt about the normal lapse rate in the previous portion. So we feel cold as we go up to higher elevations. The presence of a higher relief prevents the cold winds from entering, like the Himalayas prevent the chilly winds from entering India from central Asia.
- **Ocean currents:** Warm ocean currents raise the temperature of a place along which they flow while cold ocean currents reduce the temperature of the coasts along which they flow.
- **Winds:** Winds transport heat from one place to another, so they also affect the temperature of a place.
- **Vegetation cover:** Soils devoid of any vegetation cover receive heat more rapidly and support radiation from the Earth, while dense vegetation cover prevents heat from escaping.

- **Gradient of slope:** A steep slope will cause more angle of incidence of the sun's rays than gentler slopes.
- **Distance from the sea:** Places located near the coast will have maritime climate because there is more mixing of air masses between the sea and the coastal land. As the distance from the the sea increases, the range of temperature becomes more.

***Vertical distribution of temperature***

Temperature decreases with an increase in height in the troposphere, but the rate at which it decreases depends on the seasons, duration of day and location. As the distance from the Earth's surface increases, the temperature of air goes down. This is proof that air is heated from the surface of the Earth as there is a transfer of heat from the surface to the air above through the processes of conduction, convection and radiation.

The air in the lower layers of the atmosphere contains more water vapour, gases and dust particles, which absorb the outgoing longwave terrestrial radiation. These decrease rapidly as we go up. Thus, the temperature of the lower layers of the atmosphere is more than the upper layers due to greater absorption of terrestrial radiation in the lower layers.

***Inversion of temperature***

We know that the temperature decreases with increasing height, but sometimes, it is the opposite of the normal trend, that is, the temperature is higher in the upper layers. This occurs due to certain factors: long winter nights, clear skies, dry air and the absence of winds. This leads to quick radiation of the heat from the surface, so the air becomes cooler and denser at the surface while warm, light air floats above. This phenomenon is of shorter duration because during daytime, the Earth's surface will get heated again and will warm up the cold air near the surface. Inversion of temperature is common at the bottom of valleys. The valley floor remains colder than the top because of the descent of cold, dense air at the bottom and due to a lack of heat loss through terrestrial radiation. Inversion of temperature causes frost, which is not economically viable for fruit orchards in valleys.

***Relevance of inversion of temperature***

- Urban smog is formed due to the inversion of temperature. Fog is created due to the rising of warm air and sinking of cold air below. The warm air is cooled from below due to the presence of lower cold air. This causes condensation and tiny droplets are formed around the smoke and dust on long winter nights. Smoke and dust are generated by houses when people light chimneys to keep themselves warm.
- Gases like sulphur dioxide are poisonous and create health hazards.
- Inversion of temperature also causes atmospheric stability and anticyclonic conditions. Atmospheric stability does not promote wind circulation, and hence, rainfall is affected. This results in aridity.
- It also promotes frost conditions in lower valleys. This affects fruit cultivation in the valleys.

***Types of inversion of temperature***

Temperature inversion can be **ground surface inversion** and occurs in static atmospheric conditions with no vertical or horizontal air movement.

**Upper air inversion** can be either thermal inversion caused by the ozone layer or mechanical upper air inversion due to the subsidence of air and turbulence at higher heights in the atmosphere.

It can be also **cyclonic inversion** or **valley inversion**. Cyclonic inversion is common in temperate regions, caused due to temperate cyclones. Temperate cyclones are formed due to the meeting of two different air masses. Valley inversion occurs in hilly regions due to vertical air movements and radiation.

# 25

# ATMOSPHERIC PRESSURE AND WINDS

The weight of a column of air at a given place and time is called **atmospheric pressure**. It is measured by an instrument called the barometer. Atmospheric pressure is measured as force per unit area. The unit used for measuring pressure is a millibar.

***Factors responsible for variation in air pressure***

- **Air temperature:** There is an inverse relationship between pressure and temperature. At higher temperatures, the air becomes warmer and lighter. Lighter air expands in volume and rises, creating a vacuum. Hence, equatorial regions have low pressure and polar regions have high pressure.
- **Earth's rotation:** The Earth's rotation creates a centrifugal force. This creates deflection of air from its original place, causing pressure to decrease. The Earth's rotation causes convergence and divergence of moving air. Areas of convergence create low pressure and vice versa.
- **Pressure of water vapour:** Air with more water vapour has lower pressure and that of lower quantity has higher pressure. In winter, the continents are much colder and tend to develop high-pressure areas. In summer, oceans are cooler than the continents, so high pressure develops over oceans.

*Pressure belts of the world*

- **Equatorial low-pressure belt:** This belt is called the **doldrums** or zone of calm as there is an absence of moving surface wind here. The sun shines almost vertically throughout the year on the equator. So the air remains warm near the surface, gets heated up, expands and rises, producing low pressure. This belt extends from 0° to 10° N and S latitudes. This zone is also called the Intertropical Convergence Zone as the winds from subtropical high-pressure belts converge here. It is a zone of aridity and atmospheric stability.
- **The subtropical high-pressure belt:** This belt extends from the tropics to 35° latitude in both hemispheres. The warm air rising from the equator condenses, cools down and settles down in the subtropical belt due to the deflection of winds by the Earth's rotation. This creates a zone of high pressure. This belt is also called the **Horse Latitudes**.
- **The subpolar low-pressure belt:** This belt extends between 45 °N and the Arctic Circle and 45° S and the Antarctic Circle in the northern and southern hemispheres respectively. The belt is produced due to the deflection of winds from the subtropical high-pressure belt. This belt is more developed in the southern hemisphere because of the dominance of water bodies. There are small centres of low pressure over the oceans in the northern hemisphere. Due to great contrasts between sea and land temperature during the northern summer, the low-pressure belt becomes discontinuous and is found in small cells, while in winter, the temperature contrasts between land and sea is minimal, and so, the low-pressure belt becomes continuous in the northern hemisphere. Since this belt lies near the poles, the temperature remains low here, so the pressure is supposed to be high. But this belt is not thermally induced. It is dynamically induced as it is triggered by the rotation of the Earth and Coriolis force.

- **Polar high-pressure belt:** Very low temperature makes the air at the surface cold. Thus, cold air being heavier, it compresses and stays closer to the ground. The denser cold air creates high pressure in the poles.

> **FACT FILE**
>
> Imaginary lines joining places with the same temperature are called **isotherms.**
> Imaginary lines joining places with the same atmospheric pressure are called **isobars.**

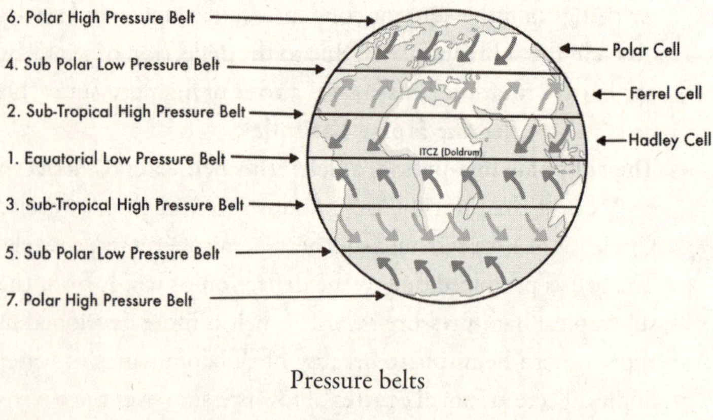


Pressure belts

### Have you ever thought?

### Why is the subtropical low-pressure belt called the horse latitudes?

As already mentioned, the subtropical high-pressure belt is a zone of calm and feeble air, so in ancient times, whenever traders would pass through this zone in their ships, they would throw away some of the horses they carried so that the weight of the ships would decrease and they could sail through the calm waters.

### *Shifting of pressure belts*

The northward and southward migration of the overhead sun causes the shifting of the pressure belts at about 5°. All pressure belts move northward during the summer solstice due to the northward migration of the overhead sun, except the polar high-pressure belt. Similarly, during the winter solstice, all pressure belts, except the polar high, shift southward. At the time of vernal and autumnal equinoxes, the pressure belts remain in almost the same position.

The reason the Mediterranean region receives rainfall in winter is the shifting of the pressure belt southward, so it comes under the influence of the westerlies that bring moist rain-bearing wind.

**Pressure gradient:** Pressure gradient means the difference in pressure between two places. The steep pressure gradient is represented by closely spaced isobars, while the low-pressure gradient is represented by widely spaced isobars. The direction of pressure movement is always perpendicular to isobars. Wind always has the tendency to blow from regions of high pressure to regions of low pressure.

> The slope of the land facing the wind is called the **windward** slope, and the slope on the other side is called the **leeward** slope.

> Wind always gets deflected due to the rotation of the Earth along its axis, as well as due to the pressure gradient. The force that deflects wind is called the Coriolis force. Due to this force, wind is deflected to the right in the northern hemisphere and to the left in the southern hemisphere. The direction of the pressure gradient is also from high pressure to low pressure.

**Fact:** We know that the speed of rotation of the Earth is maximum at the equator and decreases at the poles. When the wind reaches the equator, it lags behind because the ground beneath moves faster and ahead of the winds due to high rotational speed of the Earth and absence of Coriolis force at the equator. In contrast, when winds are travelling towards the poles, the winds move ahead of the ground as it moves slower due to lower rotational speed. This law was propounded by **Ferrel**, where he said, **'If one stands with one's back towards the direction from where winds are coming, they (winds) are deflected to the right in the northern hemisphere and to the left in the southern hemisphere.'**

***Planetary winds***

**The trade winds/easterlies:** These winds blow from the subtropical high-pressure belt to the equatorial low-pressure belt. The word 'trade' means 'track'. Due to Coriolis force, the northern trade winds move away from subtropical high in a north-east direction, and in the southern hemisphere, the trade winds move from subtropical high pressure to equatorial low pressure from the south-east direction. Trade winds are onshore winds when they blow along the eastern margins, so they bring rainfall. They are offshore when they blow along the western margins. Hence, most of the deserts of the world are found along the western margins of the continents.

**The westerlies:** These winds blow poleward from subtropical high pressure in the northern hemisphere and are deflected to the right and blow from the south-west. In the southern hemisphere, these winds are deflected to the left and blow from the north-west. Westerlies are more complicated in the northern hemisphere due to the dominance of land. They are less effective in summer and more active in winter. The westerlies bring rainfall to the Mediterranean lands in winter. In the southern hemisphere, the westerlies become vigorous due to the dominance of water bodies. They bring gale and high-velocity winds known by different names in different latitudes.

**Classification of winds**

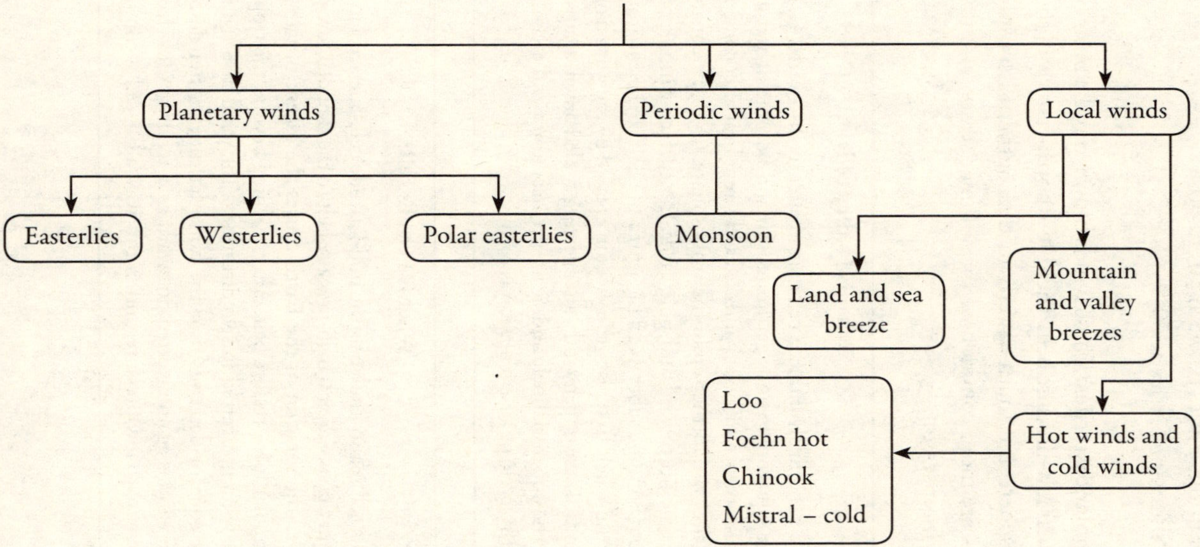

- Roaring Forties between 40° to 50°S
- Furious Fifties between 50° to 60°S
- Shrieking Sixties at 60°S

**The polar easterlies:** These winds blow from the polar high to the subpolar low-pressure belt. They blow north-easterly in the northern hemisphere and south-easterly in the southern hemisphere. Polar winds are more common in the summer season and disappear in the winter season.

**What is Hadley cell?**

It is a thermally induced cell named after its discoverer, G. Hadley. The equatorial winds get heated up and become lighter and rise. These warm and moist winds releases latent heat after condensation, so they rise further up in the troposphere. Over the equator, they diverge northward and poleward. The surface winds meanwhile blow from the subtropical high-pressure belt to the equatorial low-pressure belt to replace the vacuum created by the warm equatorial winds. These upper winds, after getting cooled down, again descend to the equatorial belt and again get heated up and ascend. So an entire cycle of air circulation is formed.

**What is Ferrel's cell?**

This cell is also known as the mid-latitude cell. Surface winds blow from the subtropical high-pressure belt to the subpolar low-pressure belt. The rotation of the Earth causes the ascent of wind at the subpolar low-pressure belt. After reaching beyond the tropopause, the wind is diverted in two directions. The wind diverted towards the equator descends near the horse latitudes. After descending, the wind is again diverted poleward as it tends to blow from high pressure to low pressure, and in this way, a full cell is completed.

**What is a polar cell?**

It involves the circulation of winds between 60° and the poles. Cold winds blow from the polar high-pressure belt to the subpolar low-pressure belt. The general direction of the wind due to Coriolis force is easterly. These cold winds meet the warm westerlies at 60° to 65°, and a front is formed. This becomes the origin of temperate cyclones. The wind ascends from the subpolar low-pressure belt, and due to the Earth's rotation, it is diverted equatorward and poleward. The poleward upper air descends at the pole, and in this way, a full cell is completed.

### *Periodic winds*

**Monsoon winds:** The word 'monsoon' is derived from the Arabic word 'mausim', meaning seasons. These winds change their direction with the change of seasons.

We cannot understand the monsoon mechanism without getting to know what our country experiences in the monsoon months. Because, after all, India is a monsoon country!

### *Origin of the Indian monsoon*

- The role of the Himalayas and the Tibetan Plateau as physical barriers.
- Differential heating and cooling of large land masses and water bodies.
- Upper air jet stream in the troposphere.

**Summer monsoons:** When the sun shines vertically over the Tropic of Cancer, intense low pressure is developed over the Indian subcontinent. This is due to intense heating of the land during April–May. The surrounding seas are comparatively cooler and develop a high pressure over them. Winds tend to blow from high-pressure to low-pressure areas. So moisture-laden winds start blowing from the sea towards the land during May–June. These winds are south-east trade winds, and when they cross the equator, they become south-westerly due to Coriolis force and rush towards India. The winds get divided into two branches – the Bay of Bengal branch and the Arabian Sea branch – due to the tapering nature of the Indian peninsula.

The Arabian Sea branches rise abruptly after getting hit by the windward side of the Western Ghats and yield heavy rainfall there while the eastern side of the Western Ghats receives less rainfall as the winds descend along the eastern slopes and are warmed due to which the relative humidity increases. This leeward side of the relief is also known as the rain shadow area.

- Now we know why Pune on the leeward side of the Western Ghats gets less rainfall than Mumbai on the windward side!
- Why is Thar a desert?
  The south-west monsoon winds of the Arabian Sea branch move parallel to the Aravallis, so it cannot shed its moisture on the Thar Desert, which lies on the leeward side of the Aravallis. Hence Thar is a desert area.

The Bay of Bengal branch of the SW monsoon winds runs along the coast of Bangladesh and Myanmar. It strikes against the Arakan Yoma and is diverted towards the Indian subcontinent. As a result, monsoon strikes India from the south and south-east. Due to the presence of the Himalayas, the Bay of Bengal branch gets diverted into two sub-branches. One moves westward along the Gangetic plains, and the other moves towards the north-east, up to the Brahmaputra Valley. The winds strike against the Garo Khasi and Jaintia hills of Meghalaya, making Mawsynram the wettest place on Earth.

The monsoon branches of the Arabian Sea and Bay of Bengal meet each other over the northern part of the Gangetic plains, bringing showers to the Delhi–NCR region and the rest of north India.

**Winter monsoon:** The situation is reversed in winter. The seas are comparatively warmer than the land mass. So a high pressure is created over the land mass while the sea develops low pressure. Wind now starts blowing from land towards the sea. Since these winds are offshore winds, they do not shed much moisture. These winds blow in a north-east direction, so they are also called NE monsoon winds. They pick up moisture while blowing over the Bay of Bengal and shed rainfall over the Coromandel coast during October–November.

Apart from the Coromandel (Tamil Nadu) coast, Punjab, Haryana and western UP also receive mild to heavy rainfall in winter and snowfall in Jammu and Kashmir.

The reason is **western disturbances.** These are temperate cyclones, which originate in the Mediterranean Sea and bring rainfall to India and Pakistan. These winter showers are extremely beneficial for rabi cultivation in north India.

**Land and sea breezes:** This is a daily cycle produced due to differential heating of land and sea, causing high and low pressure.

- **Sea breeze:** During the daytime, the land gets heated up quicker than the adjacent sea. Warm air over the land expands and rises, so low pressure develops, while high pressure develops over the sea. This difference in pressure systems causes the wind to blow from sea to land. This phenomenon continues till sunset, when the sea becomes comparatively warmer than the land. Sea breezes are onshore winds, and they are most active in summer.
- **Land breeze:** During night-time, the sea breezes weaken as low pressure develops over the sea. The adjacent land has high

pressure. So the wind starts blowing from land to sea. These winds are offshore and dry winds.

**Mountain and valley breezes:** The valley floors and slopes are more heated during the daytime due to insolation. As a result, the warm wind of the valley bottoms rises and expands. This upslope breeze during the daytime is called valley breeze. Valley breezes, once they reach up, cool down and condense. They bring rainfall to the mountain peaks. When the valley breeze condenses and cools down due to a loss of heat through outgoing radiation, it is called mountain breeze. Valley and mountain breezes cause an inversion of temperature.

**Hot winds**

- **Loo:** Hot, dry local winds that blow over the northern and north-western plains of India in May and June in the afternoons.
- **Foehn:** Strong, dry, dusty local winds that develop on the leeward side of the Alps. Foehn help in the early ripening of grapes. As they descend, they melt the snow, thus making pasture land ready for cattle grazing.
- **Chinook:** Hot, dry local winds that blow down the eastern slopes of the Rockies of the USA and Canada. They are also called snow eaters since they keep the grassland snow-free.
- **Harmattan:** These are warm and dry winds blowing across the Sahara. While blowing over the Sahara Desert, these winds pick up sand and deposit in nearby regions. Harmattan is also known as doctor wind in Guinea and western Africa as it brings pleasant weather and reduces the uncomfortably high relative humidity due to its arid and high temperature conditions.
- **Sirocco:** It is a warm, dry and dusty wind that blows in a northern direction from the Sahara to Italy, Spain and around the Mediterranean Sea. These winds are particularly very active

at the time of temperate cyclones over the Mediterranean Sea. While passing over the sea, sirocco picks up moisture and brings rainfall to the Mediterranean countries. However, this wind is very injurious to agriculture since it carries a lot of red dust with it from the Sahara.

**Cold winds**

- **Mistral:** Very cold, dry, high-velocity local winds originating in the Alps and blowing towards the Mediterranean Sea through the Rhone Valley. They bring down the temperature below freezing point in areas under their realm.
- **Bora:** It is an extremely cold and dry north-easterly wind that blows along the Adriatic Sea. It is moister than mistral as it picks up moisture while blowing over the Adriatic Sea.
- **Blizzard:** These are snowstorms that are typically found in the north and south polar regions. These are violent, stormy and chilly winds that cause sudden drops in temperature to sub-zero levels and cause permafrost conditions.

**Jet streams**

These are fast-moving circumpolar westerly wind circulations blowing in the upper layers of the troposphere. This circulation is observed between the poles and 20° latitudes in both hemispheres. They are circumpolar since they blow around the poles in both hemispheres. There is a change in the wind velocity of jet streams. They become strong in winter, and wind velocity becomes twice the velocity during summer.

***Jet streams in India***

**The easterly jet stream** plays an important role in India's summer monsoon. They are formed due to the intense heating of the Tibetan Plateau during summer, which triggers the summer monsoon.

**The westerly jet stream** brings winter rainfall to north-western and northern India in the form of western disturbances.

*Types of jet streams*

**Subtropical jet streams:** They are best developed in winter and early springtime. The subtropical jet stream weakens in the northern hemisphere during summer and is found in small cells with sporadic velocity. During winter, their velocity intensifies, and their maximum speed can reach up to 300 knots. They are most active at about 35,000 to 45,000 feet. In Asia, the subtropical jet stream is replaced by the tropical easterly jet stream. Subtropical jets bring fair and pleasant weather wherever they pass through.

**Tropical easterly jet stream:** These winds are strongest over southern India, but they are not as strong as the subtropical jet streams. They are associated with the summer monsoons of south Asia. There is a deep layer of warm air to the north of the jet and cold air to the south, over the Indian Ocean. This warm air is due to the intense heating of the Indian land mass during summer while the ocean is cooler. This difference in the pressure gradient triggers the movement of this jet stream.

**Polar night jet stream:** These winds are found over the poles in the upper stratosphere. They are most active on cold winter nights. Lack of solar radiation during six months of night-time in the poles causes excessive cooling. The horizontal temperature gradient between the equator and the poles becomes strong at that time, and the pressure gradient makes this jet stream. The temperature gradient is gentler during middle and late winter, which makes the jet intermittent at this stage. In the southern hemisphere, however, the temperature gradient and the jet stream disappear abruptly at spring.

***What is* El Nino?**

They are warm ocean winds that develop on the surface waters of the tropical east Pacific Ocean, causing global changes in the world distribution of rainfall and temperature. Low air pressure is formed in the south-east Pacific, mainly off the coasts of Peru and Ecuador (South America). Upwelling of cold seawater is stopped, warm air rises and becomes unstable, bringing rainfall after condensation.

***What is* La Nina?**

The cold phase of El Nino is La Nina when the sea's surface temperature in south-east Pacific goes down and air pressure is high.

Both El Nino and La Nina trigger heavy floods on the west coast of South America or drought in Australia and can also lead to weaker monsoons over the Indian subcontinent.

# 26

## HUMIDITY AND RAINFALL

Humidity is the amount of water vapour present in the air. Water vapour is found in only 2% of the total composition of the atmosphere, but this composition varies both spatially as well as locally. About 50% of the water vapour is concentrated in the lower layers of the atmosphere up to a height of 2,000 m. Water vapour plays a vital role in the regulation of temperature, the hydrological cycle, the amount of precipitation, the amount of loss of heat through radiation, etc. The water vapour present in the atmosphere has its source from rivers, lakes, streams, seas and oceans through evaporation.

**Evaporation** is the process of transformation of liquid water to its gaseous state. The rate of evaporation varies from place to place and depends upon several factors, such as aridity, wind velocity, temperature. The higher the aridity and wind velocity, the greater the rate of evaporation because dry air with high temperature has more capacity to hold water vapour than already humid air.

**Condensation** is the process of transformation from a gaseous state to a liquid or solid state.

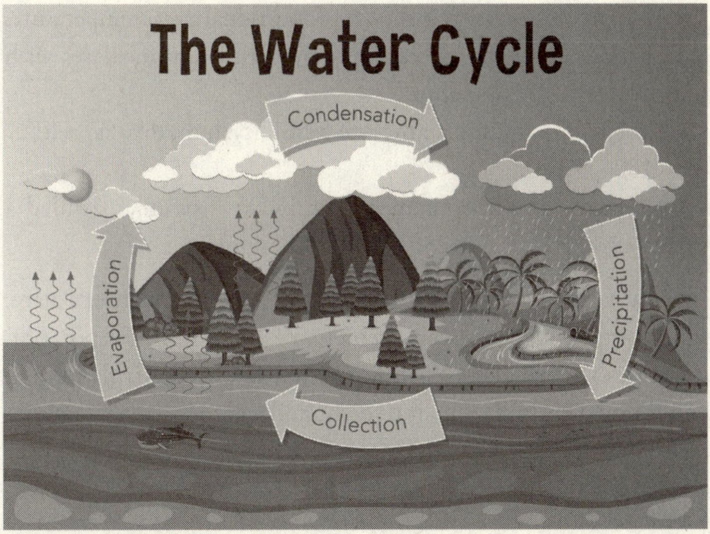


**Latent heat** is the amount of heat hidden in water vapour. The amount of heat needed for the process of evaporation is never lost; rather, it is always associated with water vapour. For example, when we sit under the fan after returning home on a sultry summer afternoon, we feel instantly cool because our sweat gets evaporated. The latent heat of condensation is the heat energy released after condensation.

**Absolute humidity** is the total amount of water vapour present in a column of air at a given temperature. Absolute humidity decreases from the equator towards the poles and from oceans to the continents.

**Relative humidity** is the ratio of the amount of water vapour actually present in the air to the maximum amount of water vapour that the air can hold. Relative humidity is expressed in percentage. When relative humidity is 100%, the air is said to be **saturated**.

- Relative humidity is inversely proportional to air temperature. It decreases with increasing temperature and increases with decreasing temperature.
- Relative humidity = absolute humidity/humidity capacity × 100
- Relative humidity is measured by an instrument called a hygrometer or wet and dry bulb thermometer.

Relative humidity (RH) helps in predicting the climate of a place. For example, high RH can predict wet conditions. Evaporation decreases with high relative humidity. It also controls human comfort and health. When it is too humid and the relative humidity is very high, we feel uncomfortable and sweaty.

## Condensation

Condensation depends on two factors:

- The percentage of relative humidity in the air
- The degree of cooling of the air

### *What is adiabatic change of temperature?*

When there is a change in the temperature of the air due to contraction or expansion of air, it is called adiabatic change of temperature. This happens when air condenses and cools down and becomes heavier. The heaviness is due to the contraction of air, but its temperature increases as it comes near the surface. This change of temperature is due to the descent and not due to any addition or subtraction of heat from it.

**Stable and unstable air:** Stable air is without vertical movement while unstable air is with any vertical movement. An air mass, when it becomes lighter, ascends and becomes unstable, while an air mass, when it descends, becomes stable.

> The temperature at which air gets saturated is called **dew point**.

The stability and instability of an air mass depend on the relationship between normal lapse rate and adiabatic temperature changes. The adiabatic temperature remains constant while the normal lapse rate might change.

***Forms of condensation***

**Fog:** Thin clouds consisting of very small water droplets, which remain suspended in the air near the ground surface and reduce horizontal visibility.

Lighter fog is called mist.

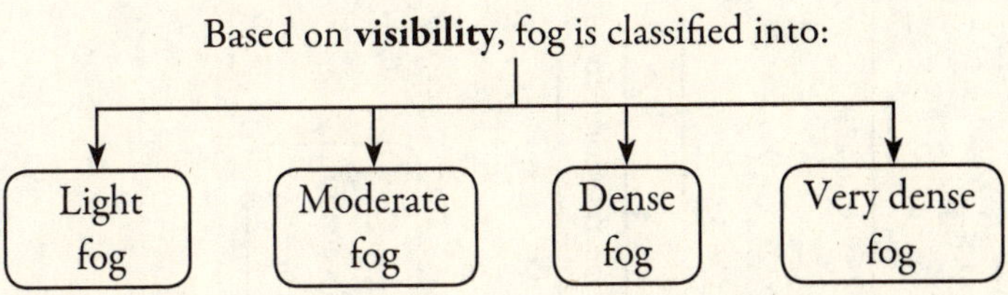


***Effects of fog***

- Fog hinders navigation and transport.
- Dense fog and smoke create smog, which creates health hazards.
- Fog also affects flight take-offs and landings causing delays in air traffic.
- Dense fog causes road accidents due to low visibility.

**Clouds:** Clouds are formed due to condensation of water vapour around hygroscopic nuclei caused by the cooling of air due to ascent. All forms of precipitation originate from clouds. Clouds are microscopically minute droplets of water, ice particles or both that remain suspended in the air above the ground. Clouds absorb and diffuse a part of incoming solar radiation and also absorb some amount of longwave terrestrial radiation.

Based on **processes of formation**, fog is classified into:

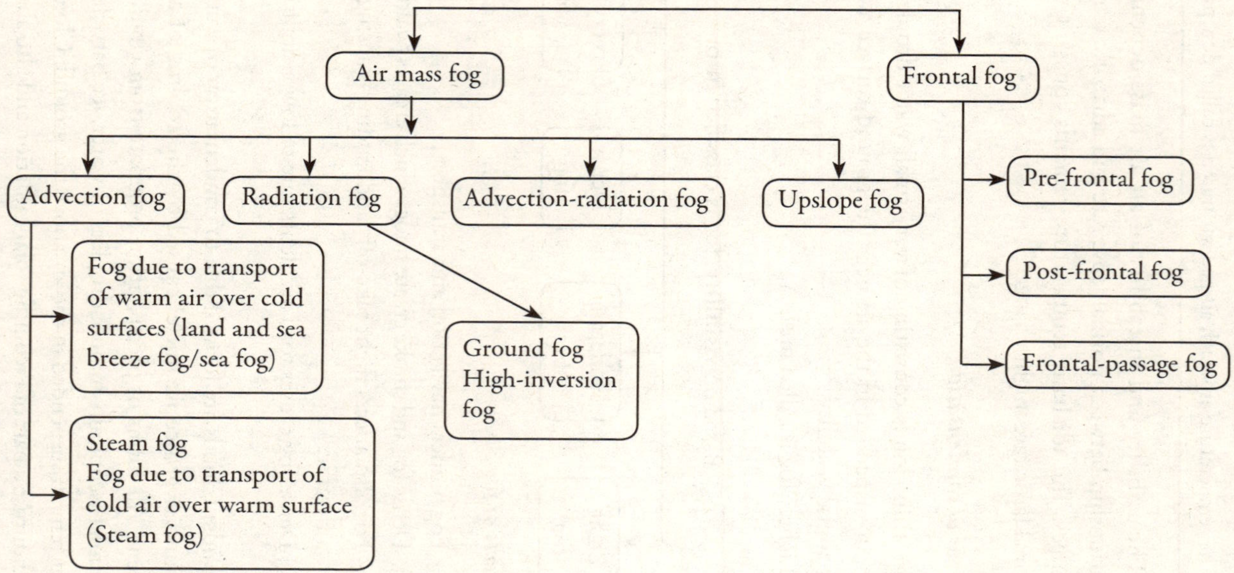

## Classification of Clouds

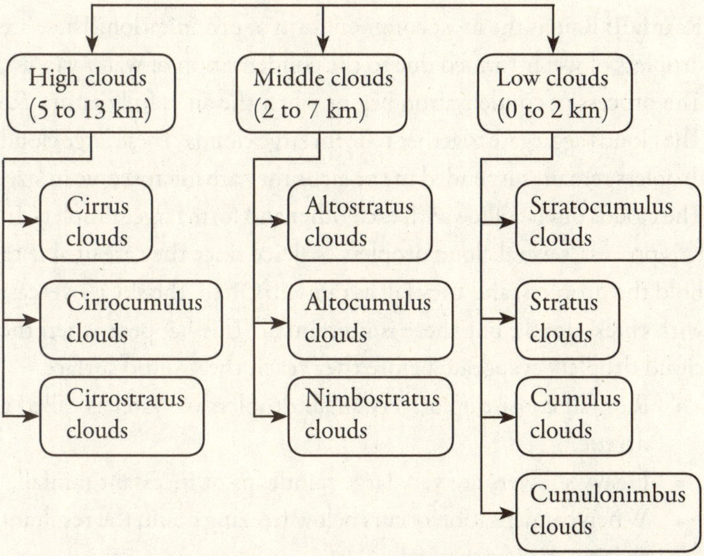

Types of clouds

### *Forms of precipitation*

**Rainfall:** Rain is the most common form of precipitation. These are droplets of water formed due to the condensation of water vapour. The process of condensation begins when the air is fully saturated. The clouds aggregate together to form large clouds. These large cloud droplets remain suspended in the air as they are microscopic in size. The clouds often collide with each other and form larger droplets. In this process, several cloud droplets coalesce since they are unable to hold the droplets, and they fall as rainfall. Often, the sky is overcast with thick clouds, but there is no rainfall. This happens when the cloud droplets evaporate before they reach the ground surface.

- Rainfall consisting of very small droplets of water is called a drizzle.
- Heavy showers are very large raindrops or incessant rainfall.
- When condensation occurs below freezing point, the resultant precipitation is snowfall.

### *Types of rainfall*

**Convectional rainfall:** This type of rainfall is most common in equatorial regions.

1. The ground surface is intensely heated due to the vertical rays of the sun.
2. The air above the surface also gets heated. It becomes lighter as it expands and rises.
3. This ascending warm air, after reaching a height, starts cooling down when its relativity humidity increases. The air becomes saturated as it further rises, and when it reaches beyond the saturation point, it condenses and precipitates in the form of rainfall.
4. When the air further ascends, it reaches a height where the temperature of the air matches the temperature of the

surrounding air, the process of condensation is doubled and thick cumulonimbus clouds are formed.

5. Convectional rainfall occurs almost every afternoon in equatorial regions, where they are called 4 o'clock showers.
6. This type of rainfall is accompanied by thunder and lightning.
7. They are associated with dark, thick cumulonimbus clouds and bring heavy showers of a short duration.

**Orographic rainfall:** This type of rainfall is triggered by the presence of high relief in the path of moisture-laden winds.

1. When moisture-laden winds strike against a mountain barrier, they are forced to rise.
2. The ascent of the air cools the air and raises its relative humidity. The air becomes further saturated after reaching a certain height, and condensation begins around hygroscopic nuclei.
3. The addition of the latent heat of condensation causes the air to ascend further. This ascending air yields precipitation. The presence of the mountain barrier and its height trigger the moist, warm air to ascend.
4. The windward side of the mountain receives heavier rainfall than the leeward side. When the moisture winds reach the leeward side, they start descending, and consequently, the relative humidity falls, so most of the moisture is lost.
5. The amount of orographic rainfall is maximum near mountain slopes, and the amount starts decreasing away from the foothills.
6. Monsoons in India are mostly orographic in nature.

**Cyclonic or frontal rainfall:** This type of rainfall occurs due to the convergence of two air masses with distinct characteristics.

1. When warm and cold air masses converge along a line, a front is formed.

2. The warm ascends along the front while the colder denser wind settles down. This type of rainfall is temperate cyclonic in nature, where cold polar winds and warm westerlies converge.
3. The warm air lying over the cold air is cooled and gets condensed around hygroscopic nuclei.
4. The process of condensation is gradual, so this type of rainfall is of long duration with weak spells. Sometimes, the precipitation occurs in the form of snowfall and hail.
5. Precipitation associated with a warm front brings drizzles of long duration, while precipitation associated with a cold front brings thunderstorms of short duration. This is because the cold air mass pushes with great force, causing the warm air mass to ascend.

***Other forms of precipitation***

**Snowfall:** When the saturation of air occurs at temperatures below freezing point, the type of precipitation that occurs is called snowfall. These are small, opaque grains of ice that fall and settle down on the ground. Snowfall is common in high-altitude regions.

**Sleet:** A mixture of snow and rain is called sleet.

**Hail:** This is precipitation of small balls of ice with diameters of 5 to 50 mm. Hailstorms are bad for agricultural crops. They fall as alternate layers of transparent and translucent ice.

**Drizzle:** This happens when numerous minute droplets of water with a diameter of less than 0.5 mm fall continuously from low-altitude clouds.

*World distribution of rainfall:*

**Equatorial region of maximum rainfall:** This region receives rainfall throughout the year, but the maximum amount is received at the vernal and autumnal equinoxes. The intense heating of the surface leads to convective currents that bring rainfall. Rainfall occurs almost daily, accompanied by thunder and lightning.

**The tropical rainfall zone:** The eastern parts of the continents receive more rainfall than the western parts. This zone is dominated by the south-east and north-east trade winds. The winds are onshore in the eastern part and offshore in the western part.

**Monsoon rain region:** This type of rainfall is mainly orographic and cyclonic in origin. The maximum rainfall occurs from July to September. Summer monsoon is caused by south-west monsoon winds, and winter monsoon is caused by north-east monsoon winds. The regions in south Asia are dominated by monsoon winds.

**Mediterranean rainfall region:** Typically, this region receives rainfall in winter and faces extreme dry summer heat. The winter rain is caused by the shifting of pressure belts when the westerlies are onshore. Summers remain dry due to the offshore trade winds.

**Polar zone region:** From 60° latitude, the amount of precipitation decreases. Most of it occurs in the form of snowfall.

**The mid-latitudinal region:** The temperate regions between 40° to 50° latitudes in both the hemispheres receive rainfall from temperate cyclones and westerlies. The western parts of continents receive more rainfall. It decreases towards the continental interiors. The southern hemisphere, due to the dominance of water bodies, receives more rainfall than the northern hemisphere.

# 27

## CYCLONES AND ANTICYCLONES

**Cyclones:** These are centres of low pressure surrounded by closely spaced isobars. The centre of the cyclone consists of low pressure, and the wind blows inward in an anticlockwise direction in the northern hemisphere and clockwise in the southern hemisphere. Cyclones are of two types: temperate cyclones and tropical cyclones.

### Temperate cyclones

These are atmospheric disturbances with low pressure in the centre and increasing pressure outward. They are formed due to the convergence of warm and cold air masses along a front. They are found in mid-latitudes as they move east under the influence of westerly winds.

Temperate cyclones are of different shapes – elliptical, oval or V-shaped. They have closely spaced isobars in which the wind blows inward. Since these cyclones are formed due to the convergence of two contrasting air masses, the temperature recorded in each part of the cyclone is different. The southern part of the cyclone records higher temperatures due to the dominance of warmer air while the north, north-western parts of the cyclones record low temperatures because of polar air masses. Notably, the warm part of the front is associated with warm air, and the cold part is associated with cold, dense air. So, there is a sudden change in the wind direction along the warm and cold fronts. This line along which the wind changes its direction is called the **wind shift line**.

Temperate cyclones, unlike tropical cyclones, occur for longer durations and in weak spells. They are generally not always associated with thunder and lightning.

### *Types of temperate cyclones*

- **Dynamic temperate cyclones:** These are the real ones, formed due to the meeting of two different air masses. They affect large areas in mid-latitudes. They are called dynamic as they are formed dynamically due to the convergence of warm tropical air masses and cold polar air masses.
- **Thermal cyclones:** These cyclones are formed due to intense low pressure developed in summers on the continents in mid-latitudes. Winds blow from all directions towards the low-pressure system. These cyclones do not develop fronts and are solely thermally induced.
- **Secondary cyclones:** These are small, stationary and feeble cyclones that develop after the occlusion of the main cyclone.

### *Tropical cyclones*

Cyclones that occur between the Tropics of Cancer and Capricorn are called tropical cyclones. These cyclones are not regular and uniform. The centre of the cyclone consists of low pressure surrounded by closely spaced isobars. The velocity of wind is very high as it moves inward. Tropical cyclones develop over the sea; they gain intensity over the sea, vigorously picking up moisture while moving towards land. Once they make landfall, they become weak and feeble. They ultimately die out in the interior of the continent.

Tropical cyclones derive their energy from the latent heat of condensation. They are not stationary. The more they stay over the sea, the more they gain moisture and cause larger destruction to life and property.

Tropical cyclones are associated with incessant rainfall of shorter duration from dark, thick cumulonimbus clouds with thunder and lightning. The average wind velocity ranges from 35 km/hour to more than 150 km/hour.

The eye of the cyclone is characterized by calm conditions, high air temperature, low wind velocity and calm weather. This situation changes very soon with the building up of cirrus and later thicker clouds. The wind velocity becomes very high, and there are heavy downpours.

Tropical cyclones are known by different names in different parts of the world. They are called hurricanes/tornadoes in the USA, typhoons in Japan, willy-willies in Australia and tropical storms or cyclones in the Indian subcontinent.

| Type | Wind speed in km/h | Wind speed in knot (mps) |
|---|---|---|
| Low pressure area (L) | Less than 31 | Less than 17 (09) |
| Depression (D) | 31–49 | 17–27 (9-14) |
| Deep depression (DD) | 50–61 | 28–33 (15–17) |
| Cyclonic storm (CS) | 62–88 | 34–47 (18–24) |
| Severe cyclonic storm (SCS) | 89–118 | 48–63 (25–32) |
| Very severe cyclonic storm (VSCS) | 119–221 | 64–119 (33–61) |
| Super cyclonic storm (Sup. CS) | 222 or more | 120 (62) or more |
| Generic name like tropical cyclone or cyclone is used to represent CS, SCS, VSCS and Sup. CS as a whole | | |

Table: The scale of tropical cyclones in the Indian Ocean

**Thunderstorms:** These are local storms characterized by heavy rainfall with thunder and lightning. In thunderstorms, the wind, instead of blowing inward, rises upward as convectional currents. The showers are heavy, like that of a cloudburst but of short duration. As the name suggests, such storms produce thundering sounds due to the sudden and rapid expansion of air columns (along the path of the lightning bolt) caused due to rapid heating by lightning.

***Weather conditions associated with thunderstorms***

- Heavy downpour of short duration. The amount of rainfall varies within the cells of the storm where the maximum rainfall occurs in the centre and minimum at the periphery.
- Thunderstorms are accompanied by thunder and lightning.
- They are often accompanied by squalls. The downward movement of cold air causing its divergence at the ground is known as a squall. The velocity of squalls is very high, and they cause huge damage to human property and vegetation.
- Condensation below freezing point causes the formation of hail. These are small ice balls that fall when the rising convectional currents become weak. Hailstorms pose a serious threat to vegetation.

**Tornado**

These are funnel-shaped storms that are violent and cause destruction. They are rotating columns of air having an upper portion of towering cumulonimbus clouds that are attached to the ground by narrow columns of air. There is dust, sand and debris present in the column of air. The centre of the tornado has extreme low pressure. A steep pressure gradient forces the wind to gush inside with a high velocity of around 600 to 800 km per hour. Tornadoes are most common in summer and spring. Intense heating of the surface causes strong convective currents that can also trigger the formation of a tornado.

Tornadoes may also develop in groups or colonies. When this happens, they cause huge damage to life and property.

**Anticyclones**

Anticyclones are characterized by high pressure in the centre and low pressure in the periphery. The wind blows outward in a clockwise direction in the northern hemisphere and anticlockwise in the southern hemisphere. Anticyclones are most common in subtropical high-pressure belts and are literally not found in equatorial low-pressure areas.

Anticyclones are calm weather phenomena. They have a sluggish movement, and they are much larger in area and size. Their average velocity is 30 km/hour to 50 km/hour. Sometimes, they may remain stationary in a particular region for several days. They bring dry spells of weather, light breeze and clear skies. Sometimes, they create a halo around the sun.

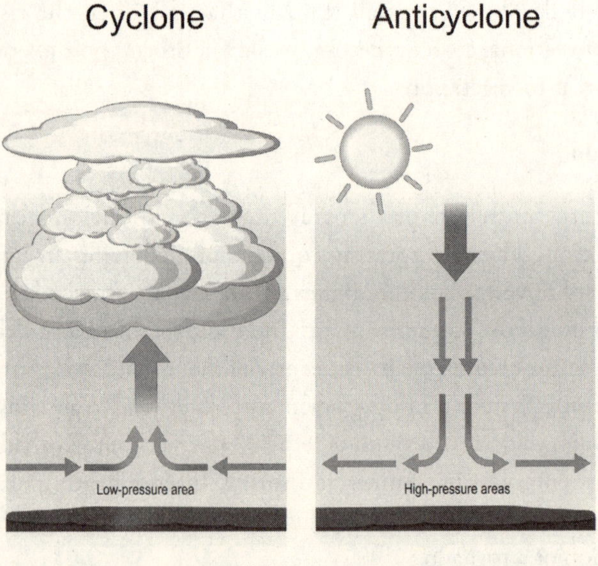


Cyclone and anticyclone

***Types of anticyclones***

- Cold anticyclones
- Warm anticyclones
- Blocking anticyclones

***Difference between weather and climate***

Weather is the short-term characteristic of a particular region with respect to its temperature, rainfall, humidity, moisture, cloudiness, etc. The weather of a particular place may vary at any time. For example, the weather in Delhi today is hot and dry.

Climate is the aggregate weather conditions in a region over a long period of time. For example, India has a tropical monsoon-type of climate. So here, we are identifying the climate of India from a broader perspective.

# 28

## CLIMATIC CLASSIFICATION BY KÖPPEN

Dr Wladimir Köppen, a German climatologist and botanist, first introduced his climatic classification in 1900, which he later modified in 1918, then 1931 and 1936.

He divided the world into five zones based on the natural vegetation of the region:

- **A climate:** This represents humid tropical climate characterized by warm and tropical conditions throughout the year, the absence of winter and mean temperature always above 18°C.
- **B climate:** Dry climate where the rate of evaporation is greater than rainfall, so there is always water scarcity throughout the year.
- **C climate:** Humid mesothermal climate found in mid-latitudes having mild winters and average temperature ranges between 8°C to 18°C.
- **D climate:** Humid microthermal or cold forest climate with severe winters. The average temperature is as low as 3°C and does not rise above 10°C.
- **E climate:** Polar climate characterized by severe winter and absence of summer. The average temperature is below 10°C even in the warmest months.

Köppen used small letters beside the above capital letters to denote the following:

- f: rainfall throughout the year, average temperature more than 18°C in the coldest month
- m: monsoon climate and short dry season
- w: winter dry season
- s: summer dry season

**The five major climatic regions along with their subdivisions are:**

| Climatic type | Subtypes | |
|---|---|---|
| Tropical rainy climate (A) | Af climate: The tropical rainforest. This is the zone of continuous heavy rainfall. It is in the Amazon basin in South America, the Zaire basin, the Guinea coast, the East Indies and some parts of coastal tropical Asia. Rainfall is heavy and the sun shines almost vertically throughout the year. The daily range of temperature is low. | |
| | Aw climate: Tropical humid and dry climate, winter dry season and high temperature throughout the year. This represents savanna climate. | |

| | | |
|---|---|---|
| | Am climate: Monsoon climate in southern Asia, Indochina and southern parts of China. The rainfall is orographic and cyclonic in origin. The most important season is the rainy season, and the climate remains hot and humid throughout the year. | |
| | As climate: An extremely rare climate type, it is found in rainshadow areas. | |
| | | |
| **Climatic type** | **Parameter** | **Subtypes** |
| Dry climate (B) Based on annual temperature | Based on annual temperature and rainiest months | Dry desert climate (BW) |
| | Semi-arid or steppe climate (BS) | |
| | BWh: Tropical desert climate, average annual temperature more than 18°C | |
| | BSh: Tropical steppe climate, average annual temperature more than 18°C | |
| | BWk: Cold desert mid-latitude climate, average annual temperature less than 18°C | |
| BSk: Mid-latitude cold steppe climate, average annual temperature less than 18°C | | |

### *Further Details on B Climate*

| | |
|---|---|
| k | Mean annual temperature less than 18°C |
| h | Mean annual temperature more than 18°C |
| a | Dry summer, more precipitation in the wettest month of the winter season than the driest month of the summer season |
| w | Winter dry, ten times more rainfall in the wettest month of summer than the driest month of winter season |
| n | Minimum fog |

| **Humid mesothermal or warm temperate rainy climate (C climate )** | **Average temperature of the coldest month is above 3°C and below 13°C. Rainfall in all seasons.** |
|---|---|
| Cf climate | Represents western European type of climate. Precipitation throughout the year. The chief regions are north-western Europe, western portions of North America from California to 60-degree north latitude, New Zealand. |
| Cw climate | Dry winters, ten times more precipitation in the wettest month of the summer season than the driest month of winter season. This is China type of climate. The chief regions are south-eastern states and Florida in the USA, China, south-eastern coastlands of Australia and South Africa, parts of Uruguay and south-eastern Brazil. |
| Ca climate | Dry summers, three times more precipitation in the wettest month of winter season than the driest month of summer season. It is Mediterranean type of climate. The regions include the areas around the Mediterranean Sea, California in the USA, central Chile in South America, the south-western tip of Australia. |

### *Further details on C climate*

| | |
|---|---|
| a | Warm summers, temperature of the warmest month above 22°C |
| b | Cold winters, temperature of the warmest month below 22°C |
| c | Cold, short summer season |

| Humid microthermal climate or cold humid climates (D) | Subtype |
|---|---|
| Df climate | Humid cold climate, no dry season. They can be Dfa ( long, warm summers), Dfb (long, cool summers) and Dfc (short, cool summers) |
| Dw climate | Humid cold climate, dry winters. They can be either Dwa (long, cool summers and continental climate), Dwb (cool, short summers) and Dwc (cold winters) |

| | Subtype |
|---|---|
| **Polar climate (E climate)** | ET climate: tundra climate, temperature of warmest month below 10°C but above 0°C |
| | EF climate: permafrost area, temperature always below 0°C |

# OCEANOGRAPHY

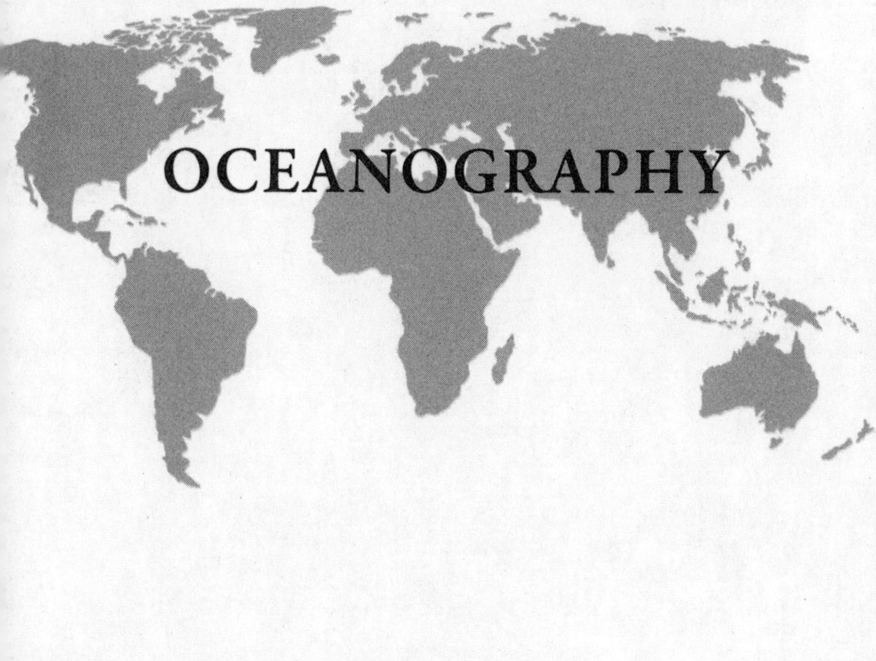

# 29

## OCEANIC RELIEF AND FEATURES

1. **Continental shelf:** The shallow, submerged extensions of continents are called continental shelves. The continental shelf slopes gently seaward with an angle of less than a degree. The shallow seawater over the continental shelf has a depth between 120 and 350 metres. Continental shelves are sources of petroleum and natural gas. They are the sources of the major fishing grounds of the world.

Continental shelves are marked by the presence of submarine canyons. These canyons are steep, sloped valleys in the seafloor. They are formed due to earthquakes or landslides underwater. The force of the moving sediments causes the valley to erode, forming canyons.

2. **Continental slope:** Steep slopes extending from the continental shelves to the deep-sea plains. Continental slopes are formed due to the erosion of sediments under the sea by the sea waves.

3. **Abyssal plains:** These are undulating deep-sea plains found at a depth between 3,400 to 5,000 m. Abyssal plains are formed of sediments. Sometimes, these plains are marked by the presence of fossils of marine life, forming sediments, which are called oozes.

4. **Submarine ridges:** High-relief features under the sea are called submarine ridges. These are oceanic mountains, which are

intersected by faults and are interconnected between oceans. The ridges are those mountain chains beneath the oceans that are frequently affected by earthquakes and volcanism.

The **Mid-Atlantic Ridge** is the largest submarine ridge that runs from the north of the Atlantic Ocean to its south.

5. **Seamounts and Guyots:** Submerged volcanoes with sharp, pointed peaks are called seamounts. Sometimes, they are visible to us as isolated islands.

Guyots are submerged volcanoes whose tops have been eroded and get covered by water.

**Ocean deeps:** The deepest part of the ocean, also called oceanic trenches, these are long, narrow, steep-sided depressions on the seafloor. Ocean deeps are not necessarily located in the middle of the ocean; they can be located parallel to the continental margins. They are the zone of tectonic activities. The Pacific Ocean has the largest number of trenches.

> The Challenger Deep in **Mariana Trench** of the western part of the Pacific Ocean is the deepest point of the Earth.

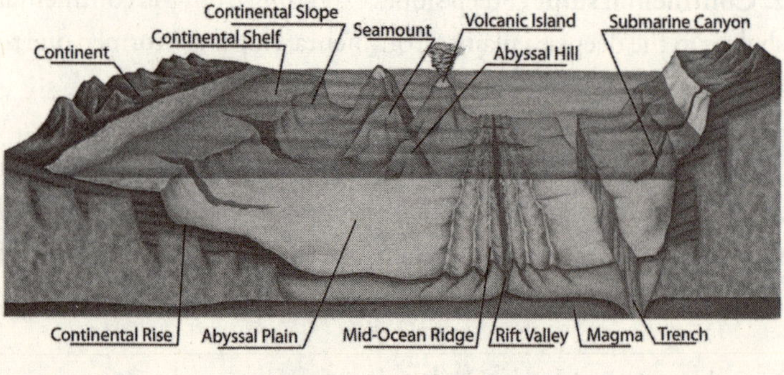


Oceanic relief and features

# 30

# THE TEMPERATURE OF OCEANS

### The importance of the temperature of oceans

- The temperature of the oceans is essential for the survival of marine plants and animals.
- It also affects the temperature of the coastal lands.

### Layers of oceanic temperature

- **First layer:** The top layer of the warm oceanic water where the temperature varies between 20° to 25°C. This layer is mainly prevalent in tropical waters.
- **Second layer:** The **thermocline** layer, characterized by a rapid decrease of temperature with increasing depth.
- **Third layer:** This is a very cold layer where no sunlight can penetrate. This layer extends up to the ocean floor.

### Factors affecting the temperature of ocean water

- **Latitudes:** We know that the amount of insolation decreases from the equator to the poles. This is due to the rays of the sun slanting more at the poles. Similarly, the temperature of the surface water of the oceans decreases from the equator to the poles.

- **Prevailing winds:** Winds, whether they are blowing from land to sea or from sea to land, also affect the temperature of ocean water. Offshore winds, which blow from land to sea, push away the warm surface water from the coast while the denser cold water from the bottom rises. Onshore winds cause warm water to pile up near the coast and thus raise the temperature.

  The trade winds, when they blow along the eastern coastal areas, are onshore, so they raise the temperature of the eastern coastal areas. Whereas trade winds that are offshore along the western margins of the continents and eastern margins of the seas lower the temperature of the western coastal areas and eastern margins of the seas.
- **Distribution of land and water:** The temperature of oceanic water will always differ between the northern and the southern hemispheres. This is due to the dominance of the sea in the southern hemisphere. Due to the dominance of land in the northern hemisphere, the oceans there receive more insolation. They are in contact with larger land masses than their counterparts in the southern hemisphere. This is also why enclosed seas in low latitudes have higher surface temperatures than open seas as the former is connected with a land mass unlike the latter.
- **Ocean currents:** Warm ocean currents, such as the Gulf Stream, raise the surface temperature of the oceans while cold ocean currents, such as the Labrador Current, lower the temperature of the oceans.
- **Other factors:** Other factors, such as incidences of storms, cloudiness, rainfall and shape of the land, also influence the temperature of oceans.

### *Distribution of temperature*

It is a known fact that the temperature of the surface of the oceans will always be higher than the bottom. This is due to the maximum amount of solar insolation received at the surface. The sun's rays can penetrate up to 20 m depth, and beyond that, there is a rapid fall in temperature with increasing depth. However, the temperature falls with increasing depth very rapidly up to a depth of 200 m, and beyond that, the rate of decrease slows down.

Oceans are divided into two zones based on **solar penetration:**

- **Photic zone:** From the surface up to a depth of 200 m. This zone receives solar rays.
- **Aphotic zone:** From 200 m till the ocean floor. This zone does not receive solar rays and is completely dark.

**FACT FILE**

There are some seas where the temperature of the seafloor also records high temperature. These seas are enclosed seas of low latitudes. For example: the Mediterranean Sea, Sargasso Sea and the Red Sea.

The enclosed seas of high latitudes remain frozen on the surface while their bottom records higher temperature!

**POINT TO REMEMBER**

The rate of decrease in temperature is not uniform from the equator to the poles. The surface temperature of seas near the equator is higher than at the poles, but the temperature of the seafloor is almost uniform from the equator to the poles. That means there is a rapid fall of temperature with increasing depth near the equator than at the poles.

# 31

## SALINITY OF OCEANS

The oceans do not contain only sodium chloride as we believe but consist of a variety of other salts as well. The dominant salts found in oceans are sodium chloride (77.7%) and magnesium chloride (10.9%). Other notable salts are magnesium sulphate (4.7%) and calcium sulphate (3.6%). The proportion of sea salts remains more or less the same due to the free movement of oceanic water, but the concentration of salts varies from one sea to another.

Salinity is defined as the following: 'The total amount of solid material in grams contained in one kilogram of seawater and is expressed as part per thousand (%).' For example: 40% means 40 gm of salt in 1,000 gm of seawater.

***The Importance of the salinity of oceans***

- The salinity of seas and oceans affects marine plants and animals.
- It also influences the physical properties of the water, such as temperature, density, waves and currents.
- Ocean currents are affected by salinity.
- The more saline seawater freezes slowly as compared to freshwater.

***From where do these oceanic salts come?***

The source of oceanic salts is land in solution form. When the rivers join the seas and oceans, they bring salts with them. Where rivers contain lesser amounts of salts (about 2%), oceans contain almost 77% of sodium chloride. Winds also blow salts towards oceans. The rocks on the sea coasts get eroded and dissolved in seawater, which is carried away by waves and ocean currents. Marine organisms may also release salts and calcium into the ocean floor.

**FACT FILE**

People seldom drown in very saline seawater, for example, the Dead Sea, as the density of such seas is always higher!

Imaginary lines joining places on a map having equal oceanic salinity are called **isohalines**.

***Factors influencing oceanic salinity***

1. **Evaporation:** There is a direct relationship between the rate of evaporation and the amount of salinity. The greater the evaporation, the more the salinity. So the salinity of oceans is always higher in seas experiencing higher rates of evaporation. Salinity is higher in the tropics than in the equator due to dry conditions over the tropics, although the rate of evaporation is high in both areas. Salinity can go down in situations of cloudiness with high humidity.
2. **Precipitation:** Abundant rainfall decreases salinity. So equatorial regions receiving heavy rainfall throughout the year record lower oceanic salinity than regions of low rainfall. The influx of freshwater from the melting of glaciers or rainwater reduces oceanic salinity.

3. **River water:** The influx of freshwater from rivers reduces salinity. That is why the mouth of the rivers record low salinity due to the mixing of more river water. Some seas have more salinity when the rate of evaporation is more than the influx of fresh rainwater.
4. **Wind direction:** Winds drive away more saline water into less saline areas, resulting in a decrease in salinity in the former. Trade winds blow away high saline water from the western margins of the continents (eastern seas) and pile them up in the western seas. This results in more salinity in the eastern seas.
5. **Atmospheric disturbances:** Incidences of cyclones can churn the salinity of seawater while anticyclonic conditions that are characterized by calm weather and clear skies may increase the salinity of the surface of seas.

The variation in sea salinity depends **on three factors**:

- How much river water and freshwater is mixing with the sea
- The rate of evaporation
- Mixing of the ocean water through currents

**Distribution of salinity**

***Latitudinal distribution of salinity***

| Regions of Low Salinity | Regions of Maximum Salinity | Regions of Low Salinity | Regions of Minimum Salinity |
|---|---|---|---|
| Equatorial regions (heavy rainfall) | Tropical region (high evaporation and low rainfall) | Temperate region (less evaporation) | Polar and subpolar regions (influx of melted fresh ice caps and glaciers) |

| Seas having above normal salinity | Seas having normal salinity | Seas having below normal salinity |
|---|---|---|
| Red Sea, Dead Sea, Mediterranean Sea, Persian Gulf | Caribbean Sea, Gulf of Mexico, Gulf of California | Arctic Ocean, Bering Sea, Japan Sea, Andaman Sea, China Sea, Baltic Sea, English Channel |

***Vertical distribution of oceanic salinity***

- Salinity increases with increasing depth at higher latitudes.
- Heavy rainfall reduces the salinity of the surface oceanic water in equatorial regions, but high salinity can be recorded below.

# 32

# OCEANIC DEPOSITS

***The sources of oceanic deposits are classified into three categories:***

1. **Terrigenous materials:** These are the rock fragments and gravel that are weathered and disintegrated, forming fine sediments. These sediments are continental in origin as they are brought down by the rivers to the seas.

   These include: Gravel, including boulders, pebbles, stones, etc. Sands, which may range from very fine sands to large, coarse sands. Silt, clay and mud.
2. **Volcanic materials:** The source can either be volcanic eruptions occurring under the seas when the sediments are directly deposited or it can be volcanic eruptions near the coast. These volcanic materials are brought down by the winds to the oceans.
3. **Organic materials:** These include remains of marine plants and animals. These are of two subtypes:

   a. **Pelagic deposits:** which include the remains of different types of algae

b. **Neritic deposits:** which include the remains of dead marine plants and animals

Pelagic deposits are called oozes. These are of two types:

**Calcareous ooze:** They consist of calcium deposits of marine skeletons. They get dissolved very fast so are seldom found at greater depths. These are generally white or grey.

**Siliceous ooze:** These are mostly made up of silica. They are not as soluble as calcium because of less calcium dominance. These oozes are found in both warm and cold waters at great depths.

4. **Inorganic materials:** The source of these materials is rainfall or surface run-off. Often, the rivers carry these sediments and deposit them into the seas. They include iron, manganese oxide, dolomite, phosphate, etc. The organic and inorganic materials are so mixed together that they cannot be isolated. These include red clay. They cover the largest area of deep-sea deposits. Red clay mostly consists of silicates of alumina and iron oxides.

***Classification of oceanic deposits***

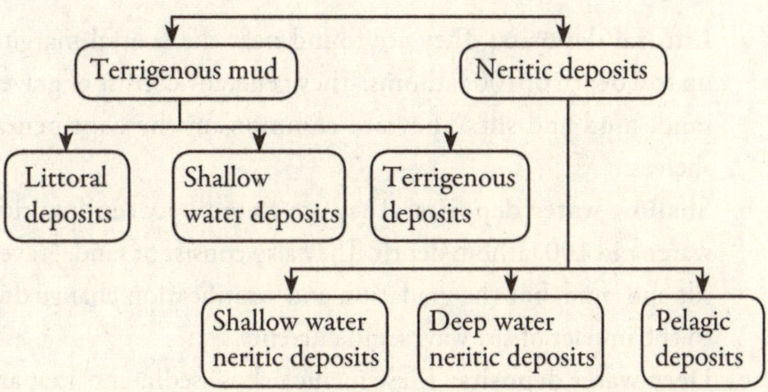

***Classification based on the origin of deposits***

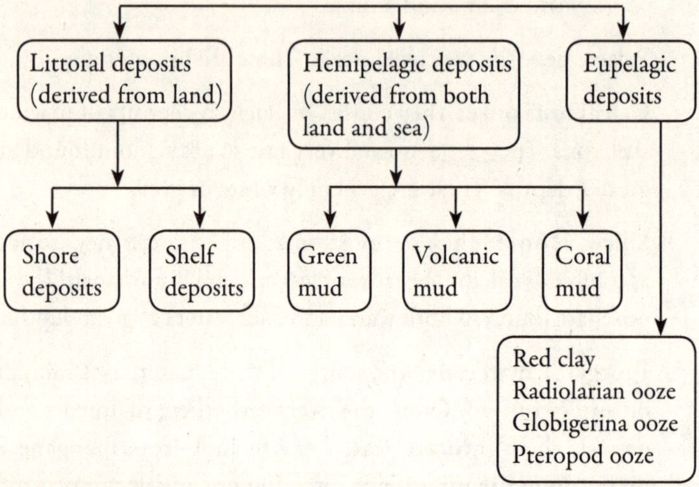


**Distribution of oceanic deposits**

**Terrigenous deposits:** These include gravel, sands, mud, volcanic materials, etc. They are obtained from the weathering and erosion of continental rocks. There is a particular sequence in the deposition of these deposits that starts from gravel, sand, silt, clay and mud towards the sea. These deposits can either be:

a. **Littoral deposits:** They are found near the coastal margins up to a depth of 100 fathoms. They generally consist of gravel, sand, mud and silt. They are common on the continental shelves.
b. **Shallow water deposits:** They are found between low tide water and 100 fathom depth. They also consist of sand, gravel, silt and mud, but the gradation and stratification change due to the impact of sea waves and currents.
c. **Deep water deposits:** These include those sediments that are deposited below 100 fathoms. The sediments become blue mud, red mud, green mud and coral mud with increasing depth.

**Pelagic deposits:** These contain the remains of dead plants and animals in the form of oozes, the most dominant one being the red ooze.

**Pteropod oozes:** They are the most dominant ones, marine deposits made up of small wing-footed snails called pteropods. The Pacific Ocean is dominated by the globigerina oozes.

# 33

## OCEAN TIDES AND CURRENTS

**Waves:** Waves are caused due to winds blowing on the surface of the seawater. As the water comes in contact with the wind, it rises up and down in the form of crests and troughs. The raised part of the wave is called a **crest**, and the low area between two crests is called a **trough**. The vertical distance between the crest and trough is called **wave height**. The horizontal distance between two crests or two troughs is called **wavelength. Wave period** is the time taken for two crests to pass through a given point. When waves are fast-moving, the wave period is shorter.

***Factors determining the force of sea waves***

1. The wind velocity
2. The time taken by the wind to blow
3. Distance the wind has travelled across the open sea (**fetch**)

When the sea waves dash up the shore after breaking down, they make a great noise. This is called swash. When the sea waves retreat backwards or seawards, it is called backswash. All waves are controlled by the velocity of the sea winds. Large-sized waves are called **stern waves.**

## Tides

The periodic rise and fall of sea levels is called tides. Such variations in sea levels occur daily and from hour to hour. At the time of a rise in sea level, the tidal water comes towards the shore as a flood tide. At the time of falling sea levels, the tidal water withdraws and is called tidal ebb. The flood tide is called high tide or spring tide, and low tide is called neap tide. Tides occur twice a day at regular intervals. It is important to note that twice a month, high tides are higher than average and ebb tides are lower than average.

### *Causes of tides*

Tides are caused due to the gravitational force of the moon and sun on the Earth. The moon and the sun exert gravitational force on the Earth. Since the moon is closer to the Earth, the gravitational pull of the moon is greater than sun. The part of the Earth facing the moon experiences high tide. The opposite side also has high tide at the same time due to centrifugal force. A low tide is seen on the upper and lower parts of the Earth.

Theoretically, the duration between a high tide and a low tide is 12 hours. Each day, the high tide arrives about 51 minutes later than the previous day. This is because each day, the rising and setting of the moon lags behind by 51 minutes. It takes 24 hours and 50 minutes for the Earth to bring the same meridian below the moon every day.

### *Types of tides*

There is a difference in the intensity and duration of tides due to the varying distance between the Earth, sun and moon. The types of tides based on these factors are:

1. **Spring tide:** These are very high tides caused when the Earth, sun and moon are in the same line. This position when the sun,

moon and Earth are in the same line is called **syzygy**. When the sun and moon are on one side of the Earth, the position is called conjunction. Conjunction occurs during new moon or Amavasya. When the Earth is between the sun and moon, it is called opposition. Opposition occurs at the time of full moon or Purnima. The height of spring tides is always 20% more than normal high tides.

2. **Neap tides:** When the sun, moon and Earth are in the position of a right angle or quadrature, low tide is caused. The height of a neap tide is 20% lower than normal low tides. The gravitational force of the sun and moon works in opposite directions, thus the low tide is formed.
3. **High tides:** When there is a normal rise of seawater due to the gravitational force of the sun and moon, it is called high tide. High tide occurs twice daily.
4. **Low tides:** When there is a normal fall of seawater due to the gravitational force of the sun and moon, it is called low tide. Low tide occurs twice daily.
5. **Apogean and perigean tides:** The position when the moon is closest to the Earth is called perigee. At this time, abnormally high tides occur due to increased gravitational pull.

   The position of the Earth when the moon is at its farthest is called apogee. Exceptionally low tides are formed at this time due to decreased gravitational pull.

   When spring tides and perigean tides occur at the same time, the resultant tide is abnormally high.
6. **Daily tides:** The tides arriving daily at an interval of 24 hours and 52 minutes are called daily tides.

***Factors affecting the variation in tides***

a. The position of the sun and moon in relation to the Earth
b. The distance between the Earth and moon and sun that is not constant

c. The shape of the coastline
d. The dominance of sea and oceans

**Important facts**

Water has the tendency to flow from tidal crest to tidal trough. If the wavelength of the wave is too long, it takes greater time to travel from the crest to the trough. At this time, the journey is affected by the Coriolis force. In the northern hemisphere, the tidal waves are deflected to the right, and in the southern hemisphere, they are deflected to the left. When the tidal waves are deflected to the right, the crest swirls anticlockwise around a point. At this point, the water remains stagnant throughout the tidal cycle. This point is called the **amphidromic** point.

Thus, the tidal range is zero at the amphidromic point, and it increases away from the point.

The Earth rotates from west to east. The speed of rotation is also not the same at every latitude. The velocity of rotation decreases with increasing latitude, so the tidal bulge is displaced furthest to the east while it is least affected at the poles.

**Newton's equilibrium theory**

Newton believed that every heavenly body has its own gravitational force. Both the sun and moon exert gravitational force on the Earth. Although the gravitational force of the sun will be more than the moon, the effect of the moon on Earth will be greater since it is closer to the Earth and sun. The water of the surface facing the moon is attracted, and high tide is caused. The opposite side of the Earth is also pulled due to centrifugal force. The sea level is lowered on the other sides of the poles due to the balancing of the gravitational and centrifugal forces along a line joining the two poles. It is apparent that each place experiences two high tides every day.

**Ocean currents:** The movement of huge masses of oceanic water in a definite direction is called ocean current.

Based on **temperature**, ocean currents are of two types: warm and cold ocean currents.

Based on **velocity**, ocean currents are of three types: currents, drifts and streams.

- **Warm ocean currents:** When the large masses of oceanic water move from warm areas to cold areas, they are warm ocean currents.
- **Cold ocean currents:** The movement of ocean water from cold areas to warm areas is called cold ocean currents.
- **Drift:** The movement of surface water of the oceans under the influence of the prevailing winds is called drift.
- **Current:** This is the movement of large volumes of oceanic water with great speed in a particular direction.
- **Streams:** These are the same as drifts and currents but with greater velocity.

***Factors affecting the movement of ocean currents***

1. **Factors related to the rotation of the Earth:** The rotation of the Earth from west to east creates Coriolis force, which deflects any moving object, winds and ocean currents. Ocean currents flowing from the equator to the North Pole are deflected to the right. The rotation of the Earth causes movement of oceanic water near the equator in the opposite direction, from east to west, and thus, equatorial currents are formed.
2. **Temperature differences between oceans:** Since the amount of insolation received at the equator is greater than the poles, the equator waters always have higher temperatures. The higher temperatures of the equatorial waters makes the water less dense because of the expansion of water molecules. The waters

at the poles are heavier due to contraction. As a result, waters with more expansion move towards denser water, that is, from the equatorial regions to the polar regions. There is also the movement of subsurface water currents from polar areas to equatorial areas to balance the loss of water in the equatorial areas.

3. **Salinity differences between oceans:** Saline water is denser than less saline water. So even if the temperature between two oceanic bodies remains the same and the salinity is different, water with greater salinity will be denser than the water with less salinity. The denser water sinks and moves as subsurface current towards areas of low density while the less denser water moves as surface current towards more saline water.

**Good to know!**

The transfer of water is evident between open seas and closed seas. For example, the Mediterranean Sea is more saline than the Atlantic Ocean, so it is much denser than the Atlantic Ocean. The denser saline water sinks in and flows as an undercurrent into the Atlantic Ocean while, in order to compensate for the loss, the less saline water of the Atlantic Ocean flows into the Mediterranean Sea as a surface current.

4. **Density differences due to the influx of freshwater:** Apart from salinity and temperature differences, the density of oceans also varies due to the influx of freshwater into the seas and oceans from the melting of ice caps or due to the joining of rivers and streams. The density of water decreases due to the influx of freshwater from melting of polar ice caps and glaciers into the oceans. But polar areas will also have highly dense water due to the low insolation and low temperature of the polar seas. The water which is less dense moves towards the denser water as surface current while the denser water moves

towards the less dense waters as subsurface current.

5. **Amount of rainfall:** Heavy rainfall with low evaporation increases the sea level, whereas if the rate of evaporation is high and rainfall is less, the salinity of the seas will increase. This will cause the movement of surface currents from low-density areas to high-density areas. Ocean currents move from equatorial regions towards the higher latitudes because, in equatorial regions, the sea level is always high due to heavy rainfall and low evaporation throughout the year. Polar ocean currents move towards the low latitudes because they have more water levels due to a low rate of evaporation and more influx of freshwater from the melting of glaciers.
6. **Other factors:** The shape of the coastline affects the movement of ocean currents. The Brazilian coast bifurcates the equatorial current into two branches. The northern branch flows as the Gulf Stream along the east coast of the USA, and the southern branch moves parallel to the Brazilian coast.

   Seasons also affect ocean currents. In India, the ocean currents follow the season of rain. In summer monsoon, the direction of the monsoon drift is north-east. And during the north-east winter monsoons, they follow the direction of east to west.

**Major oceanic currents of the world**

***Currents of the Pacific Ocean***

**Warm ocean currents**

- **The North Equatorial Current:** This originates off the western coast of Mexico and flows in a westerly direction and reaches the Philippines coast.
- **South Equatorial Current:** Due to the influence of south-eastern trade winds, it flows from east to west. This current is stronger than the north equatorial current. The volume of the water increases in the west as numerous minor currents join

from the left.

- **Kuroshio Current:** This is north-flowing on the west side of the North Pacific Ocean basin.
- **North Pacific Current:** The Kuroshio Current extends eastward and reaches the western coast of North America.

**Cold ocean currents**

- **Oyashio Current:** Also called Kurile Current, it flows through the Bering Strait in a southerly direction. It transports cold water from the Arctic Ocean to the Pacific Ocean.
- **Peru Current:** A cold current flowing along the western coast of South America from south to north.
- **Californian Current:** This is the eastward extension of the North Pacific Current. It is formed due to the movement of oceanic water from north to south along the California coast.

### *Currents of the Indian Ocean*

**Warm ocean currents**

- **North-East Monsoon Current:** This blows from land to sea in the northern hemisphere during winter and is formed between Andaman and Somali.
- **South-West Monsoon Current:** In summer, the general direction of monsoon winds is from south-west to north-east.

**Cold ocean currents**

- **West Wind Drift:** These are formed due to the westerlies, called Roaring Forties, at 40° latitude.

### *Currents of the Atlantic Ocean*

**Warm ocean currents**

- **North Atlantic Current:** It originates in the eastern part of North America and moves in a north-eastern direction towards the western coast of Europe.

- **Gulf Stream:** This originates near the Gulf of Mexico and moves towards western Europe after flowing along the Grand Banks region of North America.

**Cold ocean currents**

- **Labrador Current:** This flows between western Greenland and Baffin Bay. It meets the warm Gulf Stream off the coast of Newfoundland, making that area one of the richest fishing grounds in the world.
- **Canaries Current:** An extension of the North Atlantic Current.
- **Falkland Current:** This flows from the Antarctic region up to Argentina. It makes the east coast of South America cold.

***Effects of ocean currents***

- **Modifies climate:** The warm ocean currents when they reach the cold areas make them relatively warmer in the winter months. Cold ocean currents lower the temperature of the affected areas and cause snowfall. The Labrador Current keeps the ports frozen and causes snowfall in affected areas during

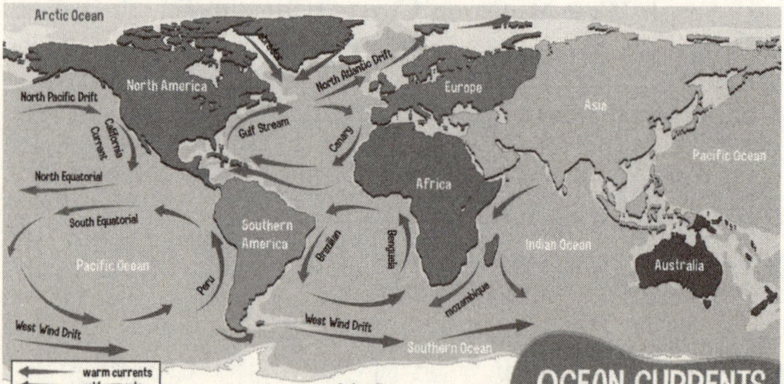


Ocean currents

winters. When warm winds blow over warm ocean currents, they pick up moisture and bring rainfall to the coastal areas. For example, the warm Kuroshio Current helps in causing rainfall along the east coast of Japan.

Cold ocean currents cause aridity, for example, the Kalahari Desert is formed due to the Benguela Current and the Atacama Desert due to the cold Peru Current.

- **Fishing and supply of plankton:** The meeting of warm and cold ocean currents makes for the best fishing grounds in the world. For example, the meeting of the warm Kuroshio Current and cold Oyashio Current makes Japan one of the richest fishing grounds in the world. Ocean currents help in transporting plankton from one part of the ocean to another.
- **Effects on navigation:** Dense fogs are formed at the meeting of warm and cold ocean currents. These affect navigation.

# 34

# CORAL REEFS AND MARINE RESOURCES

Coral reefs are formed due to the accumulation of skeletal remains of lime-secreting organisms that are called coral polyps. Coral polyps are common in tropical waters. Numerous coral polyps are grouped together as colonies and form calcareous shells around them. Coral reefs are formed due to the development of one shell over the other at a suitable depth. Coral reefs cannot survive on the surface, so they are always found at depths below the sea surface.

***Favourable conditions helping the growth of corals***

1. Corals are found mainly in the tropical seas and oceans as they require about 20°–21°C for their survival.
2. Corals flourish in sediment-free water. Muddy water hinders the growth of corals. Corals cannot flourish in freshwater also. So they are found far from coastal lands and not near the mouth of rivers.
3. Corals do not live in deeper waters. They avoid greater depths due to the lack of penetration of sunlight and oxygen.
4. Corals cannot survive in extremely saline water because saline water is poor in calcium carbonate, especially lime.

5. Ocean currents and waves bring sufficient food for the coral polyps. So corals cannot survive in enclosed seas because of the lack of supply of food.
6. Submarine platforms favour the growth of coral polyps. Corals can grow when there is a strong base of rocks and grow upward till they reach sea level.
7. Human activities like deforestation, pollution of oceanic water, overfishing and urban waste cause the death of coral polyps.

*Types of coral reefs*

1. **Fringing reef:** Coral reefs that are found along the continental margins or along islands are called fringing reefs. Here, the seaward slope is steeper than the landward slope. Fringing reefs are mainly attached to the coast, but sometimes, there can be a gap between the reef and the coast. This gap is filled with water, forming lagoons. These are called **boat channels**.
2. **Barrier reef:** The most extensive coral reefs are found here. These are generally found broken and not continuous. They are connected with the lagoons through a tidal inlet. Sometimes, the tidal inlets become so broad that ships can enter through them.
3. **Atoll:** They are formed around an island or on a submarine platform. These are rings of narrow growing corals. There is a lagoon in the middle of the ring.

Atolls are of three types.

- **Island atoll:** Having an island in the centre of the lagoon enclosed by a reef.
- **Coral island:** The island is formed due to deposition by oceanic waves.
- **True atoll:** A circular reef enclosing a shallow lagoon but no island.

**The Great Barrier Reef** in Australia is the largest in the world.

**Terms to remember**

**Coral pinnacles:** small ridges within lagoons
**Coral banks:** isolated shapeless reefs
**Faros:** chains of small atolls having several small lagoons

### *The origin of corals*

**Subsidence theory by Darwin:** According to Charles Darwin, coral polyps can only grow in shallow seawaters. Contrary to this coral reefs are also found at great depths. He believed that fringing reefs and atolls are found on land that is never stationary. In fact, these lands are always subsiding.

The stages of the formation of coral reefs and atolls are:

- **1st stage:** The formation of coral polyps on a suitable submarine platform. They grow upward and reach sea level. So a fringing reef is formed.
- **2nd stage:** The land is subjected to gradual subsidence, and coral reefs grow at greater depths.
- **3rd stage:** A lagoon is formed between the coast and the fringing reef. A barrier reef is formed.
- **4th stage:** More subsidence of the land causes further submergence of the island, and a ring of coral reef as an atoll is formed.

**Coral bleaching:** The loss of algae leads to whitening of the corals, which indicates the death of corals. A global concern, coral bleaching is the direct consequence of global warming and other human malpractices. El Nino, the outbreak of coral diseases and too much human interference, like oil spills, overfishing, etc., cause coral bleaching.

**Classification of Marine Resources**

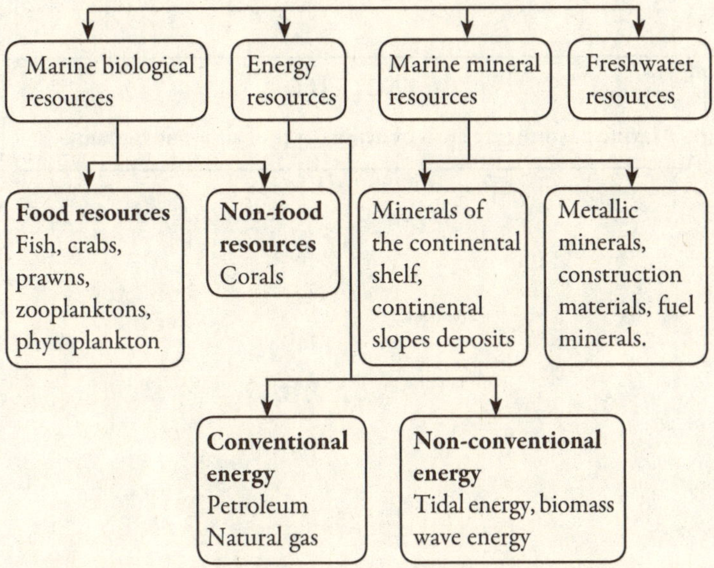


Marine organisms are divided into three categories based on **their habitats.**

1. **Plankton:** These are floating microorganisms of photic zones and are the food of marine organisms. They are divided into phytoplankton and zooplankton.
2. **Nektons:** Include algae, as well as fishes.
3. **Benthos community:** Includes all those marine organisms that live on at bottom of the seafloor. The majority of benthos include scavengers like sharks, swordfish, octopus, etc.

Corals are considered to be the most important marine organisms. They are generally called **rainforests of the ocean.** The richness of marine life depends on the variety of corals in the oceans. As we know, coral polyps grow in colonies, and these colonies form the habitat for several other marine organisms. Most of the marine fishes lay eggs in coral colonies.

**FACT FILE**

**Marine pastures** are areas of dense cover of algae and diatoms.

# BIOGEOGRAPHY

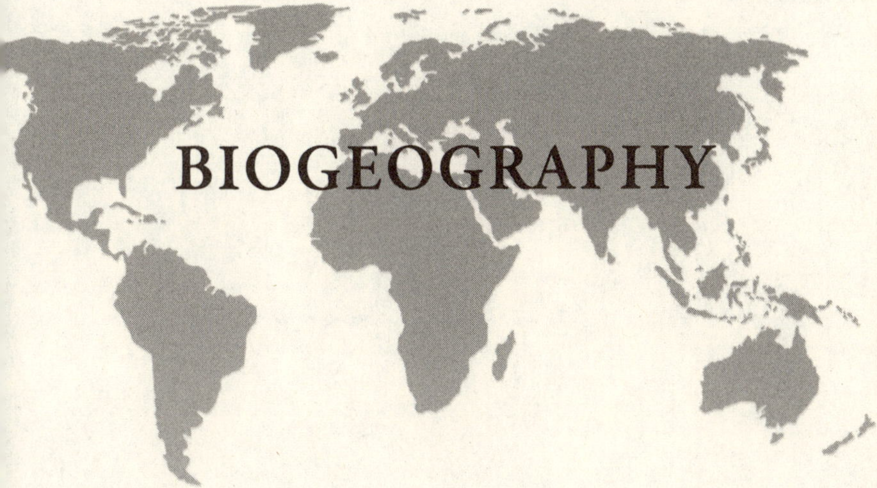

# 35

# THE BIOSPHERE

The study of the biosphere is called biogeography. Margaret Anderson has rightly remarked that biogeography is '**the essence of biological relations between man (considered as animal) and the whole of his animate and inanimate environment**.'

**Biosphere:** This is the part of the Earth that supports and contains living organisms. The biosphere consists of both living and non-living organisms, and there is constant interaction and flow of energy between the living beings and the physical environment and also within the living organisms themselves. The upper limit of the biosphere is determined by the availability of oxygen, suitable temperature, pressure conditions and moisture. The lower limit is determined by the availability of water and light that is needed to sustain life. The deepest roots of the trees that can sustain life and microorganisms, the depth of the oceans and the deepest of the oceanic trenches that can sustain marine life are the lowest extent of the biosphere.

The biosphere is always affected and modified by the constant flow of energy. These factors are called modifiers. These are of three types: physical modifiers, chemical modifiers and biological modifiers.

The physical modifiers affect the physical properties of the atmosphere in the form of climate change, temperature, humidity changes, etc. When chemical elements of soil, water or climate are modified, they are called chemical modifiers. Biological factors affect the population, land use and distribution of animals.

**Classification of Biosphere**

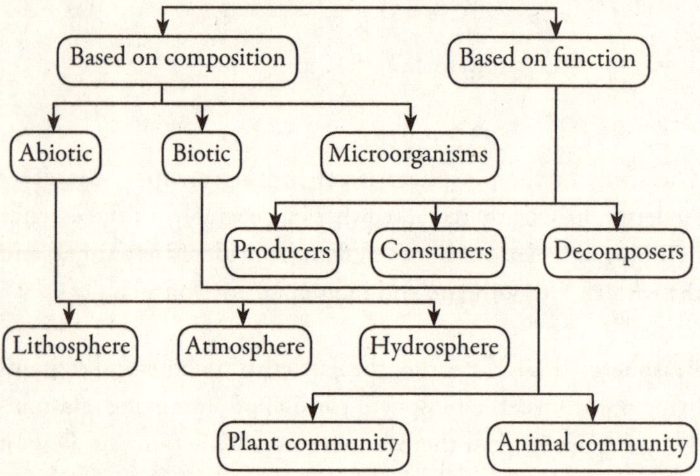


***Abiotic components***

**Lithosphere:** This consists of land, rocks, soil, minerals, erosion, transportation and depositional features produced by exogenic forces; mountains, plateaus and plains formed by endogenetic forces on and below the Earth's crust. The Earth's surface is a storehouse of minerals. Different landform features on and below the Earth's crust add to the dynamicity of the planet. The forces on and below the crust are constantly acting upon each other, leading to the creation, transformation, destruction and recreation of features. Soil is an important component of the lithosphere. It is made up of the breaking down or disintegration of rocks and its particles form the base on which plants grow. Soil acts as a reservoir of nutrients for living organisms.

**Atmosphere:** All the essential gases needed for the survival of the biosphere are provided by the atmosphere. The atmosphere filters the incoming solar radiation to the Earth by preventing the harmful UV rays of the sun from reaching the Earth. The atmosphere gives us all the weather phenomena, be it temperature, rainfall, humidity, air pressure, winds, cyclones, anticyclones, air currents, etc.

**Hydrosphere:** Water is an essential component for all forms of life. Water is needed for the circulation of nutrients among the different components of the ecosystem. Water is available as surface water or groundwater. Surface water is found in seas, oceans, lakes, rivers, streams, ponds, tanks and reservoirs. Groundwater is found in underground reserves called aquifers. The hydrosphere also includes deep-sea features such as continental shelves, continental slopes, abyssal plains, oceanic trenches, coral reefs, atolls, etc.

***Biotic components***

**Plant community:** The social groupings of plant species are plant communities. Plants are the primary producers since they produce their own food through the process of photosynthesis. A plant community includes plants of different species or a single species. There is a constant interaction between plants and their physical environment and also within themselves. Plants develop their own habitat depending on several factors of the environment. While soil and climate are the most significant ones, plants also control and affect the soil and climate of their physical habitat. For example, an area with dense vegetation will always support heavy precipitation and the presence of moist soil. Plants can be found in the form of naturally grown large areas covered with vegetation such as forests, meadows and grasslands, or they can be planted by man in the form of gardens, sanctuaries and nurseries.

***The importance of forests***

- Forests increase precipitation.
- They help in controlling soil erosion, erosion by wind, surface run-off and floods. The dense root system of trees helps in binding the soil particles together.
- Forests help in recharging underground water reserves.
- Forests are the natural habitats of rich wildlife.
- Forests act as the natural sink of carbon dioxide. They help in absorbing greenhouse gases and help in moderating temperature. They purify the air. They are a source of food and shelter for both humans and wildlife.
- They help in controlling air, water and land pollution.

**Animal community:** The animal community consists of autotrophs or plants and heterotrophs that depend on autotrophs for their food. The heterotrophic animals are also called primary consumers. These animals are further classified into:

- **Saprophytes:** Animals that feed on the decayed remains of dead plants and animals. Example: plant fungus.
- **Parasites:** Organisms that depend on other plants and animals for their survival. Example: protozoa.
- **Holozoic:** Those that consume their food through their mouths. All animals are included in this category.

**Microorganisms:** They decompose dead plants and animals and other organic matter. During this process of decomposition, the microorganisms feed on the decayed parts and break down the organic matter so that they can be utilized again by primary producers for making food. Bacteria and fungi come under microorganisms.

**FACT FILE**

**Producers:** Green plants that manufacture their own food through photosynthesis and nutrients from the soil through their roots.

**Consumers:** Includes man and other animals. They can be herbivores (primary consumers that feed on plants only), carnivores (secondary consumers that feed on primary consumers) and omnivores (that feed on both)

A deer is a herbivore, a lion is a carnivore, and man is an omnivore!

**Decomposers:** These decompose and feed on dead plants and animals.

# 36

## ECOLOGY AND ECOSYSTEM

**Definition:** Ernst Haeckel has rightly defined ecology as 'the **study of the reciprocal relationship between living organisms and their environments**'. The word 'ecology' is derived from the combination of two Greek words – 'oikos' meaning 'home' and 'logos' meaning 'study'.

The concept of ecology can be applied in various fields, whether it is population, human behaviour, climate, human genetics, meteorology, etc. Ecology is divided into two broad categories: autecology and synecology.

- **Autecology:** Auto means self, so this ecology studies a particular species.
- **Synecology:** Syn means together, so this ecology studies a group of organisms. Basically, autecology studies a particular species and its relation to the physical environment, the habitat in which it grows. Synecology is concerned with the study of the composition, characteristics, structure and distribution of groups of organisms.

*Fields of ecology*

- **Paleoecology:** Studies the origin of plants and animals, past geological periods and the different eras of evolution of flora and fauna.
- **Population ecology:** Studies the number of species in the ecosystem, their interrelationships, the factors influencing their distribution and growth.
- **Habitat ecology:** The study of habit that includes forests, grasslands, oceans, rivers, deserts, etc.
- **Cytoecology:** Studies the cytological details that are the microscopic cell structure of the organisms of the population species in relation to their physical environment.
- **Ecosystem ecology:** Studies the structure and function of an ecosystem, how they are interrelated, the function and interrelationship between the biotic and abiotic components.
- **Conservation ecology:** Studies the protection and management of natural resources so that the needs of the future generation are not jeopardized.
- **Production ecology:** Deals with the production of energy, conversion of energy and the flow of energy through organisms, which is essential for the survival and growth of organisms.
- **Radiation ecology:** The study of radioactive substances and the positive and negative impacts of radiation for human welfare.
- **Gene ecology:** Studies the genetics of the population, the origin and evolution of species.

*The principles of ecology*

1. Man being the most important member of an ecosystem has the power to modify the natural environment by using resources efficiently or inefficiently. He can either introduce new farming techniques, cause deforestation, construct buildings, cultivate and introduce a new breed of vegetation or change habitats.

2. Ecological study depends on the study of the ecosystem, which is the most vital unit.
3. Living organisms are always interacting with each other and influence each other. Similarly, they also interact with their physical environments.
4. The sun is the prime source of energy for all organisms. Solar energy is needed for the process of photosynthesis. The flow of energy from the sun is non-cyclic and unidirectional. This flow also helps in the circulation of nutrients within the different trophic levels.
5. There is a constant loss of energy as one moves up the trophic level.
6. The productivity of an ecosystem refers to the rate at which biomass is produced by the organisms per unit time by green plants through photosynthesis with the help of solar energy. It depends on how much solar energy is used or available and the efficiency of the plants to convert the solar energy into chemical energy.
7. The ecosystem productivity decreases from the equator towards the poles due to fewer solar rays received at the poles.

**What is climax vegetation?**

It is the vegetation community that develops at the end of succession. This happens when vegetation passes through several phases and ultimately derives an equilibrium. Now this vegetation community will remain unaltered unless disturbed.

**Ecosystem**

**Definition:** Ecosystem has been defined by E.P. Odum (1971) as '**living organisms and their non-living (abiotic) environment are inseparably interrelated and interact upon each other. Any unit**

**that includes all of the organisms (i.e. the community) in a given area interacting with the physical environment so that a flow of energy leads to clearly defined trophic structure, biotic diversity and material cycle (i.e. exchange of materials between living and non-living parts) within the system in an ecological system or ecosystem**'. So in simpler words, we can say that an ecosystem is the process of interaction between organisms and their environment.

*Types of ecosystems*

| Natural ecosystem | Artificial ecosystem |
|---|---|
| Operate all by themselves without any human interference. They can be terrestrial ecosystems, such as forests, grasslands, deserts, or marine ecosystems, such as oceans, rivers, etc. | These are maintained by man and his activities such as agriculture – the cultivation of crops, which modifies both the physical and social environment. |

*Characteristics of an ecosystem*

- An ecosystem is the sum of all living organisms and their physical environment in a given area.
- It is composed of abiotic and biotic components.
- It occupies a well-defined area.
- There is always an interaction between the organisms and among the organisms.
- These are natural resource systems.
- There is a continuous input and output of energy and matter.
- The sun is the prime source of energy.
- An ecosystem has a dimension or a particular unit area. It can be a small space, such as a little pond, or as big as a desert.
- It is well-organized and structured.

### *Structure of an ecosystem*

The structure of an ecosystem is related to the diversity of species. The greater the species diversity, the more is the complexity of the ecosystem. The structure of an ecosystem includes the species, their composition, numbers, history, space and distribution, as well as the distribution, quantity and nature of non-living things.

### *Functions of an ecosystem*

The functioning of an ecosystem depends on energy flow. The flow of energy is unidirectional, while matter flows in a cyclic path. The sun is the primary source of energy. Green plants or primary producers absorb solar energy to produce food through the process of photosynthesis, which converts solar energy into chemical energy. This chemical energy helps in the production of food by autotrophs. This is called **trophic level 1**. Some amount of energy is lost through respiration by plants. This energy of the autotrophs is consumed by animals of the first order or herbivores or primary consumers. Herbivores use this energy to build their own tissues. This is called **trophic level 2**. These are again transferred to carnivores (secondary consumers). This is called **trophic level 3**.

- It is important to note that not all energy is transferred from plants to herbivores or from herbivores to carnivores. Some amount of chemical energy is lost through respiration.
- The higher the level of animals, the more complex will be the transfer of energy as animals of a higher order will need more energy to perform their activities than animals of a lower order.

Some portions of the energy are then transferred from trophic level 3 to **trophic level 4**, that is, omnivores. They are also called tertiary consumers. Man is an important example of an omnivore.

- Man takes energy from trophic level 1, as well as 2.

Some portion of energy is lost through respiration by omnivores. The stored chemical energy of the remains of dead plants and animals is transferred to decomposers. These decomposers absorb the energy released by both plants and animals. The decomposers then release a substantial amount of energy to the atmosphere.

Matters or nutrients flow in a cyclic manner. Both organic and inorganic substances move in the biosphere, hydrosphere, lithosphere and atmosphere through systems of cycle in such a way that the total mass of all the substances remains the same. The inorganic elements comprise waste materials, as well as the dead remains of plants and animals. Plants derive energy from the sun, as well as from the roots and soil through root osmosis. This is used to produce food and for the development of tissues. The nutrients derived through the roots of plants are then transferred to the various components of the biosphere through a biogeochemical cycle.

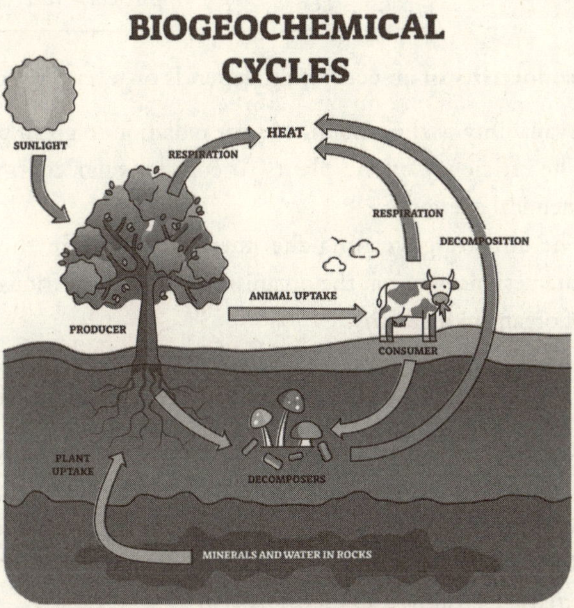


Biogeochemical cycle

**Types of productivity of an ecosystem**

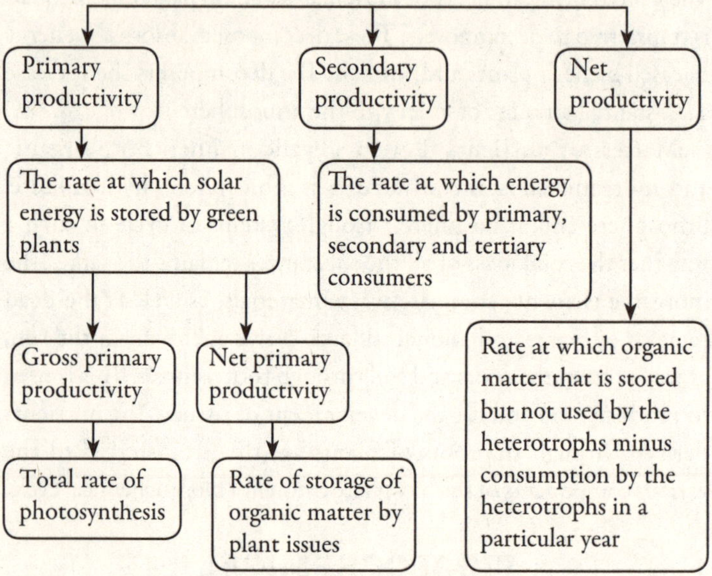


**The productivity of an ecosystem depends on a few factors:**

- Availability of the amount of solar radiation to green plants.
- The efficiency of the plants to convert solar energy into chemical energy.
- The climate governing the nutrient supply in the area, interactions between the organisms, the role of various levels of organism hierarchy.

**There are three levels of primary productivity in the world.**

1. **Regions of high primary productivity:** tropical rainforests, shallow water bodies, alluvial plains, intensive cultivated areas
2. **Regions of low primary productivity:** permafrost areas
3. **Regions of intermediate productivity:** grasslands, lakes, extensive farming areas

# 37

## BASIC CONCEPTS OF FOOD CHAIN, FOOD WEB AND TROPHIC LEVELS

**Trophic level:** This is the chain of transfer of food energy from one group of organisms to the other.

> **What is a food chain?**
>
> It is the chain of transfer of energy from one group of organisms to another in an ecosystem.

- **Trophic level 1:** This is the base of the food chain. It is composed of green autotrophic plants. Green plants use the chlorophyll in them to absorb solar energy, water, carbon dioxide and nutrients to produce food through the process of photosynthesis. They use the energy to build plant tissues. Green plants are the source of food for all organisms of the upper trophic levels.
- **Trophic level 2:** These include organisms that cannot produce their own food but depend on green plants for their survival. They are herbivorous or primary consumers. This includes cattle, goats, sheep, grasshoppers and deer.

- **Trophic level 3:** These are the carnivores or secondary consumers. They feed on the primary consumers. They can be either land animals, such as lions, tigers and eagles, or animals living in soil, such as bacteria and fungi, which feed on the decomposed and decayed remains of dead animals and marine animals such as sperm whales and sea otters.
- **Trophic level 4:** These animals are called omnivores. They take food from all the other levels as tertiary consumers. Man is the perfect example of an omnivore since man derives energy from either plants or by feeding on animals on second and third trophic levels.

**What is a food web?**

The process of transferring food energy from one level to another is not simple; it is a complex process. There are several interconnected, overlapping food chains. Such food chains are called food webs. For example, grass is eaten by grasshoppers. Grasshoppers also feed on grains. Rats feed on both grains and grasshoppers. Owls feed on both grasshoppers and rats. Similarly, rabbits can feed on both grass as well as grains.

Food webs maintain the stability of the ecosystem. The more complex the food web, the more the interdependence between organisms and the more the stability of the ecosystem.

The complexity of a food web depends on certain factors.

**Length of the food chain:** The food chain becomes longer if there is more diversity in the organisms.

When a particular level acts as an alternative to animals belonging to multiple trophic levels, this will make the food web more complex.

**Ecological pyramids:** As already mentioned, at each step in the food chain, the organisms never consume the total amount of

Food chain and food web

energy from their previous level. Some amount of energy is lost through respiration. So every organism passes on a lesser amount of energy to the next level. The higher the trophic levels, the lesser the energy available for the final members. This decrease in the amount of energy at higher levels creates a tapering form in the shape of a pyramid. This is called an ecological pyramid. The base of the pyramid is broad because it contains many organisms, while as one goes to the top, the number of organisms decreases.

*Types of ecological pyramids*

**Pyramid of numbers:** When only the number of species is included, it is called a pyramid of numbers. The base of the pyramid consists of autotrophs, which are larger in number. Above it lie the primary consumers at trophic level 2, which are larger in size and comparatively less in number. (For example, at trophic level 1 lies grass. Grasses are found in thousands of blades, which are consumed by a single cow at trophic level 2). Similarly, at level 3 lie the secondary consumers, which are less in numbers than trophic level 2, but the size gets bigger. Thus, in this kind of pyramid, the size of the animals gets bigger as one goes up, and the numbers also decrease towards the top.

- **Exception to the law:** This happens in forest ecosystems. Forests consist of many large trees. A single tree can be fed on by large numbers of herbivores at trophic level 2. So the base of the pyramid is tapered and broader at trophic level 2 due to many herbivores. A single tree can be consumed by many birds, hyperparasites and parasites as primary and secondary consumers.

**Pyramid of biomass:** When the weight of the organisms is taken into consideration, it is called a biomass pyramid. The shape of the pyramid implies the decrease in the biomass at each trophic level from the base to the apex. The total biomass of the producers is more than the primary consumers, and the biomass of the primary consumers is more than the secondary ones. Since some amount of energy is always lost at each trophic level, the amount of biomass difference depends on the rate at which the energy is stored below.

**Pyramid of energy:** When the total amount of energy used at each trophic level is taken into account, it is called a pyramid of energy. At trophic level 1, the amount of energy will be more than at trophic level 2. The primary producers may have smaller biomass, but the amount of energy conserved and transferred may be greater than the organisms of trophic level 2, which may have a bigger biomass. The loss of energy through respiration is also maximum at the base and decreases towards the top.

# 38

# CIRCULATION OF MATTER

## Hydrological cycle/water cycle

The hydrological cycle involves the following steps:

- Evaporation of water from oceans, seas and lakes through insolation.
- The conversion of water into water vapor through the process of condensation.
- The movement of atmospheric moisture overseas and continents by air circulation.
- The release of water back to the Earth through precipitation either in the form of snowfall or rainfall.
- The eventual return of the water to the seas and oceans.

When there is precipitation, water that directly falls on the oceans and seas is called **direct falls**. Some amount of rain also falls on vegetation and reaches the ground. The amount falling on the ground gets lost through surface run-off or can get percolated through the pores and crevasses into the underground.

## Carbon cycle

There are three phases in the transfer of carbon in the biosphere.

a. **Gaseous phase:** carbon in the form of carbon dioxide in the atmosphere
b. **Liquid phase:** dissolved carbon dioxide in water
c. **Solid phase:** carbon stored in fossil fuels, organic matter

There are two ways in which the movement of carbon takes place. Either it takes place as a gaseous phase in which the carbon dioxide moves as gas in the atmosphere and in dissolved form in water or as a non-gaseous phase in which the carbon is stored in fossil fuels or rocks.

- The carbon dioxide enters the biosphere from the atmosphere through the process of photosynthesis with the help of sunlight by green plants. The component that provides energy is called the donor component and the one receiving the energy is called the recipient component. The transfer of carbon from the donor to the recipient components is a two-way process. The amount of carbon dioxide absorbed by the plants depends on the density of vegetation, activities, other natural factors and the concentration of $CO_2$ in the atmosphere.
- The carbon dioxide absorbed by plants is stored in the tissues and barks of trees as an organic reservoir. This carbon is released due to the breakdown of carbohydrates during respiration from living organisms. Respiration converts the carbohydrates to gaseous carbon dioxide that returns to the atmosphere.

**FACT FILE**

The hydrological cycle involves the movement of water across oceans, continents and the atmosphere, but around 95% of the total moisture of the biosphere is never available to the cycle. Only 5% is available. Out of this 5%, 97% is stored in oceans, 2.15% stored in the form of polar ice caps, 0.62% in the form of groundwater and 0.03% in the form of freshwater lakes, rivers and ponds.

- Some amount of carbon dioxide is released back when there is a breakdown of the carbohydrates by animals of trophic levels 2, 3 and 4.
- Even decomposers break down carbon to carbon dioxide.
- The sedimentary reserves store carbon in the form of fossil fuels and organic matter for a long geological period. When these rocks are weathered or eroded and fossil fuels are burnt, this carbon dioxide is released back into the atmosphere.

**FACT FILE**

It is important to note that in the carbon cycle, the amount of carbon that is released back into the atmosphere is more than the amount removed. This is due to human interference, where deforestation and burning of fossil fuels increase carbon dioxide concentration, leading to global warming.

## Oxygen cycle

Oxygen is a vital element for living organisms as it supports life. It is a chemically active element because it easily combines with most elements in the biosphere. There are different forms of oxygen from the atmosphere to the biosphere: molecular oxygen, water, carbon dioxide and inorganic compounds such as oxides (ferrous oxides, calcium carbonates).

- Green plants release oxygen into the atmosphere at the time of photosynthesis.
- Some amount of oxygen is released into the atmosphere through volcanic eruptions.
- This oxygen is then utilized by animals of terrestrial and marine ecosystems for respiration.
- Some amount is consumed during the burning of fossil fuels.
- Some amount enters the sedimentary rock reservoirs through oxides.

# 39

## MAJOR NATURAL REGIONS OF THE WORLD

> **What is a biome?**
>
> A large natural ecosystem consisting of an assemblage of plant and animal communities is a biome.

***Tropical evergreen rainforest biome***

- **Location and extent:** This biome extends between 10°N and 10°S latitudes. It is the richest one in terms of its luxuriant plant growth and diversity in animal life since it remains hot and humid throughout the year. The equatorial regions of the Congo basin, the Amazon basin and the forests of the SE Asian countries come under this biome.
- **Climate:** The mean annual temperature remains about 20°C throughout the year. The average annual rainfall is about 200 cm. There are no seasons, and the diurnal range of temperature is low. The length of days and nights are almost equal. Rainfall is of the convectional type. It rains almost every day in the late afternoon, called 4 o'clock showers.

- **Plant life:** Numerous species of plants are found in this biome. Mostly evergreen, hardwood and broad-leaved trees are found here. The rainforest is covered with big trees, creepers, climbers and epiphytes. Each vertical layer of the forest presents new and different strata of plants from the soil surface to the uppermost forest canopy. The typical trees found here are mahogany, ebony, rosewood, rubber and cinchona.
- **The first layer or the topmost strata:** It is the uppermost canopy of the tallest trees of the forest. The canopy looks like an umbrella. This layer receives the maximum amount of rainfall and sunshine. The height of the tallest trees can be as high as 60 m. This is the emergent layer.
- **The second layer or the canopy layer:** It is found below the first layer and has a height of about 20–35 m.
- **Third layer:** Here, the height of the trees is about 15 to 20 m. The leaves are broad in the surface area to trap as much sunlight as possible. The amount of sunshine and rainfall decreases at this layer due to the thick and dense growth of the trees above. This is the understorey.
- **Lowest layer or the forest floor:** The absence of sunlight makes the ground layer very dark and moist. It consists of only a few shrubs, grasses and creepers that grow on taller trees.
- **Animal life:** This biome is full of different varieties of animals. The animals in this biome have some typical characteristics: Since there is an abundant supply of food throughout the year, the animals found here are the least mobile. They are larger and bulkier in size and occupy the various strata of the forest. The floor of the forest is filled with large ground animals like deer, elephants, bison, gorillas, wild pigs, leopards, tigers, etc. Most of the animals are arboreal, like monkeys, squirrels, etc. There are varieties of birds, too, like parakeets, toucans and barbets.

***Monsoon deciduous forest biome***

- **Location and extent:** This biome is associated with the monsoon biome and is found in the belts of south and south-east Asia, except the equatorial zone, northern Australia and eastern Africa.

  Apart from this, a few localized pockets are found in South Africa, southern Brazil and south-eastern USA.
- **Climate:** The maximum temperature during dry season ranges between 38°C and 45°C. The average annual temperature during warm summers, which are hot and humid, stays between 20°C and 30°C. Rainfall mainly occurs during the south-west monsoon period from July to September, and there is spatial variation in the amount of rainfall received. The mean annual rainfall is around 150 cm. The winters are cool and dry. Only a few regions receive rainfall during winter from the retreating monsoon winds.
- **Plant life:** Most of the trees found here are deciduous. The height of the trees ranges between 12 m to 30 m. Trees are found in pure stands and are broad-leaved that is the leaves are broad enough to absorb as much water as possible during the rainy season. The trees shed their leaves during the dry season to conserve moisture. The barks of the trees are thick, hard and rough. There are also climbers in the form of epiphytes. The typical trees found here are sal, teak, rosewood, mango, neem and shisham.
- **Animal life:** The variety of animal species in the tropical deciduous forests is less than in the equatorial rainforest. The animals range from small-sized ones like squirrels and rats to large and bulky ones like bison, elephants, tigers, wild pigs and wild buffaloes. There are different species of birds, too. This region also sees a lot of migratory birds from the Arctic during its cool, short winters.

***Temperate grassland biome***

- **Location and extent:** The temperate grasslands are mainly found in the interior of continents where the offshore westerlies keep the climate hot and dry. The grasslands are treeless. In the northern hemisphere, the grasslands are hot and dry, while in the southern hemisphere, they have a comparatively better climate due to the maritime influences of the surrounding seas.

  The different names of the world temperate grasslands:

  - Prairies: North America
  - Pampas: South America
  - Veldts: Africa
  - Downs: Australia
  - Canterbury: New Zealand
  - Steppes: Europe

- **Climate:** In the northern hemisphere, the temperate grasslands have an extreme climate because of their interior location and scanty rainfall, while in the southern hemisphere, the climate is maritime. Summers are warm, and temperature ranges between 20°C to 30°C. Winters are very cold and severe in the northern hemisphere. The temperature in January is from –18°C to 10°C. The average annual rainfall ranges between 25 cm to 75 cm throughout the year in different locations of the temperate grasslands. Winter sees snowfall in the landlocked areas of the extreme north.
- **Plant life:** Grasses dominate the grasslands. The lack of rainfall makes the grasslands almost treeless. Different species of grass are found in the temperate grasslands depending on the rainfall, location, temperature and soil. The Australian Downs comprise a mixture of grasses with eucalyptus trees. Winter is warmer here than their counterpart in the northern hemisphere.

The North American Prairie is found between the foothills of the Rockies and the temperate deciduous forest in the east. The tall grass prairies have a height of 1.5 m to 2.5 m (bluestem), mixed prairies have grasses of heights of 0.6 to 1.2 m (needlegrass/little blue stem) and short grasses of about 60 cm.

- **Animal life:** Herbivores mainly dominate the grasslands. Large mammals, such as buffaloes, deer, antelopes and gazelles, kangaroos, and emu (Downs) are found here. The mammals are large and bulky in order to protect themselves from predators like wolves and leopards. Burrowing animals, such as rats, moles, and mongoose, are found. They dig holes in the soft soil to store food and protect themselves from the extreme winter. There has been a modification in the animal life of the grasslands. Large-scale hunting and deforestation to make way for agriculture have led to the disappearance of animals from this region.

**Savanna**

- **Location and extent:** Found between 10° to 20° latitudes in both the hemispheres, it includes the Llanos of Venezuela and Columbia, Brazil and Paraguay in South America and Sudan and other parts of central and east Africa.
- **Climate:** The temperature remains high throughout the year with abundant sunshine. The cold dry season is characterized by day temperatures of about 26°C to 32°C and nights are around 20°C. The warm dry season is marked by temperatures of 32°C to 38°C. The amount of rainfall depends on the distance from the equator. The savanna grasslands close to the equator, for example, the savanna grasslands of Brazil, get an annual rainfall of about 70 to 200 cm.
- **Plant life:** The savannas are dominated by tall grass and herbaceous plants. The grass is hard, rough, dominates the

ground layer and generally attains a height of about 80 cm and sometimes 500 cm, like the African elephant grass. Some trees of the savanna have distinct characteristics that help them reduce water loss through evapotranspiration, so they remain green even during dry periods. The roots are long to penetrate deep into the ground to absorb underground water. The baobab tree is a significant tree found in the savannas.

- **Animal life:** The African savanna has the most variety of animals. Large herbivorous mammals like zebras, giraffes, buffaloes, elephants and antelopes are found here. The Australian savanna is dominated by marsupials like kangaroos and wallabies. Toucans, parakeets, kingfishers, woodpeckers and doves are common in South American savannas. There is also a large variety of invertebrates found in the savannas, like insects (locusts, grasshoppers, crickets) and arthropods (scorpions, spiders).

**Tropical desert**

- **Location and extent:** Tropical deserts are found on the western margins of the continents between 15° to 30° latitudes north and south of the equator. The flow of offshore trade winds in the western margins of the continents makes the regions dry and hot. The regions include the Sahara Desert (Africa), Namib and Kalahari (southern part of Africa), the deserts of Thar, Iran, Arabia (Asia), Peruvian (South America), Californian, Sonoran, and the Australian Outback in Australia.
- **Climate:** Extremes of temperature are found in deserts. The summers are hot, and the winters are cold. In summer, the temperature ranges between 30° to 45°C, while in winter, the temperature sometimes goes down to less than 15°C. The diurnal range of temperature is also very high. Frost is common in winter. In some areas, the summer temperature

shoots up to 58°C. The reason for high temperatures during the day is the absence of vegetation cover because of which the land absorbs heat very fast. However, at night, the cloudless skies promote high terrestrial radiation, causing a drop in temperature. Rainfall is scanty with less than 25 cm annual rainfall. The offshore trade winds and cold ocean currents make the climate dry. Local winds like sirocco, mistral and bora may bring pleasant weather conditions and cause short wet spells in the coastal parts.

- **Plant life:** Because of the scanty rainfall and dry conditions, the kind of natural vegetation found in deserts is of the **xerophyte** type. They are adapted to the natural arid conditions as they have long roots, thick barks and waxy leaves. They are mostly stunted trees that are leafless and have a strong odour to protect themselves from grazing animals. The typical plants are cacti, date palms, prickly pear, acacia, grasses and shrubs.
- **Animal life:** Burrowing animals are found in large numbers, like rats, snakes and squirrels. These animals protect themselves from the heat by staying indoors. Apart from these, camels, jackals, hyenas and antelopes are common.

**Mediterranean biome**

- **Location and extent:** This biome extends between 30 ° to 45° N and S latitudes in the western parts of the continents. The regions are lands around the Mediterranean Sea, central Chile of South America, central and southern California, USA, the coastal lands of Africa and Asia bordering the Mediterranean Sea and some coastal parts of western and southern Australia.
- **Climate:** Summers are hot and dry, while winters are cool and wet. Summers are sunny, and the temperature ranges between 20°C to 27°C. The temperature in winter ranges between 5°C

to 10°C. Rainfall is received in winter due to the shifting of pressure belts, ranging between 30 to 60 cm.

- **Plant life:** The vegetation of this biome naturally adapts to survive the hot dry summers. The trees have long roots, thick stems and waxy, smaller leaves to prevent the loss of water through evapotranspiration. The common trees found here are karri, jarrah varieties of eucalyptus, oak, chaparral shrubs and several varieties of garden flower plants. With the advent of modernization, today, the Mediterranean lands are known for the widespread cultivation of citrus fruits, such as grapes, olives and oranges.
- **Animal life:** The animals found here are mainly mule deer, wood rats, squirrels, coyotes, lizards, snakes, foxes and rabbits. Most of the native mammals have now disappeared due to the clearing of forests for farming. The Australian region has kangaroos, wallabies and mice. The typical birds are whistlers, honeyeaters, robins, etc.

**Taiga region**

- **Location and extent:** It lies between 55° to 60°N in the northern hemisphere. It merges with the tundra in the north around the Arctic Circle. The region experiences a continental climate, so only conifers are found on the uplands of Europe, Russia and North America. The regions include northern Siberia (Asia), southern Canada, southern Alaska (North America), Sweden, Norway and Finland (Europe).
- **Climate:** The winters are very long and severe, and the summers are shorter and warmer. Summers last for only three to four months, and rainfall ranges between 25 to 100 cm. It mainly occurs as snowfall in winter since the temperature remains below freezing point. Frost occurs in August. Rainfall

is evenly distributed throughout the year. Cold anticyclones in the form of blizzards or snowstorms all occur during winter.

- **Plant life:** The most dominant trees are evergreen conifers. These are naturally adapted to survive in the long, chilly winters. They are found in a continuous belt from North America to Asia. These trees are soft-wooded, have needle-shaped leaves and downward-drooping limbs, which help in snow shedding. Some broad-leaved trees, such as birch and willow, are also found. The dominant trees are pine, spruce, cedar, oak, elm and maple. The southern part of the taiga sees a smooth transition from conifers to temperate mixed vegetation due to a slight rise in temperature.
- **Animal life:** The extreme winter makes wildlife difficult in the taiga. Only a few species are found in the boreal/taiga forests, such as Siberian fox, salamander, Canadian toad, wood frog, etc. They mostly hibernate in winter. Large numbers of herbivore mammals are found, such as caribou, reindeer, wild boar and snow sheep. Small mammals, such as beaver, squirrel and chipmunk, and predatory mammals that travel long distances to catch prey are also found, such as European lynx, Siberian weasel, wolf, red fox, arctic fox, polar bear, black bear, Siberian tiger, etc. Many migratory birds from the taiga region migrate to the warmer south to escape the harsh winters.

### Tundra region

- **Location and extent:** The word 'tundra' means 'barren land'. It includes parts of Alaska, northern parts of Canada, northern Siberia and the coastal strips of Greenland. The severity of climate causes rapid changes in the vegetation below the tree line. The tundra is found between the southern limit of the permanent ice caps in the north to the northern limits of the taiga in the south.

- **Climate:** The climate is characterized by severe winters, very low temperatures throughout the year and little insolation. The tundra remains a barren land due to the severity of the climate. The below-freezing-point temperature leads to permafrost. Precipitation occurs as snowfall below 40 cm. Winters are very long and severe, and summers are cool. The region experiences six months of daylight and six months of night due to its location at the poles.
- **Plant life:** During summers when the temperature rises a little, mosses and lichens grow on the soil. The vegetation found in tundra is **cryophytes** – ones that are naturally adapted to survive in the harsh cold weather. Most of these are stunted plants with a height of about 5 to 8 cm. These plants do not grow tall and remain stuck to the surface to protect themselves from blizzards.
- **Animal life:** Both resident, as well as migratory animals, are found in this biome. The resident animals have thick, furry coats that protect them from the severe winter. The thick coat acts as an insulator that is impervious to cold. For example, the American musk ox. The musk ox shed their heavy coats

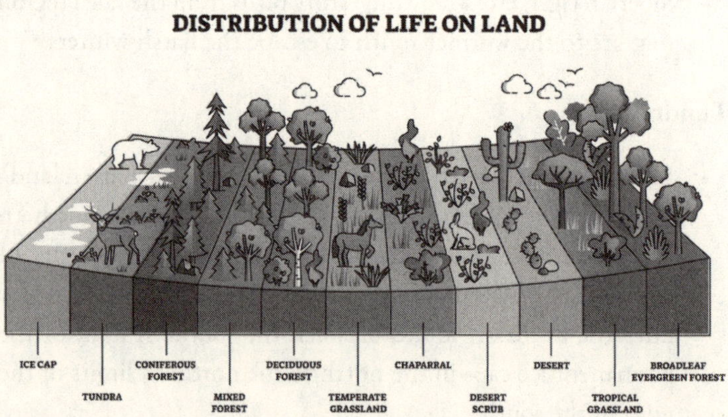

in summer to adjust to the warm summer. The arctic fox has a much thicker fur coat to withstand the winter. Arctic foxes can survive and remain active even during long winters. The resident birds have feathers that work as insulators.

Migratory birds leave the tundra in autumn and are the first ones to return in early spring. These include geese, ducks and swan. These birds do not have special features to protect themselves from the severe winter. The Arctic tern is the longest-flying migratory bird. It flies from the Arctic tundra all the way to Antarctica in the southern hemisphere. The migratory animals include reindeer and caribou. These animals come down to the taiga biome to spend the winters.

# PEDOLOGY

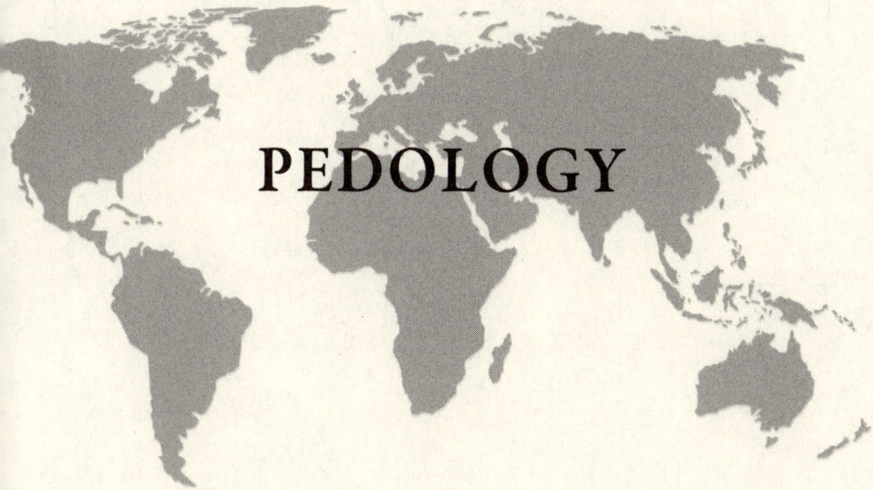

# 40

## WORLD SOILS

Soil can be classified based on several factors.

Let us first see the classification of soil based on **climate.**

- **Arid soils:** As the name suggests, these types of soils are found in arid or desert regions with little precipitation and high rates of evaporation. They have a sandy texture and less organic matter.
- **Semi-arid soils:** These are found in semi-arid regions with minimum precipitation. They contain more clay and organic matter as compared to arid soils.
- **Subtropical soils:** They are found in subtropical regions with warm and humid summers.
- **Tropical soils:** Found in tropical regions where the amount of rainfall is more. The heavy amount of rainfall leaches the soil, that is, the nutrients from the topsoil may get removed.
- **Temperate soils:** These soils are fertile as they are found in temperate climates, where both temperature and rainfall are moderate.
- **Boreal soils:** Found in cool or taiga climate. These soils can be acidic and may contain high amounts of organic matter.

- **Polar soils:** Found in the polar regions – extreme low-temperature regions that keep the soil permafrost for most parts of the year. They contain limited organic matter.

***Classification of soil on the basis of global location***

- **Zonal soils:** These soils depend on climate as the main factor for their formation.
- **Intrazonal soils:** These soils depend on any particular local factor for their formation.
- **Azonal soils:** They are poorly developed or immature soils.

Let us go through the subtypes of each of the above soils:

**Zonal soil:** As said before, this type of soil is formed primarily depending on the climate and natural vegetation of the region. Its subtypes are:

1. **Podzols:** They are found to the south of the tundra region and are associated with taiga vegetation. The humus is washed down and accumulated (podzolization) as humus-rich B horizon. There is a high concentration of iron oxide at the B horizon. The E horizon is bleached.
2. **Brown Earth:** They are found to the south of the podzol region and especially cover Great Britain. They support deciduous vegetation and are less leached than podzols. They are also less acidic and are rich in organic matter.
3. **Tundra soils:** There is presence of a peaty layer due to the slow rate of plant decomposition in stable slope conditions. In active slope conditions, the soil is thin. In extreme cold climates, the soil remains permafrost and does not support vegetation.
4. **Sierozem:** These are found typically in arid and semi-arid regions. The upward capillary action forces the lime and gypsum to come up to the surface. The amount of organic

matter is low due to less leaf fall. The plants growing in these soils are mostly xerophytes.

5. **Chernozem soils:** They are common in temperate grassland regions or the prairies. They are rich in calcium due to less leaching. The dark colour of the soil is due to the presence of alkaline-rich minerals. The humus content is low, and the primary parent material of this soil is loess.
6. **Prairie soil:** It occurs at the transition zone of increasing precipitation between the chernozems and forest brown Earth.
7. **Chestnut soil:** It occurs in the arid belt of chernozem soil. It has low organic matter content.
8. **Grumusols:** They are dark clayey soils, and they have a tendency to develop cracks during the dry season. They are common in the dry savanna that has warm, dry summers. The soil is rich in calcium, which gives it its dark colour.
9. **Ferralsols:** Tropical soil that is rich in ferric oxides. The colour of the soil is occasionally red, brown or yellow due to the presence of sesquioxides of iron and aluminium. These soils are not fertile as they are poor in humus.

**Intrazonal soils:** Here the main soil-forming factors are relief, parent material and age rather than only vegetation and climate.

1. **Hydromorphic soils:** These soils are associated with the presence of underground water tables. They are associated with marshes, wetlands and poor drainage.
2. **Calcimorphic soils:** They are formed from calcium-rich parent material. They are of two subtypes: terra rossa, which are found in the Mediterranean region, and rendzinas, which are rich with dark organic matter, found in Britain.
3. **Halomorphic soils:** These are saline soils found in deserts. They can be of three subtypes:

a. **Solonchak:** found in depressions and form white salts in dry periods
b. **Solonetz:** formed by intense alkalization and consist of sodium carbonate
c. **Sodic soils:** bleached soil formed due to the leaching of clays and sesquioxides.

**Azonal soils:** These soils lack a well-developed soil profile and are poorly developed.

***Soil profile***

The soil profile is the vertical profile of soil that extends from the surface to the parent material below. Each of the horizons has a distinct characteristic that runs horizontally to the soil surface and is different from the adjacent layers above or below. There are five master layers in the soil profile. However, one must remember that all soil profiles may not have five horizons.

1. **The O horizon:** Surface horizon comprising organic matter at different stages of decomposition. It is most developed in forested regions due to the high amount of leaf fall.
2. **The A horizon:** Surface horizon mostly consisting of sand, silt and clay and also organic matter. It is the surface layer of grassland soils and cultivable lands.
3. **The E horizon:** Subsurface soils that have been leached. It is found beneath the O horizon. It is lighter in colour.
4. **The B horizon:** It is an accumulated horizon developed due to the deposition of minerals that have leached from the upper layers.
5. **The C horizon:** Subsurface horizon. It consists of unconsolidated parent material and is the least weathered region.

# HUMAN GEOGRAPHY

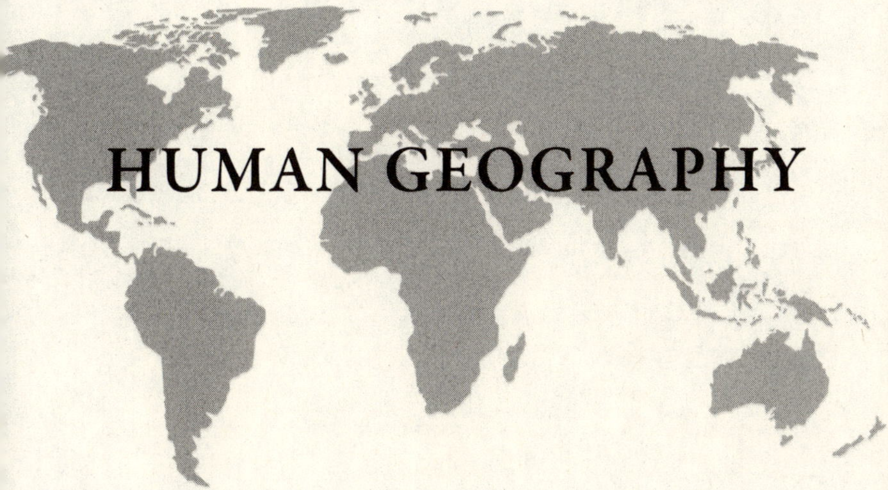

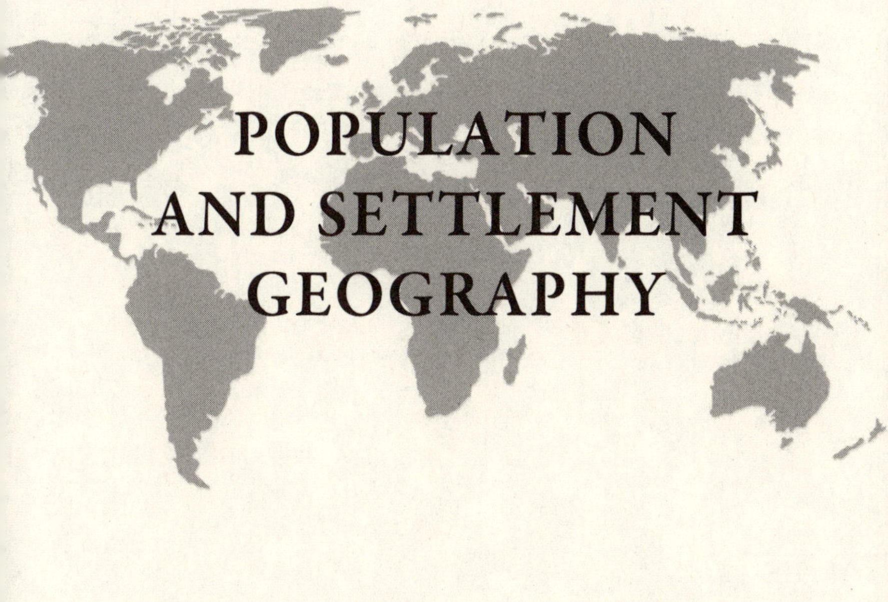

# POPULATION AND SETTLEMENT GEOGRAPHY

# 41

# THE CONCEPT OF POPULATION

Population geography is geography that deals with the Earth's population. Here, population includes the geographical distribution, composition, migration and various social and demographic attributes of a region.

## POPULATION DENSITY

Asia remains the continent with the highest population density of 145 persons per square kilometre. Europe, with 116 persons per sq. km, comes second. Among the countries, higher densities are found in relatively smaller nations like Hong Kong and Singapore, where the population densities are about 6,000 persons per sq. km. Among the larger countries, population densities are higher in Bangladesh (1,237), South Korea (533), Netherlands (532), India (382) and Japan (348).

Even within a country, there is spatial variation in the distribution of population.

### *The world can be divided into two population zones*

**Areas of high population density:** In this region, population density is about more than 300 persons per sq. km. The areas that are mostly dense are south-east Asian and south Asian countries and the European cluster.

- **South-east Asia:** About 25% of the world's population is concentrated in this region. It includes the countries of China, Korea, Vietnam, Japan and Indonesia. The majority of the people here are engaged in agriculture and other allied activities. The fertile river soil, suitable climate, irrigational facilities and well-developed transport system have contributed to the population growth in these countries.
- **South Asia:** Nearly one-fourth of the world's population is found in this cluster, where India is the most populous one. However, Bangladesh has a higher population density than India owing to its smaller size. This zone comprises India, Pakistan, Bangladesh, Myanmar and Sri Lanka. Agriculture is the most important occupation here due to the availability of fertile alluvial soil, fresh river water, an appropriate tropical climate to grow a variety of fruits and vegetables, port facilities, a transport network and a readily available market.
- **European clusters:** High population density is found in the European cluster from the British Isles to European Russia. The development of industries and the availability of oil and mineral resources have supported a large population in this cluster. Agriculture is also developed in this region, but food production capacity is not much in this zone, especially in some countries, owing to climatic restrictions.

**Areas of moderate population density:** The population density is between 100 to 300 persons per sq. km. Although this region has medium population density, the density in these areas is comparatively larger. Owing to their relatively small size and area as compared to the major clusters, they fall under the category of medium population density. This region has witnessed rapid population growth mainly after the Industrial Revolution.

- **North-east USA and south-east Canada:** Large concentrations of minerals and agricultural resources have contributed to the population in this region. The region also supports industries, and a dense transport network provides support to urbanization.
- **South-east Australia:** The region is rich in industries, mineral resources and suitable climate and soil for agriculture.
- **The Nile Valley region:** Fertile deltaic soil, irrigation and a strong agricultural base have contributed to the growth of population in this region.

**Point to note**

Since ancient times, the largest concentration of population has been in the cradles of ancient human civilization, mainly India and China.

Approximately 40% of the world's population is found in the tropical belt, despite experiencing highest levels of temperature, rainfall and humidity on Earth.

**Areas of low population density:** The very hot or very cold areas, infertile lands and rugged terrains have a very low density of population. The large deserts of Sahara, Atacama and Kalahari are sparsely populated. Similarly, the cold, arid regions of Siberia and northern parts of Canada, the tundra regions, are also least populated. The rugged mountainous regions of the Rockies, Himalayas and Alps are uninhabited. The densely forested regions of the Amazon rainforests are also least populated.

*Factors affecting population growth*

**Physical factors:**

- **Terrain:** Plain areas will always support higher populations as compared to plateaus and mountainous regions. Plain lands are suitable for growing crops and for the construction of roads, bridges and buildings. They can also support the growth of industries, which can generate employment opportunities.

- **Suitable climate:** Moderate climate – neither too hot nor too cold – will always attract more population. Desert regions and mountainous terrain, which pose difficulties in cultivation and transport and communication, do not attract large populations. Similarly, regions receiving extremely heavy rainfall, like the areas of dense rainforests, are also sparsely populated. They produce very humid and oppressive conditions of survival.
- **Availability of fertile soil:** Agriculture has always been the most important economic activity since time immemorial. Agriculture needs fertile soil throughout the year. From ancient times, the cradles of human civilization have been laid along riverbanks due to the availability of fertile soil.
- **Supply of freshwater:** River valleys have always attracted population growth. In fact, in deserts, the population seems to grow around any water body, like an oasis. Water is essential both for domestic as well as non-domestic uses.
- **Mineral resources:** The availability of mineral resources is needed for the development of industries. Sometimes, in mountainous regions, high population densities are seen due to the mining of precious minerals. In India, the Chota Nagpur Plateau is highly industrialized owing to the availability of minerals, which has led to the growth of several towns and cities in this region.

**Economic factors**

- **Government policies:** Favourable government policies and peaceful and conducive socio-economic environments will help in supporting population growth.
- **Employment opportunities:** The growth of industries in a particular region will attract people towards it as it will help

in generating employment opportunities. So the population growth is always higher in cities and towns.

***Important terms related to population***

- **Census:** A source of data for population studies.
- **Crude birth rate:** The number of births per 1,000 of total population.
- **Crude death rate:** The number of deaths per 1,000 of total population.
- **Natural increase:** The difference between crude birth rate and crude death rate expressed as % in a year.
- **Reproduction rate:** The average number of girls born per woman.
- **Fertility rate:** The birth rate per 1,000 women from 15 to 49 years old.
- **Fertility:** The actual number of live births produced by a woman in a population.
- **Fecundity:** The actual number of healthy babies born to a woman in a population.
- **Infant mortality rate:** The number of infant deaths in a year per 1,000 live births during a year.
- **Maternal mortality rate:** The annual number of maternal deaths per 1,00,000 live births.
- **Life expectancy:** The number of years a person is expected to live based on statistical average.
- **Population density:** The number of persons per unit area.
- **Age dependency ratio:** The ratio of people who are dependent (0–15 and 64 and above) to the persons who are economically independent (15 to 64) years in a population.
- **Population pyramid/age-sex pyramid:** A bar chart arranged vertically that shows the distribution of population by age and sex. In the pyramid, males are shown to the left, and females

are shown to the right. The younger age groups are shown at the bottom.

- **Neonatal mortality rate:** The number of deaths of infants under 28 days of age per 1,000 live births in a year.
- **Perinatal mortality rate:** The number of fetal deaths after 28 weeks of pregnancy, plus the number of deaths of infants under 7 days of age per 1,000 live births.
- **Postneonatal mortality rate:** The annual number of deaths of infants from 28 days to one year per 1,000 live births in a year.
- **Sex ratio:** The number of females per 1,000 males in a population.

# 42

# POPULATION COMPOSITION AND POPULATION PYRAMID

## POPULATION COMPOSITION

**Rural-urban composition:** The composition shows the proportion of rural people and urban people to the total population. The rural population is the number of people living in small-sized settlements in the countryside. Urban population is the number of people living in cities and towns.

An important indicator of social and economic development is the number of people living in rural or urban areas. In India, since Independence, there has been a steady increase in population in urban areas than in rural areas.

**Religious composition:** The cultural and political life of a nation is always influenced by the religious composition of the population.

| Religion | Percentage of Global Population |
|---|---|
| Christians | 31.6% |
| Muslims | 25.8% |
| Hindus | 15.1% |

| | |
|---|---|
| Unaffiliated | 14.4% |
| Buddhists | 6.6% |
| Jews | 0.2% |
| Folk religions | 5.6% |

(*Data: Global Surveys 2022*)

**Sex composition:** The sex composition of a population is indicative of the balance between males and females in a country. A low sex ratio in any country is due to:

A. lack of fair treatment given to women
B. superstitions attached to female children as the male child is considered an asset and the female child as a liability
C. poor medical facilities
D. sex determination before birth, leading to termination of pregnancy

**Age-sex pyramid:** An age-sex pyramid is the graphical representation of the population composition of a region in terms of age and sex. Males are shown to the left of the pyramid and females are shown to the right. The age is shown on the y-axis, and the population is shown on the x-axis. This graphical representation takes the shape of a pyramid because it represents the growth of the population.

**Types of population pyramids:** Population pyramids are of three types: expansive, constrictive and stationary.

**Expansive population pyramid:** This pyramid represents the growing population. In these countries, the fertility rates are higher, but life expectancy is low. Typically found in developing countries, these pyramids have a broader base that tapers narrowly to the top. The proportion of the population belonging to younger and reproductive age groups is the maximum. India almost has an expansive population pyramid.

**Constrictive population pyramid:** This pyramid represents a declining population. Here, the fertility rates and mortality rates are lower, life expectancy is higher. The pyramid is broader in the middle and has a narrow base. These are typically found in developed nations like Japan. The proportion of the population belonging to the elderly group and post-reproductive stage is higher.

**Stationary population pyramid:** This pyramid represents a stationary population. Here, the population is neither growing nor declining. The fertility rates and mortality rates are more or less the same. It is in the shape of a bell. Typically found in developed nations like the USA, the pyramid has a larger percentage of its population in the working age group.

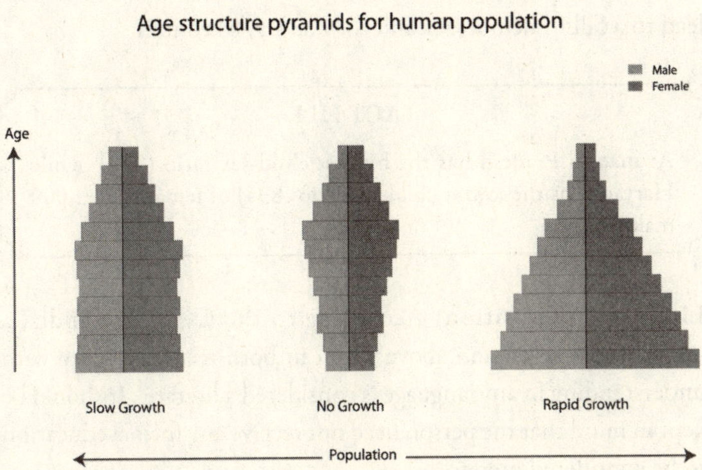


Age-sex pyramids

**Significance of the population pyramid**

- The population pyramid tells us about the number of dependants and the working population in a region.
- It gives information about whether there is a balance in the sex composition of a nation.
- It tells us about the birth rates and death rates.
- It helps in predicting the future growth in population and population policies.

**Child-sex ratio:** It is defined as the number of females per 1,000 males in the age group of 0 to 6 years. There was a fall in the child-sex ratio in India when it dropped to 918 in 2011 from 927 in 2001.

[The reasons for low child-sex ratio have already been discussed in the segment of reasons for low sex ratio.]

**Consequences of low child-sex ratio:** The lack of balance between males and females in a population can lead to greater violence against women. Women's lessened participation in political matters can lead to a fall in democracy and the country's economy.

**FACT FILE**

Arunachal Pradesh has the highest child-sex ratio (972), while Haryana has the lowest child-sex ratio (834) of females per 1,000 males.

**Literacy composition:** According to the Census of India, a 'person aged seven and above who can both read and write with understanding in any language is considered a literate'. It should be kept in mind that the person need not receive any formal education to be considered literate.

**Crude literacy rate:** the number of literate persons/total population × 100

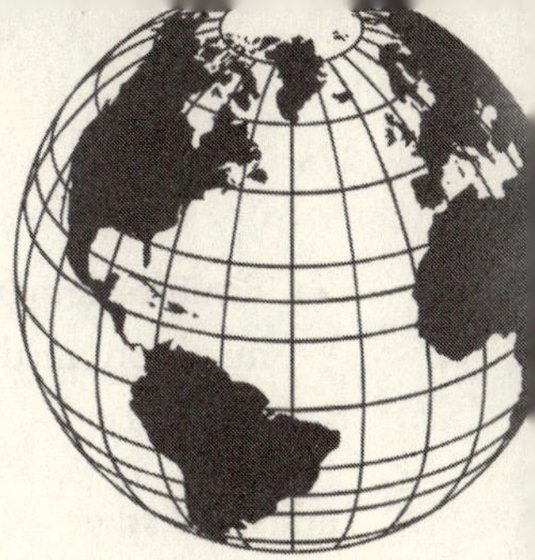

# 43

# THE THEORY OF DEMOGRAPHIC TRANSITION

**The theory of demographic transition** deals with the transformation of a society characterized by high fertility and mortality rates/ agrarian economy to a more developed and urbanized society. The theory was propounded by Thomson and Notestein. It shows the sequence of events of population growth. The stages of demographic transition are:

**Agrarian stage**

- In the first stage of demographic transition, the economy is agrarian or pre-industrial.
- At this stage, both the birth rates and death rates are high, so the growth rate of the population is low or fluctuating. Life expectancy is low.
- Agriculture is the most important economic activity; labour is abundant due to high population.
- Agriculture is mainly intensive in nature – mostly labour-intensive and traditional ways of farming on small plots of land are practised.
- The per-hectare productivity is low; farmers mainly grow crops for their own consumption.
- There is a high incidence of illiteracy.

- Famines, droughts and regular crop failures are common. Poor nutrition, medical and hygienic facilities lead to high infant mortality.

**Industrial stage**

- This is the early industrial stage when the birth rates show a decline and there is a sharp fall in death rates. Life expectancy also goes up.
- This is the stage of population explosion since the decline in mortality is much more than that of fertility rates, so the gap between the two increases, leading to rapid population growth.
- The fall in death rates is due to improvement in medical, health and sanitation facilities.
- Growth of industries starts, which makes way for better living standards.
- Better division of labour and use of technology in agriculture lead to better productivity.
- Spread of education leads to higher literacy.

**Urban stage**

- This is the late industrial stage or urban stage when there is a slow growth rate of population.
- Mortality rates continue to fall while fertility rates also show a sharp decline due to which there is a low and stable growth rate.
- High life expectancy is seen; remarkable improvements are made in the medical field.
- Use of technology in agriculture and industries. Generation of employment opportunities from the setting up of new industries.
- Development of towns and cities and better educational facilities lead to higher literacy and also higher cost of living.
- Higher cost of living leads to growing preferences for smaller families.

# 44

## MIGRATION

Migration refers to the movement of people from one region to another, which can be within or across nations.

Migration can be of the following types:

- **Internal migration:** The movement of people within a country due to work, health, education or any social purpose. Internal migration can be inter-regional or intra-regional, where the former means the movement of people between two regions within a country, and the latter means the movement of people within a specific region of a country.
- **International migration:** The movement of an individual across nations.
- **Immigration:** When a person settles down in a new country and leaves his country of origin.
- **Forced migration:** Sometimes, a person has to leave his place of origin forcefully and settle down somewhere else. They are also termed as refugees.

  Migration can also be :

  a. Rural to rural migration

  b. Rural to urban migration

c. Urban to urban migration
d. Urban to rural migration

*Causes of migration*

The causes of migration can be classified as push factors and pull factors.

**Push factors** are the negative factors that force a person to leave his place of origin.

**Pull factors** are positive factors that attract a person to settle down in the place they have migrated to.

*Push factors*

- Lack of proper medical facilities
- High cost of living and lack of employment opportunities
- Political instability, war, famine, crop failure and faulty government policies
- Inhospitable climate, poor soil and lack of freshwater supply
- Lack of proper educational facilities
- Prone to natural disasters like earthquakes, floods, cyclones, etc.

*Pull factors*

- Proper medical facilities in the form of doctors, medical practitioners, hospitals, clinics
- Generation of employment opportunities
- Habitable climate, fertile soil, freshwater
- Developed transport and communication facilities
- Educational facilities and friendly government policies
- Encouraging loans and incentives for research and career growth

### *Consequences of migration*

People always have a tendency to migrate from less advanced or less developed regions to more developed or advanced regions. The sole purpose of most migrations is the desire to lead a better life.

**Economic consequences:** Remittances sent by migrants to their home country add to the national income of the country. This money helps in raising the standard of living. However, it may also lead to overcrowding and the growth of slums and squatter settlements in the destination country. Overcrowding causes poor health and sanitation and a lack of proper housing. Often, people working in a new place displace the people who originally belong there from their workplaces, leading to unemployment.

**Demographic consequences:** An unbalanced sex ratio is seen in the home country as men leave their homes to work in different cities. This also negatively impacts development in the home country.

**Social consequences:** When migrants return to their place of origin, they bring with them lots of ideas, innovation, life skills, etc., which can be applied in different fields. At the same time, their social outlook is broadened because of the intermixing of different cultures and races. However, it also results in missing out on family life, loneliness, fierce competition and depression that affect their mental health.

**Environmental consequences:** Overuse and exploitation of natural resources due to migration in destination countries often lead to pollution and environmental degradation.

***Some major migrations of the world***

- In the post–World War II period, a large number of Jews migrated to Israel between 1948 and 1951. Most of the Jewish migrants were from Russia and other European countries.
- Forced migrants were sent to America from African nations.
- In the mid-1970s, a large number of European settlers of the Portuguese African colonies migrated back to Europe and others went back to South Africa. This migration was caused due to civil war in Angola followed by its independence.
- The partition of India in 1947 caused the biggest migration in Indian history, where lakhs of people were displaced from their lands overnight and were migrated forcefully to newly formed India, Bangladesh (East Pakistan) and West Pakistan.

**Brain Drain:** When talented and skilled individuals leave their country of origin and settle down in foreign countries for better exposure, pay and working conditions, it is termed as brain drain.

Brain drain is caused mainly due to a lack of facilities, lack of proper career growth and political instability in the home country. All these act as push factors while better facilities, money and exposure in developed countries act as pull factors.

***Advantages and disadvantages of brain drain***

**Advantages:** Brain drain causes migrants to send remittances to their families in their home countries, which adds to the national income of the country. When professionals return to their own country, they bring with them lots of expertise and skills that can be used. Brain drain is advantageous for countries experiencing the gain due to the influx of skilled workers. Emigration will also increase the wages of the workers staying back in their place of origin.

**Disadvantages:** Brain drain causes a loss of talented professionals from the country. It signals a lack of economic development and failure in government policies over time. There is an economic loss in terms of human capital. Critical fields like medicine suffer a setback due to a lack of skilled professionals, which will hamper the country's growth.

***How to avoid brain drain***

- Changing the education system in the country to be more vocational will teach life skills and be student-friendly
- Research infrastructure should be invested in
- Better educational facilities, schools and colleges offering more professional courses
- Proper pay cheques and a better work culture

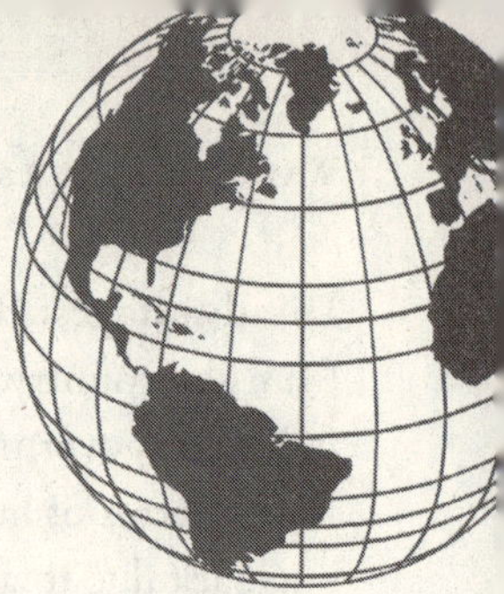

# 45

# POPULATION PROBLEM AND POLICIES

## Population problem

1. **Overcrowding:** When the carrying capacity of a region is less than its population, the area suffers from overcrowding. This leads to the exploitation of resources as there is increased pressure by the population on resources.
2. **Growth of slums and squatter settlements:** Developing nations mainly face rural to urban migration. Shortage of proper housing, health and sanitation facilities in the cities lead to the growth of slums and squatter settlements. These are temporary settlements made up of tin or cloth shades without any proper sanitation, drinking water or electricity. They continue to grow along railway tracks, roads and under-bridges in cities and their surroundings. These people neither have any permanent settlements nor do they have any legal ownership over the land where they build their settlements.
3. **Lack of employment opportunities:** Overpopulation in developing nations leads to a lack of job opportunities as the workplaces are already overburdened with too many people. All these lead to people getting involved in criminal and illegal

activities, such as theft or dacoity, to escape poverty and hunger.

4. **Low standard of living:** Poverty and unemployment increase the cost of living in cities. This leads to improper and incomplete education to get jobs early and a lack of proper health care and medical facilities.
5. **Pollution:** One of the biggest problems faced by Indian cities and towns is the alarming rate of pollution. Over-exploitation of resources, heavy vehicular traffic, unplanned setting up of factories within residential areas, cutting of trees to make way for more development, release of untreated waste into water bodies and soil lead to the pollution of air, water or soil.

***Population policy of a developed nation (USA)***

The main strategy of USA was to obtain a healthy and educated population. The population policymakers' strategy helps the US government to support women's health and family planning and provide assistance to combat HIV/AIDS, maternal health, etc. According to the US government, the ideal family size is to be decided by the couples and not by the government. So the US government does not promote family planning programs.

The United States supported the Program of Action of the 1994 International Conference on Population and Development (ICPD), which was accepted by 179 countries. According to the program, they made decisions and acted on several population issues, such as the promotion of maternal health, gender equality, the protection of children, and the right of couples to decide on the spacing between children. It does not consider abortion as a method of family planning.

It also engages on diplomatic levels on global population issues and provides assistance to advance the US government's goals to achieve a healthy and educated population. It includes working with the UN and other intergovernmental forums to ensure resolutions adopted in the UN through outreach and talks with the stakeholders, multilateral organizations, NGOs and other bodies engaged in demographic family planning, gender equality and reproductive health issues.

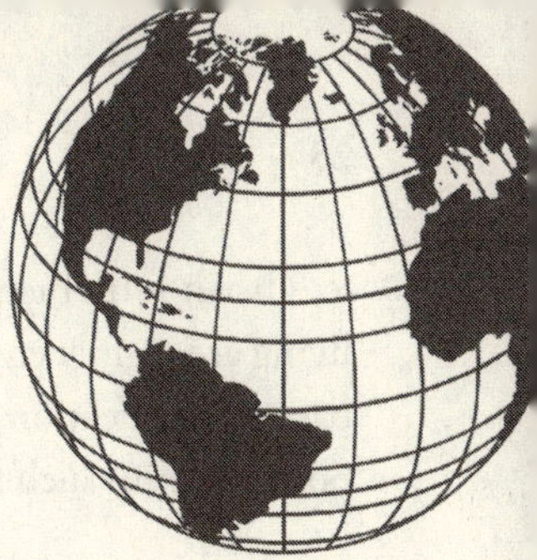

# 46

# SETTLEMENTS: RURAL AND URBAN – THEIR MORPHOLOGY

The growth of human settlements started with the domestication of animals, agriculture and permanency in living in a particular region. Previously, humans were mostly nomads; they practised hunting and grazing of animals, so they moved from one place to another in search of greener pastures. Human settlements refer to a permanent collection of houses, huts or buildings.

The growth of settlements is controlled by a few factors, such as the availability of plain lands or suitable terrain, favourable climate, the availability of fresh, clean drinking water and mineral resources or forest resources.

Human settlements can be either temporary or permanent. As the name suggests, temporary settlements are those where people move or wander from one place to another in search of food or water. These are basically nomadic hunters or pasturers.

Permanent settlements are all those houses or buildings, especially in cities or towns, in which the inhabitants live permanently or for a long period of time.

Settlements can either be rural or urban. Rural settlements are found in villages, where agriculture, fishing and forestry are the main occupations. Most rural settlements are permanent in nature.

Urban settlements are seen in cities and towns, where people living are mainly engaged in secondary and tertiary sectors, such as banking, education, medicine, law, industries, etc. The density of population in such settlements is always very high.

*Different types of settlements*

**Nucleated settlements:** These are clustered settlements that comprise many houses in compact form surrounding temples, important religious centres, water bodies or farmlands. Nucleated settlements are common in the Indo-Gangetic plains, the Nile Valley, etc. These settlements generally grow along river valleys and on flat terrain.

**Dispersed settlements:** Inhospitable areas, such as forests, rugged terrain, and arid areas, are marked by these types of settlements. The houses are located far from each other and are mostly found in remote villages, where farmers have to walk long distances to reach their fields. This may be due to an absence of proper roads or because of dense forests or hilly terrain.

*Patterns of rural settlements*

- **Rectangular pattern:** The roads are almost straight, meeting each other at right angles. These settlement patterns are mostly seen in fertile alluvial plains or valleys.
- **Linear pattern:** Houses are arranged along a major road, stream, railway line or canal.
- **Star-like pattern:** These develop when metalled or unmetalled roads converge at a point and houses spread out along the sides of the roads in all directions.
- **Triangular pattern:** At the confluence of rivers, settlements take a triangular shape following the course of the rivers.
- **Nebular pattern:** The settlement is in the shape of a nebula, where houses are built around a nucleus. This nucleus can be

a temple or water body. The roads are arranged in an almost circular way, which ends at the nucleus.

- **Semicircular pattern:** These settlements are occupation specific. Often, people engaged in fishing build their houses on the sea coasts, far from the village. This often takes the shape of a semicircle.

***Problems of rural settlements***

- Rural settlements in developing nations are mostly plagued by bad road conditions, broken bridges or lack of them and inadequate transport. These conditions make it difficult for rural people to commute from one place to another and also to transport goods from their farms to the markets, to handle medical emergencies, to send children to school and to avail public services.
- Not all villages are electrified in countries like India, Bangladesh, Pakistan, Sri Lanka, etc. These remote villages still live under the dark skies and are yet to enjoy the benefits of quality power.
- People living in rural areas face the health burden of poor water quality. Most children suffer from waterborne diseases. It is estimated that about 1.5 million children die of diarrhoea alone each year. Chemical contamination is a major problem in a country like India, where the underground water is affected by arsenic and fluoride.
- There is a wide gender disparity in the literacy rate. A low literacy rate has a propounding effect on family planning and belief in superstitions. It also has an impact on the rate of unemployment in the country and consequent family planning.
- Rural populations in developing countries are always associated with poverty. Most of them are agricultural farmers who suffer from crop failures, droughts, erratic rainfall and several other problems.

- Youth migrate to urban areas in search of jobs or better lifestyles, and the aged stay back in the villages. The use of machines in agricultural fields is increasing the problem of unemployment. Agricultural land remains static, but the population keeps growing.
- Because of a lack of educational facilities and medical facilities and in search of a better lifestyle, people migrate from rural to urban areas. Lack of housing and proper jobs in urban cities leads to the problem of slums, squatter settlements, indulgence in criminal activities, etc.

***General trends in urbanization***

The trend in urbanization varies between eastern and western countries. The Industrial Revolution caused a massive upheaval in urbanization in Europe. Urbanization was associated with the production of surplus food by farmers. This allowed farmers to make profits and use machinery in their agricultural fields. The towns became the focus of production, and selling of goods. There was a diversification of work as more and more people got involved with other economic activities, such as pottery, art, etc.

***Important terms related to urbanization***

- **Metropolis:** Urban areas having a population of more than 1 million.
- **Megalopolis:** Urban areas having a population of more than 10 million.
- **Satellite city:** An urban area typically smaller in size that grows near a metropolis. They are economically or socially independent completely or partially from the main city but well connected with the main city. Satellite cities are mainly developed to reduce the stress of population in the main city.
- **Smart city:** A city that uses advanced technology in its social, economic and physical infrastructure. Sustainable

development, enhanced connectivity, online government services, and cybersecurity are the basic components of a smart city.

- **Edge city:** A concentration of firms, factories, entertainment and shopping centres in a previously known rural or residential area is called an edge city. Edge city is an American term, where the most common type of edge cities are called boomers. A boomer is an edge city that develops gradually around a road or a shopping mall.
- **Rural-urban fringe:** It is the boundary zone where urban and rural land use intermixes. It is the area where there is a transition from city to village. The rural agricultural fields slowly change into medium-sized houses and then eventually bigger buildings.
- **Suburb:** A suburb develops on the outskirts of the city and is a mixed-use or residential area existing as a part of the city. The population density in a suburb is generally lower than the main city. People living in the suburbs mostly commute daily to the main city for work.
- **Ghetto:** An urban district in which the population mainly consists of a particular ethnic group.
- **Urban sprawl:** The rapid expansion of the geographical extent of cities or towns characterized by low-priced land, low population density, social segregation and the use of private automobiles.

***Functional classification of towns***

- **Administrative towns:** These include the capital city/town, centre of a state, province, district, tehsil, etc. All the government bureaucrats, officers and public buildings are located in administrative towns. For example, New Delhi in India.

- **Defensive towns:** They are located far away from the main city to maintain security. They contain cantonments, military base camps, training areas and barracks for the armed forces. For example, Vishakhapatnam.
- **Cultural centres:** They can either be religious centres or educational towns. For example, Oxford (England) or Kota in Rajasthan are educational centres while Mathura and Haridwar are religious towns.
- **Production centres:** Urban areas where production or manufacturing are the most important economic activities. For example, Jamshedpur in India is considered to be the steel city for its iron and steel industry.
- **Collection centres:** Mining towns and fishing towns, come under this category. For example, Raniganj in West Bengal.
- **Distribution centres:** The main function of these towns is trade and commerce. Market towns, financial towns or port cities come under this category. They mainly include port cities. Some of the world's largest cities have developed as ports. For example, Mumbai, New York, Tokyo. Some towns have developed as financial centres.
- **Resorts:** Towns that have developed for the recreation needs of the people are resorts. These places are known for their natural beauty, historical monuments, sports, cultural attractions, mountain climbing and trekking, health treatments, etc. For example, Darjeeling, Srinagar.
- **Residential towns:** These are towns mainly used for inhabitation. The land use comprises houses, schools and hospitals. Residential towns are connected to the main city, which enables daily commuters to go to work.

**FACT FILE**

India's three megacities where the population is more than 10 million are: Greater Mumbai urban agglomeration, Delhi and Kolkata.

***Mega cities of the world: (According to population)***

| | |
|---|---|
| • Tokyo (Japan) | 37.4 million |
| • Delhi (India) | 29.3 million |
| • Shanghai (China) | 26.3 million |
| • Sao Paolo (Brazil) | 21.8 million |
| • Mexico City (Mexico) | 21.6 million |
| • Cairo (Egypt) | 20.4 million |
| • Dhaka (Bangladesh) | 20.2 million |
| • Mumbai (India) | 20.1 million |
| • Beijing (China) | 19.4 million |
| • Osaka (Japan) | 19.2 million |

(*Data source: BBC* )

***Characteristics of urbanization***

- The level of urbanization is an indicator of the economic development of a nation because as the economy develops, the purchasing power of an individual also develops. There is an increase in the per capita income of an individual.
- Industrialization leads to urbanization. Land use mainly comprises manufacturing units, factories, mills and industrial set-ups.
- An urban settlement consists of high population density caused due to natural increase, as well as the migration of people from surrounding rural areas.
- The cost of living is high in urban areas, which causes the disintegration of joint families and impersonal relations.
- The problem of overpopulation causes the growth of slums, lack of housing facilities, pollution and growth in crime rates.
- Urban centres have easy availability of inputs like skilled labour, capital and repair services from which profits are earned.

- There are ample job opportunities in urban centres as workers can easily switch from one job to another as there are wider choices. So rural people often settle down near urban centres.

**What is repatriation?**

A government policy of returning immigrants to their country of origin.

**What is counter-urbanization?**

The movement of people from urban areas back to rural towns or villages to seek a better quality of life in the countryside (maybe after retirement).

### *Morphology of towns*

Morphology means the physical shape of towns. The difference in population groups within towns causes morphology. People belonging to a particular ethnic group, caste or linguistic group tend to live together because of their common backgrounds.

The difference in income also causes segregation in the population. The suburbs consist of larger houses and big lawns that are inhabited by high-income groups, while the older houses near the centre of the towns are the homes of the middle-income groups.

In the model of general growth and land use pattern, the most distinctive feature is the presence of the central business district (CBD). The CBD has tall buildings, offices, headquarters, offices, stores and major crowded streets. The fringe of the CBD consists of warehouses, transportation terminals, light factories, durable commodities stores, etc. Beyond the CBD are the residential areas.

The following are the five concentric rings of a model town.

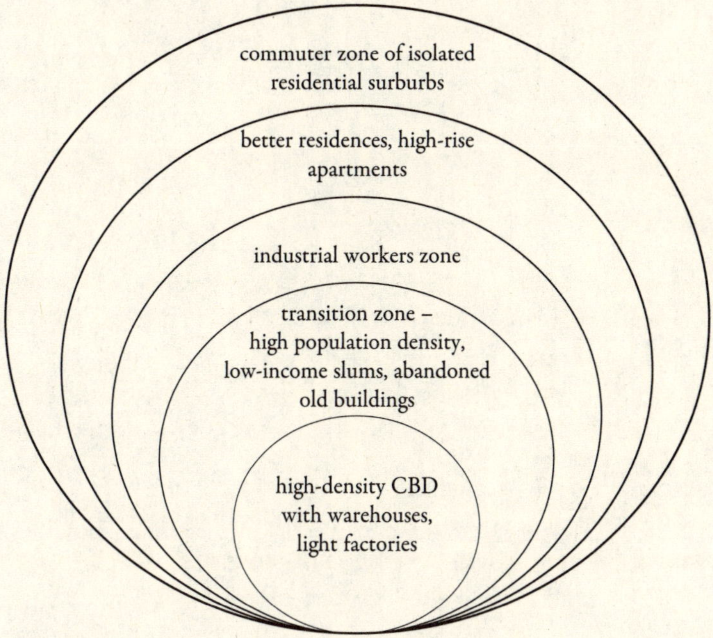

# ECONOMIC GEOGRAPHY

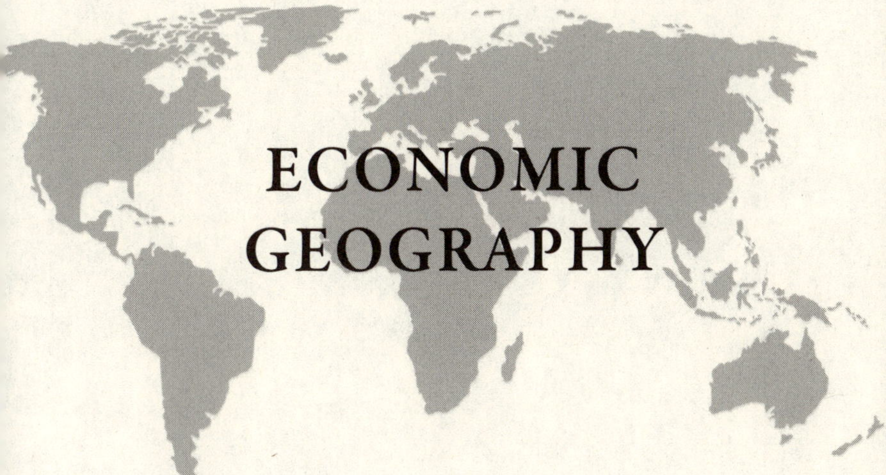

# 47

# SECTORS OF AN ECONOMY

**Sectors of an economy**

**Primary sector:** This involves primary activities, such as hunting of animals, cattle grazing, fishing, harvesting of crops and trees, obtaining minerals from the Earth's crust, etc. These activities are directly obtained from nature. The people engaged in this work are called red-collar workers.

**Secondary sector:** This involves processing and shaping commodities already obtained through primary activities, which includes the production of steel goods, the production of textiles by processing animal or plant fibres, such as wool or cotton, respectively. Workers in this group make use of machinery and capital and are termed blue-collar workers.

**Tertiary sector:** This includes the service sector, such as barbers, secretaries, clerks, etc. These include a range of business and personal services.

**Quaternary sector:** This comprises professional and administrative services, including teaching, legal services, doctors or health professionals, entertainment services, etc. These workers are called white-collar workers.

**Quinary sector:** They include chief executives and top professionals in government, as well as in the private sector. Researchers, financial planners, advisors and consultants come under this category. These people are called gold-collar workers.

**Pink-collar sector:** Activities primarily involving women come under this category. This includes jobs in beauty, nursing, social work, teaching and the childcare industry.

***Agriculture and other allied activities***

Agriculture is the most basic of all primary activities.

World agriculture is of the following types:

**Nomadic herding:** Nomads move from one place to another in search of water or pastures. It is the simplest form of pastoralism.

**Livestock ranching:** Animals are raised and taken for grazing on ranches. Ranches are more permanent than herding. The rearing of animals is done commercially, using scientific techniques.

**Shifting agriculture:** Also called the slash-and-burn method, a small plot of forested land is cleared by fire and used for growing crops. When the land loses its fertility, the farmers abandon the land and move to a fresh plot.

**Intensive subsistence farming:** Here, the farmers cultivate small plots of land using simple and primitive tools. They mainly produce crops for self-consumption. It is a labour-intensive method practiced in high-population-density regions. The landholdings are small and uneconomical due to being fragmented.

**Commercial farming:** This is capital intensive, with the use of modern machinery, irrigation methods, fertilizers and pesticides. Farming is mainly done on large plots of land with the motive of earning profit.

**Plantation farming:** A single crop is grown on large plots of land. The crops are mainly grown for profit, and the methods of farming are mechanized. It requires large amounts of capital. Irrigation methods, fertilizers and high-quality seeds are used extensively.

**Dairy farming:** Long-term production of milk for commercial sale of dairy products.

**Commercial grain farming:** Farmers grow grains for selling in the market. It is done on large plots of land using better machinery and huge capital investment.

**Organic farming:** An agricultural method that uses organic fertilizers and methods for environment-friendly produce. It reduces human health hazards by using natural inputs. It also decreases the cost of production and enhances soil fertility.

**Market gardening:** Fruits, vegetables and flowers are grown on a smaller scale to sell to consumers directly. Often, farmers practice market gardening to earn some additional income.

***Fishing***

Fishing is concentrated mainly in countries that lie close to the sea or oceans or have a good network of rivers. Fishing can be either inshore fishing or coastal fishing. The largest fishing industries are found in Japan, Russia, China and the USA. The major fishing grounds of the world where fishing is done on a commercial scale are Grand Banks near Newfoundland, the north of Japan and the sea around Iceland. Fishing grounds are mainly concentrated in the temperate latitudes due to the following reasons:

- Cool waters contain more phytoplankton than warm water, so more fish are produced.
- The continental shelves are more developed in the temperate latitudes.
- Fish storage is easier in cooler climates than in tropical climates as there is no storage problem.
- Coastal regions in higher latitudes do not grow many crops due to restrictions, so they consider fishing an important occupation.

**FACT FILE**

**Florida**, home to Universal Studios and Disney World, is also the fishing capital of the world with its great resources, variety of fish and use of modern techniques.

### *Forestry*

Forestry not only involves cutting or lumbering wood but also industries related to forests, such as the harvesting of timber, as well as forest management. Forestry includes the paper and pulp industry, the sports equipment industry and the cosmetic industry in the form of essential oils, flavours, fragrances, camphor, gum and resins. Forestry has been a major environmental concern as lots of trees are being cut down for lumbering. The ever-increasing demand for wood and timber for the growing population is one of the reasons. The dense forests of the world are found in areas of heavy rainfall and long warm seasons. The luxuriant growth of vegetation is hindered by drought conditions or aridity.

Trees, both hardwood and softwood, are found in forests. Hardwood trees are mainly deciduous or tropical evergreen trees.

They are found in both temperate and tropical latitudes. Temperate latitudes contain broad-leaved and deciduous trees like oak, beech and elm. Tropical forests contain hardwood trees like teak, ebony, rosewood and mahogany. Softwood trees are mainly conifers. These trees are needle-shaped and evergreen, such as pine, deodar, fir, spruce, etc.

Forestry is a major economic activity in the northern hemisphere. The entire belt of coniferous vegetation flourishes in the temperate latitudes from Alaska in North America to Labrador and Newfoundland. This zone is known as the taiga and extends from northern Europe through Scandinavia and Russia and across Asia through Siberia. Tropical hardwoods are found in areas of Africa, the equatorial regions of south-east Asia and Brazil in South America.

Productive function of forests: Forests provide us with a variety of products. The most important is timber, followed by pulp for paper. Other than these, many products are also extracted from trees, which do not require felling. These are gums, resins, rubber, latex, turpentine, essential oils, fragrances, spices, etc. Many plants with medicinal properties are also obtained from forests, such as cinchona, cocoa and castor oil. Cinchona is used for treating malaria and stomach bloating and for increasing appetite. A variety of fruits and nuts are also derived from forests. For example, Brazilian nuts are hard nuts used for making buttons and studs.

**Agroforestry:** It is the method where crops are cultivated along with forest trees and animal rearing on a plot of land. The main aim of agroforestry is to earn additional income for farmers and to ensure the most efficient land use in accordance with the sociocultural practices of the local people. Agroforestry is practised to:

- reduce the pressure on forests
- check soil erosion and deforestation
- maintain ecological balance and the natural fertility of the soil

- ensure maximum utilization of the available land to obtain a variety of products, such as wood, timber, fodder, livestock, etc.

**Social forestry:** This is people-oriented and joint management of forests with the major objective of satisfying the needs, desires and aspirations of both the people and the government. It includes the management of forests and afforestation on barren lands to help in social and rural development.

The objectives are:

- Providing food, fodder, timber for rural people
- Developing cottage industries
- Generating employment opportunities to rural people
- Efficient conservation of land and water
- Fulfilling the recreational needs of the people
- Adding aesthetic value to the place

# 48

## MINERALS AND ENERGY RESOURCES

Minerals are considered to be a valuable natural resource. They are not distributed equally in all parts of the world. There is an inverse relationship between the quality and quantity of minerals. The best quality minerals are found in smaller quantities and vice versa. There are several factors, such as climate, location and accessibility, that determine how and whether the minerals can be exploited commercially or not.

### Major minerals of the world

**Iron ore:** When a particular mineral is derived from a mixture of different minerals, it is called an ore of that mineral. Iron ore provides the base for the development of basic industries, such as the iron and steel industry. Australia is the largest producer of iron ore in the world. In India, iron ore is mainly concentrated in the Odisha belt. The types of iron ore are haematite, magnetite, limonite and siderite. Haematite is a black ore – the most superior variety consisting – of more than 70% iron content.

**Manganese:** Manganese is used as a raw material in the iron and steel industry to make steel stronger. It is also used in dry cell batteries, bleaching powder, paints and emulsifiers, railway tracks and shipbuilding. South Africa is the largest producer in the world and Odisha in India.

**Copper:** The first metal known to man. It is a good conductor of electricity, so it is mainly used in electrical equipment, industrial machines and for construction purposes. It is both ductile and malleable. Chile is the largest producer in the world. In India, copper reserves are found in Madhya Pradesh, followed by Rajasthan and Jharkhand.

**Aluminium:** It is mainly used to make alloys as it is strong, light and ductile. It is used in the aircraft industry, and to make jewellery, everyday items, foil, etc. It is also free from corrosion, so it is used for making high-rise buildings and bridges. The main producers are China, Russia and India. Bauxite is used in making aluminium metal. It is used to make chemicals, steel and cement and as a building material.

**Zinc:** Paints, rubber, pharmaceuticals, cosmetics, soaps, batteries and garments are manufactured using zinc oxides. China is the largest producer in the world, while in India, Rajasthan is the largest.

**Diamonds:** It si most precious of all minerals. South Africa is the leading producer in the world. Diamonds are famously used in the jewellery industry, glass industry, cosmetics industry, etc. It is the hardest of all metals. Diamonds are mined in Madhya Pradesh in India.

**Gold:** Another precious metal, the largest reserves of gold mines are found in Australia. Gold is durable and non-corrosive, so it is used in the jewellery, aerospace, automotive, dentistry and medical tools sectors. In India, gold mines are found in Karnataka and Andhra Pradesh.

**Silver:** Silver is also a precious metal. It is found either in pure form or in combination with gold, copper or lead. Silver is a malleable, soft metal. Since it is a good conductor of electricity, it is used for making batteries, ornaments, mirrors, dental alloys, etc. Mexico is the leading producer in the world, while in India, Rajasthan leads.

**Classification of minerals**

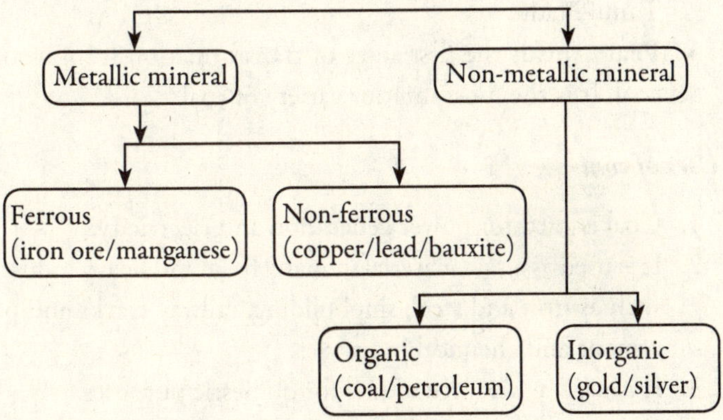


## Conventional and non-conventional sources of energy

**Conventional sources of energy:** These are energy resources that are non-renewable in nature. These energy resources have been used by man since time immemorial. The most important ones are:

**Coal:** One of the most important sources of energy, coal is a sedimentary rock formed by the action of pressure and heat on the vegetative remains of dead plants and animals. Coal is also termed as a fossil fuel. The major types of coal are:

- **Anthracite coal:** Best quality coal in which the carbon content is about 92%. It is black and lustrous. It is smokeless, burns for a long time, has high calorific value and does not contain moisture. In India, anthracite coal is found in small quantities, especially in Jammu and Kashmir.

- **Bituminous coal:** The carbon content is about 50% to 80%. Its colour ranges between dark brown to black. It is the most abundantly used coal and is primarily used for domestic purposes or as a coking coal and for blasting furnaces.
- **Lignite:** The carbon content ranges between 25% to 35%. It has a low calorific value due to its high moisture content. It is a poor-grade coal. In India, lignite is mined from Neyveli in Tamil Nadu.
- **Peat:** This is the first stage of transformation from wood to coal. It is the most inferior variety of coal.

***Uses of coal***

1. Coal is used for power generation and electricity.
2. It is used as a raw material in many basic and heavy industries, such as iron and steel, shipbuilding, railway tracks and parts, cement and chemical industries.
3. It is used as a source of fuel for domestic purposes.
4. Coking coal is used for smelting iron ore into iron and to make steel.

**FACT FILE**

- The oldest coal field in India is the Raniganj Coalfield (West Bengal).
- The largest coal field is Jharia in Jharkhand.
- The oldest oil refinery in India is Digboi Oil Refinery in Assam. The largest oil refinery in India, as well as in the world, is Reliance Industries' oil refinery in Jamnagar (Gujarat).

**Petroleum**

The term 'petroleum' is derived from 'petra' and 'oleum', which means rock oil. Petroleum is a fossil fuel derived from below the Earth's crust that is refined into fuel from its crude form. It is formed due to the decomposition of fossil fuels over millions of years. Petroleum forms the base of the transport sector. Crude oil is refined in refineries to make petrol, diesel, kerosene, LPG, gasoline, lubricating oil, paraffin wax, etc.

***Uses of petroleum***

1. Petroleum is used as a source of fuel for vehicles as petrol and diesel.
2. Liquefied petroleum gas or LPG is used for cooking purposes.
3. Petrol and diesel are used for dry cleaning and for running electric generators.
4. Paraffin wax is used for making candles, ointments, crayons and printing ink.

***What are petrochemicals?***

These are derived from petroleum, as well as its products, which are used as major raw materials. Petrochemical products are lighter, durable and cost-effective. The raw materials are also easily available and are not dependent on agriculture, as in the case of natural fibres like jute. So they are now fast replacing traditional products. Some of the common petrochemical products used in our daily life are synthetic rubber, synthetic fibres, plastic, detergents and resins. The petrochemical industries are located close to oil fields due to the easy availability of raw materials and to reduce the cost of transportation.

**Did you know?**

Why can we detect cooking gas leakage at home?
Since LPG is highly inflammable but odourless **ethyl mercaptan** is added to it, which gives a strong, foul odour so that we can easily detect that there is a leakage of gas!

**Natural gas:** These are generally associated with oil fields or as an independent source. It mainly consists of methane. Natural gas is considered to be a safer option than coal because it is environment-friendly and does not leave ash behind. It is a mixture of hydrocarbon compounds formed under the Earth's crust for millions of years due to the decay of plant and animal remains under extreme heat and pressure.

***Uses of natural gas***

1. Used as fuel in vehicles such as autorickshaws as CNG (compressed natural gas).
2. Used in making chemicals and fertilizers.
3. Used for generating electricity, cooking and heating.
4. Used in making paints, plastic, fabric, steel.

**Hydel power:** One of the cheapest sources of energy, hydel power is renewable. Hydroelectricity is produced when water is made to fall from a certain point with great force that flows through a turbine that spins it, activating the generator to generate electricity. Hydel power is environment-friendly and does not emit any greenhouse gases.

The major hydroelectric projects of India that are also multipurpose river valley projects are the Bhakra Nangal Dam project built on River Sutlej, benefitting Punjab, Haryana and Rajasthan, the Hirakud Dam project built on River Mahanadi in Odisha and the Damodar Valley Corporation on River Damodar, benefitting West Bengal and Jharkhand.

***Uses of multipurpose river valley projects***

1. To prevent soil erosion and promote afforestation
2. To control floods
3. To promote pisciculture

4. Generation of hydroelectricity
5. To provide irrigational facilities
6. To provide for the recreational needs of the locals

**Advantages and disadvantages of conventional sources of energy**

***Advantages of coal***

- It is the most traditional source of fossil fuel.
- It is used in rural households for cooking purposes.
- It provides raw materials to several industries, such as iron and steel, automobiles, chemicals, cement industries, etc.
- Several by-products, such as phenol, benzene and tar are obtained from coal.

***Disadvantages of coal***

- Indian coal is mostly bituminous coal, that too, concentrated in specific regions, and is not widely distributed all over the country.
- Coal is an exhaustible natural resource, so there is always a risk of it getting depleted fast.
- Burning of coal releases harmful gases that cause the greenhouse effect.
- The transportation cost is quite high, and there is a lot of corruption in the form of coal smuggling.

***Advantages of petroleum***

- Petroleum is used for power generation.
- Petrol, diesel, kerosene, gasoline and LPG are used as fuel in the transport sector.
- It is easy and convenient to transport petroleum over long distances through pipelines or vehicles.

- Petrochemicals that are derived from petroleum have a wide range of uses as they are cheaper and durable.

***Disadvantages of petroleum***

- Petroleum is an expensive fuel and cannot be extracted from anywhere.
- It is an exhaustible resource and takes millions of years to form.
- It is highly inflammable.
- It causes harmful gases while burning, which can cause the greenhouse effect and pollution.
- It can damage marine life through oil spills in oceans.

***Advantages of natural gas***

- It is a cheaper and cleaner fuel.
- There is no storage problem, and it can also be transported safely through gas lines.
- There is an abundant supply.
- It is colourless, odourless and lighter.
- CNG is used as an alternative to fuel which is eco-friendly.
- It is a reliable source of energy used for running electrical appliances.

***Disadvantages of natural gas***

- Natural gas leakage cannot be detected as it is odourless. So inhalation of natural gas is harmful to the human body as methane is more dangerous than carbon dioxide.
- It is a non-renewable source of energy.
- The mileage given by CNG-run vehicles is less than petrol and diesel.
- It is a highly volatile gas.
- Natural gas is mainly found near petroleum reserves, so their distribution is not widespread.

*Advantages of hydel power*

- It is the cleanest and cheapest source of energy as it does not emit any harmful gases.
- It is a renewable and sustainable source of energy.
- Apart from generating electricity, hydel power has multiple uses.
- The maintenance cost is less.

*Disadvantages of hydel power*

- The cost of installation of hydel power projects is quite high.
- These projects often lead to the displacement of people from their lands for the construction of dams, reservoirs, barrages, etc.
- They may also cause deforestation as huge plots of land are required for their installation.
- Serious geological damage can lead to earthquakes, such as for bursting of dams, or due to human negligence.

**Non-conventional sources of energy:** These are energy resources that are renewable, eco-friendly and inexhaustible in nature. They are expensive at the time of installation but are cheaper in the long run. These include solar energy, wind energy, tidal energy, nuclear energy, biogas and geothermal energy.

**Solar energy:** The sun is the prime source of energy. In a tropical country like India that receives a long duration of sunshine almost throughout the year, solar energy can be generated and put to great use. Solar energy is used for cooking, heating water and generating electricity. Solar energy is derived from solar voltaic cells. These cells make up the solar panels. Each solar cell converts light energy into electrical energy by trapping the sun's rays. Solar cells are used for running calculators, street lights, traffic lights, watches, etc.

*Advantages of solar energy*

- It is the most renewable, cleanest and safest source of energy.
- It has a wide variety of uses as it can be used for cooking, heating, running electrical appliances, water pumps, street lights, etc.
- Its maintenance and repair costs are low as there is no wear and tear.
- It saves electricity bills and can be installed easily in houses, especially in rural areas.

**Wind energy:** It is a clean, environment-friendly form of energy. Wind energy can be harnessed in coastal areas or grasslands where there is an uninterrupted flow of wind. Electricity is generated from windmills. The wind turns the blades of the mills, which in turn rotate the turbines that run the generator. The installation cost of wind farms is quite high. The largest wind farm in India is found from Nagercoil to Madurai in Tamil Nadu. Windmills that are offshore are stronger and generate greater electricity than their counterparts.

*Advantages of wind energy*

- It is a clean form of energy as it does not emit any harmful gases.
- Farmers often lend a part of their land for installing wind mills, which helps them earn some extra income.
- The electricity bills are also cut down.
- Wind energy is renewable and does not require water.

**Tidal energy:** High tides generate electricity in the form of tidal energy. There are tidal stream generators that turn turbines by using the kinetic energy of tidal water. The turbines run the generator like that of wind energy, but the intensity is higher in tidal energy due to the greater density of water. The difference in height between high tides and low tides generates the potential energy used in the tidal barrages. Tidal barrages are the most traditional method of harnessing tidal energy.

***Advantages of tidal energy***

- Tidal energy does not release any harmful gases, so it is clean and eco-friendly.
- It is a renewable source of energy.
- The maintenance cost is low.
- Tides are easy to predict and thus reliable. Even if the tidal waters are low, there is no difference in the generation of power.

**Nuclear energy:** Nuclear energy is generated by nuclear fission. The splitting of uranium atoms produces heat that forms steam. This steam turns the turbines that generate electricity.

***Advantages of nuclear energy***

- It produces zero carbon emissions and so is pollution-free.
- It is safe and reliable and is not dependent on weather.
- Used in a wide range of industries from medicine and scientific research to consumer products.
- It is cheaper and more convenient to use.

**Geothermal energy:** The term 'geothermal' is derived from the combination of two terms: 'geo' meaning 'Earth' and 'thermos' meaning 'heat'. So, geothermal energy is the energy derived from within the Earth's crust. Geothermal energies are often associated with volcanic areas. Hot magma along with steam comes out of the surface in the form of lava through fissures and cracks. This heated lava is very hot and full of energy. This energy is tapped using geothermal power plants. Generally found in areas of hot lava, pipes are fitted, which go down and pull up the required lava along with steam. The steam that comes out from below is used to turn the turbines that run the generator.

***Advantages of geothermal energy***

- Environment-friendly and does not have carbon emissions.
- Easy to maintain and reliable,
- Renewable source of energy.
- Cheaper in the long run and produces less electricity bills.

**Biogas:** A reliable source of energy used in rural households, biogas is derived from the decomposition of organic matter, animal waste, manure and vegetative matter without the presence of oxygen, thus producing combustible gas. Biogas plants use cow dung in rural areas so they are called gobar gas plants.

***Advantages of biogas***

- It is a clean, convenient, cheaper source of energy.
- There is no storage problem as there is a direct supply of gas to the plant.
- It is a renewable source of energy and is eco-friendly.
- The sludge left behind is used as an organic fertilizer for crops in rural areas.
- Organic manure is also produced.

# 49

# INDUSTRIES

Industries form the basis of the economic development of a nation. Industries are made to cater to human needs as they convert raw materials to more usable commodities. An industry can be a small cottage unit to a huge multinational unit with many factories.

***Factors supporting the growth of industries***

**Climate:** Needless to say, harsh climatic conditions can never support any industrial growth. For example, cotton textile mills have flourished in the Mumbai–Ahmedabad belt due to its humid climate. Humidity keeps the thread strong. Extreme conditions can lead to a decrease in human labour efficiency and will also discourage capital investment.

**Availability of raw materials:** Proximity to the source of raw materials cuts down transportation costs. Industries can develop around a region where there is an easy availability of raw materials. For example, iron and steel industries flourish in regions that are rich in minerals like coal, limestone, manganese, iron ore, bauxite, etc.

**Power:** The location of industries depends on an uninterrupted supply of power. For example, the location of iron and steel industries depends on regular and uninterrupted supply of coal. Similarly, many industries, such as the electrical industry, aluminium industry, ores industry and textile mills, use hydel power as their source of power.

**Labour:** Both skilled and unskilled labour is required for the location of industries. Labour-based industries benefit if there is an abundant supply of cheap labour. Most of the iron and steel plants in India are concentrated in the Chota Nagpur Plateau region, which gets an abundant supply of cheap labour from the neighbouring densely populated states of Bihar, Jharkhand, West Bengal and Odisha.

**Water:** Most industries develop in regions that are close to freshwater, which can be a major river, canal or lake. Industries, such as textiles, iron and steel, chemical, paper and pulp, require large quantities of water at the processing stage.

**Transportation:** A well-developed transport system is required both for the supply of raw materials, as well as for the distribution of finished goods to the market. A huge hinterland in Kolkata and Mumbai has been conducive for the growth of industries in these regions. Port facilities also work as an added advantage as ports are needed both for the import of raw materials, machineries and the export of finished goods.

**Market:** Proximity to markets is needed for the sale of finished goods. It is of no use if the markets are located far from the production site. It unnecessarily raises the cost of the commodity to the final customer. Heavy and perishable goods, such food items or dairy products, must be sold at nearby markets.

**Capital:** Major industries always require huge investments. That is why most industries in the world have developed in the major cities, where there is a regular flow of funds and capital.

**Banking and loan facilities:** Often, industries require a huge investment. Banking, loan and insurance facilities help any new start-ups. This provides a protective umbrella to the manufacturers, labourers and investors from any kind of unavoidable losses.

**Government policies:** In India, the policies set by the government for industrial growth in the Five-Year Plans provide the base for the economy of the nation. Government policies should aim to remove regional imbalances in industrial growth, generate employment opportunities, eliminate air, land, noise and water pollution and look for a more sustainable use of resources.

***Based on size***

- **Large-scale industry:** They use advanced technology and large capital investments. Example: iron and steel industry, aluminium industry.
- **Small-scale industry:** They require smaller capital investments and simpler machines. These industries mainly use manual labour. Example: pottery and handicrafts.

***Based on raw materials***

- **Agro-based industry:** These industries use agricultural and plant-based products as their raw materials. Example: the tea industry, sugar industry, food processing industry.
- **Mineral-based industry:** These use mineral ore as their raw material and provide raw materials to other industries. They provide machines and building materials to the other sectors. Example: iron and steel industries.
- **Forest-based industry:** They use forest products as their raw

**Classification of Industries**

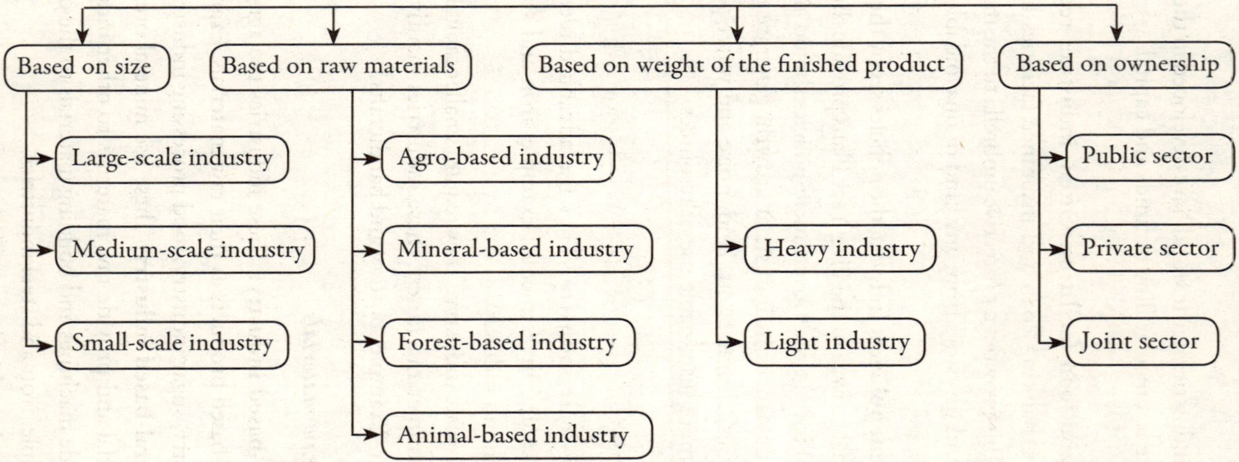

materials. Example: paper and pulp industry, timber industry, furniture industry.

- **Animal-based industry:** They use animal skin, meat and hides as their raw materials. Example: meat processing, woollen industry.

*Based on the weight of the finished product*

- **Heavy industry:** These industries use huge capital, advanced machinery, large plots of land and a lot of labour for their production and post production. Example: the shipbuilding industry, aeronautical industry.
- **Light industry:** Just the opposite of heavy industry, they use simpler machines, more manual labour and smaller capital investments. Example: the bicycle industry, food processing industry, consumer goods.

*Based on ownership*

- **Joint sector enterprise:** The ownership and management of such units are jointly done by the government and the private sector. Example: Ipitata Sponge Iron Ltd with TELCO.
- **Public sector enterprise:** The ownership and management of such units are exclusively done by the central/state government. Example: Steel Authority of India Ltd (SAIL).
- **Private sector enterprise:** The ownership and management of such units are done by individuals or groups of individuals. Example: Reliance Industries.

**Major industries**

**Iron and steel industry:** Overall industrial development depends to a large extent on the growth of the iron and steel industries of a country. This is chiefly because iron and steel provide the raw materials for numerous other industries. The location of iron and

**Important terms to remember**

**Basic industry:** Depends on other industries for the manufacturing process.
**Consumer industries**: Manufactures commodities that are directly sold to the consumers.
**Tertiary industries**: Provide public utility-based services.
**Ancillary industry**: Production of spare parts, which are used for manufacturing in large heavy industries. Example: spare parts used in automobiles.
**Consumer durables**: Commodities that are sold to the consumers and do not have to be purchased frequently and can be used for a long period of time. Example: washing machines, television sets.
**Enterprise:** An organization meant to earn profit that employs people.

steel industries is governed by several factors, such as the availability of capital, raw materials, power, water and cheap labour, proximity to a port and markets. Iron and steel industries have flourished mostly in China, South Korea, Brazil and India. The growth of the iron and steel industry in China has been phenomenal. Today, China produces 17% of crude steel and 24% of pig iron. Japan is the second leading producer of crude steel and pig iron. Although there is a dEarth of raw materials in Japan, the country mostly uses its port facilities to import raw materials. The finished products are sold in readily available markets.

India has a long history of iron and steel plants. The first steel plant (**Tata Iron and Steel Company Ltd [TISCO]**) was set up by Jamshedji Tata in 1911 in the town of Sakchi (now Jamshedpur) in then Bihar.

**Mini steel plants:** These are decentralized secondary units that use cheaply available raw materials like scrap iron and electric arc furnaces for processing. Mini steels help in eradicating regional imbalances in industrial growth. They generate employment opportunities and reduce the pressure of production from large integrated steel plants. They are easy to construct and do not require much capital investment as their gestation period is shorter. They mainly produce alloy steel and stainless steel.

**Textile industry:** The cotton textile industry is the most important among all the textile industries. The locational factors of climate, supply of raw materials, power, water and cheap labour contribute to the growth of this industry. The major cotton textile industry countries are India, China, Pakistan, Japan and Egypt. The early cotton textile mills flourished in the New England region of the USA. The early development of the industry in New England, the presence of hydel power and marine climate made this industry flourish there.

China is probably in the second spot. Like in India, China's cotton textile industry is hand spun and machine spun. The most important centre is Shanghai. It enjoys the facilities of cheap power supply, labour force, large cotton growing areas and output and a vast market. Pakistan is the fourth largest producer of cotton textiles, but it faced the wrath of Partition, when a majority of the cotton textile mills remained with India while long staple cotton-growing areas went to Pakistan.

**FACT FILE**

Mumbai is called the Cottonopolis of India and has the largest number of cotton textile mills.

Gujarat is the world's second-largest producer of cotton with Ahmedabad as the second largest city in cotton textile production. Ahmedabad is called the Manchester of India.

**Special mention**

**Silk industry:** India is the second largest producer of silk after China. Mainly four types of silk are produced in our country – mulberry, tussar, muga and eri. Raw silk is a very light material, so it can be transported very easily. China is the leading supplier of silk to the international market. Uzbekistan, Brazil, Iran and Thailand are the leaders of the silk industry in the world. The process of growing silkworms and processing them is called **sericulture**. Tamil Nadu is the leading producer of white silk in the world while Assam leads in muga silk. Several by-products are also obtained from sericulture apart from silk. Mulberry fruits are rich in vitamins and minerals, the roots, barks and leaves are used for making herbal medicines, they are used as fodder for animals, and mulberry branches are used for burning as fuel.

**FACT FILE**

Bhagalpur in Bihar, known for its Bhagalpuri silk, is known as the silk city of India.
Kanchipuram in Tamil Nadu is called the silk capital.

**Sugar industry:** The sugar industry is India's second largest organized industry. India is also the leading producer of sugar in the world now, followed by Brazil. An important cash crop, the sugar industry produces sugar, gur and khandsari by crushing sugarcane. The other by-products are molasses, bagasse and press mud. The major sugar-consuming countries are Brazil, India, China, the USA, Indonesia, Russia and EU.

The world demand for sugar depends on the availability and price of artificial sweeteners, the per capita income, population composition and concerns for health.

**FACT FILE**

Uses of the by-products:

**Molasses:** It is used for the distillation of rum and ethyl alcohol, as cattle feed, fertilizers.

**Bagasse:** It is used as fodder or as a source of fuel for sugar mills. Bagasse is used as a substitute for wood, so it is used to make printing paper, white writing paper, newsprint, tissue paper, bags and cardboard, biogas or sludge.

**Press mud:** It is used for making animal feed, fertilizers, tooth powder and board chalk.

**Handloom and khadi industry:** Khadi means when a cloth is woven using hand-spun yarn, and handloom means when a cloth is woven using machine-spun yarn. The handloom industry is one of the largest unorganized industries in India and also one of the oldest traditional industries, upholding the rich cultural heritage of our country through its usage of vibrant colours and patterns that are unique to India. It provides employment to millions of rural households. It also helps the country earn foreign exchange. The government is promoting this industry globally by organizing fairs and exhibitions across world platforms.

**Jute industry:** India is the leading producer of jute in the world market, followed by Bangladesh and China. This **golden fibre** helps India earn foreign revenue and provides employment to more than 40 lakh farmers. The jute industry in India has mainly flourished in the eastern part of the country (West Bengal, Assam, Bihar) due to several factors like hot and humid climate, which helps in producing high-quality jute, abundant supply of labour, water from the Ganga and its tributaries, a sizable market in and around Kolkata and power from the nearby coalfields of Raniganj and Jharia.

Why is jute called the **golden fibre?**

Because of its lustrous texture, it is 100% biodegradable and helps in earning foreign revenue.

**Aluminium industry:** The second largest industry after iron and steel is aluminium. Aluminium is a good conductor of electricity, so it is primarily used in making electrical equipment, aeroplanes, defence equipment, rail coaches, household utensils, etc. The chief factors influencing the location of such industries is the availability of cheap labour, power and supply of bauxite ores to obtain alumina.

**Electronics and information technology:** The newest entrant to the list, electronics and IT are spreading very fast in India. Bengaluru is known as the IT hub of India. Apart from this, Bengaluru, Hyderabad and Pune form the apex of the silicon triangle. In the world, the major IT hubs are Washington State, Washington, D.C., Atlanta (Georgia), San Francisco and Chicago. The USA is known for its Silicon Valley, which is home to the headquarters of major companies like Apple, Microsoft, Google, IBM, etc.

# 50

# TERTIARY ACTIVITIES: TRADE, TRANSPORT AND COMMUNICATION

Trade involves the exchange of goods, services, ideas and innovations. It encompasses both import and export, that is, the movement of goods and services from countries having a surplus to countries having a deficit.

***Reasons to trade***

- Trade happens when there is a difference in the production of manufactured goods since natural resources are not evenly distributed all over the world. There are many places that are not well-equipped with the basic necessities required for survival. So, all these regions have to buy those items from other countries.
- Due to differences in climatic factors like temperature, rainfall and humidity, agro-based and forest-based products differ between countries. The agro-based products of tropical countries like India will always differ from those of temperate nations like Canada. So both these countries have to trade to buy each other's items.
- The tastes and preferences of consumers also differ from one country to another, which induces trade.

- Differences in the stages of industrial development are also a factor for trade. All countries are not equally industrially developed. First-world countries like the USA and Japan are highly industrialized, countries like India are developing, and African nations are mostly least developed countries (LDCs). These differences cause trade. Goods from modern countries are bought by the less-developed or developing countries in exchange for raw materials and agro-based items.
- Trade is always controlled by transportation. Transportation means have also evolved through civilizations, so the need for trade has also evolved. Every country cannot possess the same set of skilled or semi-skilled labour forces. Every country is known for its own inherent skills of people, as well as products that represent the culture and heritage of that nation. In the same way, the level of technological development is also not the same in every country. Trade arises when there are differences in the culture, skill and expertise of people.

**Types of trade:** Trade can be either internal – when trade happens within a country or international – when trade happens across nations.

***Common items involved in international trade***

| Category | Items of trade |
|---|---|
| Food items | Grains, pulses, spices, beverages, fruits |
| Raw materials | Scrap iron, minerals, cotton, jute, tea, coffee, rubber, timber |
| Fuel | Coal, petroleum, natural gas |
| Consumer goods | Textiles, medicines, chemicals |

## World's major trading zones

**Europe:** The most industrialized and densely populated countries of Europe are found in its western part. International commercial centres at London, Paris and Rotterdam are considered to be the hub of international trade.

**North America:** Large volumes of trade take place across the USA and Canada. The developed economy, varieties of consumer durables produced and the richness of natural resources provide impetus for exports in these nations.

**World Trade Organization (WTO):** The major objectives of WTO are:

- To dissolve trade disputes
- To keep transparency in international trade agreements
- To enforce rules for international trade
- To provide a platform for international negotiations
- To cooperate and coordinate with the other organs of world trade

***Other international trade organizations***

- Asia–Pacific Economic Cooperation (APEC)
- Association of Southeast Asian Nations (ASEAN)
- Organization of the Petroleum Exporting Countries (OPEC)

## Transport and communication

**Transport:** The movement of goods and people from one place to another takes place through transportation. The transport network of a nation works like the arteries of the heart. Just like the arteries pump blood to the body, similarly, transport plays a vital role in production and consumption.

- Producers produce goods by transporting the raw materials to their production units. These raw materials are processed and made into usable consumer goods. These goods are then transported to the market centres, where they are bought by the final consumers.
- The social, cultural, political and economic development of a nation depends largely on the availability of quick and smooth transport.
- Transport has also helped in decreasing fluctuations in prices.
- The success of the Industrial Revolution in Europe paved the way for revolutionizing transport.
- Roads were developed, followed by railways. The primitive method of boats carrying people and goods was also modernized by introducing steamships, cruise liners, etc. Then came air transport, which further shortened the distance between countries.

### *Modes of transport*

There are three principal modes of transport:

**Land transport:** Both roadways and railways come under this category. A vast network of major roads as highways and expressways has been constructed throughout the world.

Roadways are more comfortable than railways for shorter distances. They provide feeders to railways as people have to get down at railway stations and use road transport to reach their destination. Roads provide door-to-door services and are good for transporting perishable goods.

When masses of people and bulky commodities need to be transported, then railways are the most convenient. They are the main movers of goods and freight. Rail transport is comfortable for old people and children.

> Inflammable objects like oil, petroleum and natural gas can be transported through pipelines across nations.

**Air transport:** Though it is the most expensive and is also weather dependant, it crosses every barrier, be it mountains or vast seas and oceans, with ease. It helps in reaching far-flung countries in the shortest time possible.

**Water transport:** It is of two types: inland waterways (rivers, canals, lakes) and oceanic waterways (seas and oceans).

Water transport is one of the oldest and cheapest means of transport. It is suitable for carrying bulk commodities and can also carry large numbers of people. However, there can be several limitations in the form of bad weather conditions, river siltation, unnavigable rivers, etc.

### *Communication*

Communication means the exchange of ideas, information, thoughts, opinions and experiences either verbally or non-verbally between two people.

Verbal communication means when we use words to communicate with each other face to face, by email or text or over the telephone.

Non-verbal communication is when we use sign language or gestures to communicate.

Radio, telephone, fax and email are different modes of communication used in our daily life.

# 51

## RESOURCES AND ITS TYPES

Resource refers to any natural substance that is used for human benefit and prosperity. Resources can be land, water, forest, soil, minerals, fish, agriculture, etc. Resources are classified into the following:

**Renewable resources:** Are those that can be renewed regularly. For example, water, forest and land are renewable. There are some renewable resources that are inexhaustible as they have unlimited supply. For example, solar energy and wind energy. Some renewable resources can become inexhaustible if they are not taken care of. For example, fish, forests, freshwater, etc.

**Non-renewable resources:** Are those that are not easy to form and take many years for their formation. Minerals such as coal and petroleum are non-renewable resources.

**Abiotic resources:** Resources that are non-living in nature. For example, land, soil, water, sunshine, minerals, etc.

**Biotic resources:** Resources that are obtained from the biosphere. For example: plants, animals, human beings, microorganisms, fish from water bodies, birds, etc.

**Energy resources:** Every human activity, as well as work by nature, depends on a constant flow of energy. Energy can be classified into conventional (coal, petroleum) and non-conventional sources of energy (solar energy, wind energy).

**Raw material resources:** These include raw materials needed for manufacturing goods. For example, iron ore, manganese and limestone are used as raw materials in the iron and steel industry.

**Actual resources:** Resources that are known to us and are being used by us at present. For example, coal.

**Potential resources:** Are those that are known to us but are not being used to the fullest potential at present due to their limited availability. For example, uranium.

**Ubiquitous resources:** These are available all over the world and are widely distributed. For example, water.

**Localized resources:** These are only concentrated in a particular area, like minerals in the Ruhr region of Germany and the Chota Nagpur Plateau region. Several natural factors govern the availability of such resources.

**Human resources:** Refers to the quality, skills and number of people who have the ability to transform goods, situations and services into anything that has more utility. Human resources are considered assets for a country's economy. Man, with the help of his expertise, skills, efficiency, labour, judgment and intellect, has the power to transform society into something conducive for human prosperity.

**Economic resources:** Resources that are used for the production of goods and services. These include land, labour, capital and entrepreneurship. Both natural and man-made resources are needed for the growth of an economy.

**Capital resources:** These include human capital, natural capital and physical capital. Human capital includes skills, intelligence and the expertise of man. Natural capital includes land, water, soil, forests, minerals, etc. Physical capital includes machines, tools and equipment needed for manufacturing.

***Resources that are assisted by technology***

1. **GIS:** A geographic information system is used to create maps. It is used to collect, store, manipulate, interpret and analyse geographical data.
2. **GPS:** A global positioning system is a satellite-based system used for navigation, to find locations and track movements on the Earth's surface.
3. **Remote sensing:** This is used to collect data on the Earth's surface and to study land use patterns, create maps and images and study environmental issues.

***Conservation of resources***

Safeguarding our precious resources should be a top priority for us. All natural resources, such as land, soil, water, air, minerals, wildlife and forests, should be conserved so that the needs of future generations are not jeopardized. This is called **sustainable development.**

Conservation of resources happens in two ways: ex-situ and in-situ conservation.

**In-situ conservation:** This is where the resources are taken care of and conserved in their place of origin. For example, the conservation of species, habitat and ecology.

**Ex-situ conservation:** This is where conservation takes place out of their natural habitats.

Conservation of resources in which there should be a judicious use of the resources to avoid any form of wastage can be done in the following ways:

- Preservation and maintenance of biological hotspots
- Maintaining and creating buffer zones between man-made and natural land use
- Conservation and protection of threatened species of plant and animal life
- The three Rs: Reduce, Reuse and Recycle.

1. **Reducing:** Here, reducing means reducing the amount of wastage or judicious use of resources. For example, we should only buy things that are enough for us to live. Reducing our needs would also mean reducing the amount of garbage, thereby reducing wastage. We should reduce our uses of polythene, plastics, disposables, etc., which are harmful to the environment.
2. **Reusing:** This is when we reuse something for its original purpose or for some other purposes without dismantling its originality. For example, when we read our daily newspaper, and after reading, instead of disposing of it, we use that paper to wrap small furniture, crockery items or any household items. Similarly, when we donate our old books and clothes to underprivileged children, it is an example of reuse.
3. **Recycling:** When we change the form of an already used commodity to make something new and fresh that might enhance its utility, it is called recycling. For example, we recycle our plastic bottles, soda cans, make paper bags out of newspapers, make gardening pots from old containers, etc.

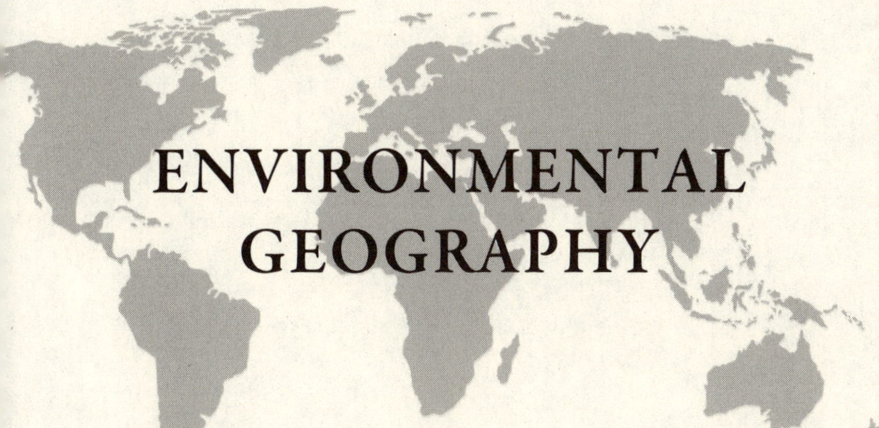

# ENVIRONMENTAL GEOGRAPHY

# 52

## MAJOR ENVIRONMENTAL ISSUES OF THE WORLD

**Global warming:** The gradual rise in the temperature of the Earth is called global warming. Global warming is related to the **greenhouse effect**. A greenhouse is a special glass house used in temperate regions where plants are kept. The glass traps the incoming solar rays and does not allow them to radiate back. This keeps the room warm and suitable for plant growth. Similarly, the increased concentration of several gases, such as carbon dioxide, methane, carbon monoxide, chlorofluorocarbons, water vapor and nitrous oxide, allows solar rays to penetrate but does not allow outgoing terrestrial radiation. This results in a rise in global temperature. The rise of greenhouse gases is due to the burning of fossil fuels, deforestation, mining, burning of biomass, etc. It is estimated that if greenhouse gases continue to rise in this way, then the global temperature will rise by about 1.5°C to 4.5°C in the next 50 years, which will pose a serious threat to life.

***Major greenhouse gases and their sources***

| Greenhouse gases | Sources of the gases |
| --- | --- |
| Carbon dioxide | Fossil fuel burning, deforestation, land use changes, release by plants and animals during respiration |
| Methane | Garbage dumps, freshwater swamps, biomass burning, flooded paddy fields, enteric fermentation in cattle |
| Chlorofluorocarbons | Non-toxic stable compounds used in making refrigerators, aerosol propellants in spray cans, insulators, fire extinguishers, air conditioners, production of plastic foams |
| Nitrous oxides | Biomass burning, agriculture (use of nitrous fertilizers), nylon production, livestock waste, contaminated groundwater |

***Consequences of global warming***

- **Rise in sea levels:** Global warming causes a rise in sea levels due to the melting of polar ice caps and glaciers. The melting of ice caps leads to global changes in water circulation. This is because the melted ice causes influx of freshwater in seas and oceans. The freshwater, which is less saline and less dense, forms a layer on the surface, thus preventing the pattern of deep ocean currents from rising to the surface.
- **Rise in surface temperature of the oceans:** This causes coral bleaching and changes the pattern of rainfall distribution.
- **Change in weather patterns:** Global warming causes extremities in climate – either desertification or severe floods. It causes stronger and more frequent storms. Warmer weather causes a higher rate of evaporation of water, leading to cloudbursts or severe rainfall. There will be areas experiencing incidences of drought due to rainfall failure.

- **Effects on animals and humans:** Warmer winters lead to death among animals who are adaptable to cold weather. The human health complications cannot be avoided. Agriculture will be affected as, with a rise in temperature, many places that were previously used for growing a particular type of crop will experience crop failure.

**Ozone ( $O_3$) depletion:** Ozone is an inorganic compound consisting of three atoms of oxygen, instead of two. The stratospheric ozone is useful for us as it prevents the harmful ultraviolet rays of the sun from reaching us. However, the excessive use of CFCs and HFC (hydrochlorofluorocarbons) act as ozone-depleting substances. They release chlorine and bromine into the atmosphere, which removes an oxygen atom from the ozone molecule with the help of sunlight. The $O_3$ depletion leads to exposure to UV rays, skin cancer, eye cataracts, crop failure and the spread of tropical diseases.

**Urban heat island:** This is a metropolitan area that is comparatively warmer than its surrounding rural areas due to human activities. This difference in temperature is felt more at night than in the day and when the wind is weak. Urban areas are considered concrete jungles. They promote surface run-off, cutting down of trees for the construction of bridges and buildings generating heat. Furthermore, increased concentration of pollutants in the lower layers of the atmosphere causes lesser outgoing terrestrial radiation.

***Consequences of urban heat islands***

- The air quality deteriorates by increasing the concentration of pollutants like carbon monoxide and ozone.
- Length of growing seasons is increased and cloud bursts or severe storms can occur.
- Excessive humidity in the air leads to human discomfort and extended summers.

**Pollution:** Certain substances, when added to air, water and soil, are responsible for causing harmful or undesirable effects and are called pollutants. These pollutants tend to cause damage to human or animal life and can pose a serious threat to the comfortable enjoyment of life, health and society. Pollutants can either be from natural or man-made sources. Let's know more about the sources and levels of **air pollution**.

| Sources of air pollutants | Examples |
|---|---|
| Natural | Volcanic eruptions, natural forest fires, dust storms |
| Man-made | Factory smoke, burning of fossil fuels, combustion, transport |
| Point sources | Volcanic eruptions, forest fires, industrial activity, power plants, chemical units, oil refineries, incineration plants, etc. |
| Non-point sources | Hospitals, residential areas, disposal of wastes, agricultural operations, transport sector, emission of smoke |

| Local level | Regional level | National level | Global level |
|---|---|---|---|
| Waste disposal, sewage, burning of wood, coal | Large-scale industries, transport, emission of smoke | Acid rain | Global warming, ozone depletion, radioactive pollution |

**Sources of water pollution**

| Sources of water pollutants | Examples |
|---|---|
| Natural | Run-off, volcanic activities, earthquakes, landslides, mudslides |
| Man-made | Domestic and medical sewage, industrial effluents, municipal waste, radioactive waste, mining waste |

**Natural disasters of the world**

Earthquakes, hurricanes, floods and typhoons are always considered to be major natural disasters that cause havoc to mankind. Let us look at a list of major natural disasters of the world in 2023 below:

| Natural disaster | Country/ countries affected | Date/time | Casualties/ number of people affected |
|---|---|---|---|
| Twin earthquakes of 7.8 and 7.5 magnitude | Southern Turkey, near the Syrian border | 6 February 2023 | 14 million people affected and about 58,000 people reportedly died |
| earthquake of 6.8 magnitude | Western Morocco | 8 September 2023 | 2,900 people reportedly died |
| Typhoon Doksuri | North-east China | 29 July 2023 | Flooding in at least 16 cities |
| Drought | Horn of Africa (Ethiopia, Kenya, Somalia) | Still ongoing | More than 43,000 people have died. The numbers are still on the rise. |

| Heavy floods | Himachal Pradesh, Uttarakhand (India) | August 2023 | 25 deaths recorded |
|---|---|---|---|

**International treaties to combat environmental issues**

**Montreal Protocol:** The aim of the protocol was the reduction in the production and consumption of ozone-depleting substances (ODS). This landmark agreement was signed in 1987. ODS are substances that are commonly used in manufacturing air conditioners, refrigerators, fire extinguishers, aerosols, etc.

**Kyoto Protocol:** An international agreement linked to the United Nations Framework Convention on climate change, which commits to setting internationally binding emission reduction targets. Since developed nations are recognized to be principally responsible for the high levels of greenhouse gas emissions in the atmosphere because of their old industrial activities, the protocol lays emphasis on developed nations under their principle of **'common but differentiated responsibilities'**. The protocol was adopted in Kyoto, Japan on 11 December 1997 and has been in operation since 2005.

**The Paris Agreement:** The Paris Agreement along with the 2030 Agenda for Sustainable Development and the Sendai Framework for Disaster Risk Reduction provides the foundation for sustainable, low-carbon emission under the broader umbrella of climate change. It is important to note that climate change is the single biggest threat to sustainable development and is affecting the poorest sections of society, who are the most vulnerable. The primary goal of the Paris Agreement is to keep the average global temperature rise below 2° Celsius and as close as possible to 1.5° Celsius. This can be achieved by bringing all the countries together to a single common cause, which is to reduce or cut down greenhouse gas emissions and build resilience and adapt to the impact of climate change by providing necessary support to developing nations.

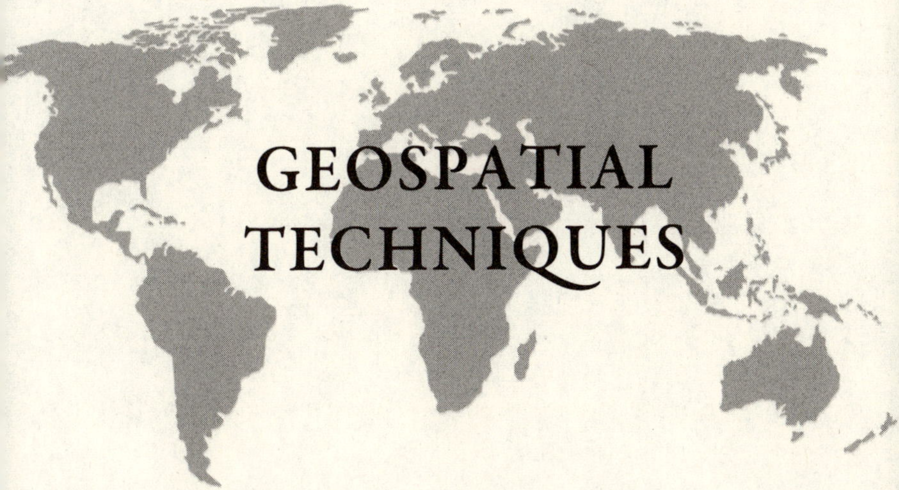

# GEOSPATIAL TECHNIQUES

# 53

# GEOGRAPHICAL TECHNIQUES AND METHODS OF MAPPING

A **map** is the most important tool of a geographer. The person who makes maps is called a cartographer, and the art of map making is called cartography.

**FACT FILE**

Some important terms to remember:

- **Contours:** imaginary lines joining places having equal elevation above sea level
- **Isogones:** imaginary lines joining places having equal compass declination
- **Isoseismal:** imaginary lines joining places having equal seismic strength
- **Isochrones:** imaginary lines joining places having equal time
- **Isobaths:** imaginary lines joining places having equal depth at the seabed
- **Isohels:** imaginary lines joining places having an equal duration of sunlight
- **Isonephs:** imaginary lines joining places having equal cloudiness
- **Isopleths:** imaginary lines of equal value of any particular phenomena

The modern world has replaced the application of traditional map making with the use of digital images, remote sensing and the global positioning system (GPS). Despite that, we must have an idea of what traditional maps are since they are the stepping stones of learning for every geographer. Maps are two-dimensional models of the Earth. Not only locations but maps also give us a vivid idea about natural, man-made and sociocultural features of a place.

**Types of Maps**

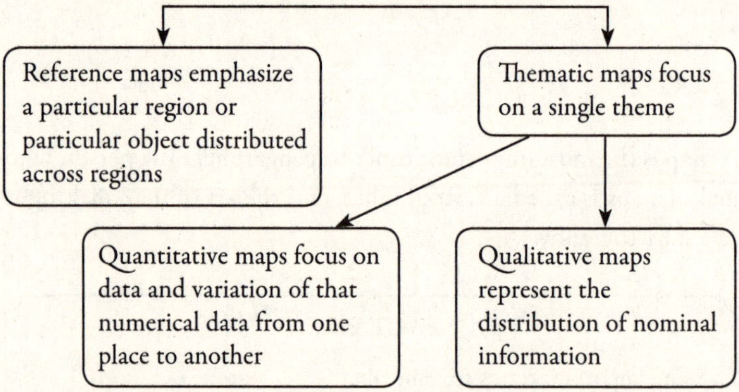


***Techniques and methods of map making***

**Isopleth maps:** As we know, isopleths lines show equal value of any particular phenomena, so isopleth maps show clear-cut regions on the basis of any particular phenomena or objects.

**Choropleth maps:** Here, distribution is shown using various colours or shades of the same colour. The density of the shading varies with the density of the distribution. This technique is called the choropleth method. It is different from isopleth maps as here, the area is given importance and not the distribution.

**Dot maps:** Absolute numbers on a map are shown by dot maps. The total population of a region can be shown by a dot map, where the value of each dot will represent a particular number of people based on a given scale. (For example, one dot represents 1,000 people). The scale is decided keeping in mind the smallest and highest figures in the data and the size of the map. The size of the dot would also depend on the size of the map and the number of dots to be placed in a particular space.

**Isarithmic maps:** These are used to depict three-dimensional values, such as elevation, on topographical maps. These maps use contour lines to depict continuous values, such as rainfall, snowfall, etc.

**Chorochromatic maps:** These are qualitative area maps, used to display nominal data with various colours or patterns. Colours are mapped according to the data. For example, soil maps and biome maps.

**Dasymetric maps:** These are refined versions of choropleth maps, where the administrative areas are divided into smaller spatial units in which demographic data (for example, population density) is shown by averaging the population to calculate a rate.

**Flow maps:** They are used to depict the flow or movement of any phenomena or objects, such as the migration of people, trading of products, etc. The direction of flow is depicted by using arrows from the point of origin to the point of destination. The flow can be unidirectional or multidirectional.

***What is remote sensing, and what are its applications?***

When we collect information without any physical contact with an object or phenomenon, it is called remote sensing. Remote sensing observations are made using satellites or aircraft. Aerial photography is the most common form of remote sensing. It is used for topographical studies, engineering and environmental studies.

*Applications*

1. **Soils:** to map soils and their distribution, classify soils, to study soil conservation and soil moisture
2. **Geology:** mapping of rock structure, rock types, igneous intrusions and bedrock, mapping of recent volcanic deposits
3. **Water resources:** measurement of water depth, distribution of watershed, mapping of floods and flood plains, riverbanks and coastal erosion
4. **Agriculture and natural vegetation:** study and monitor the extent, distribution of different vegetation types, the cropping patterns, assessing forest fire damages, drought and other hazards

**Digital imaging: the use of GPS**

The global positioning system is a satellite-based navigation system that provides detailed information on all weather conditions across the world in 3D format. GPS consists of satellites that are powered by solar cells, ground control stations and receivers that transmit and receive radio signals.

*Applications*

GPS is used for defence, navigation, astronomy, disaster relief, weather forecasting, etc.

**GIS database:** The geographical information system (GIS) is a technology that is used to collect and use geographical data.

**Components of GIS**

The various elements of GIS are:

- **Hardware:** It is the component on which the GIS works.
- **Software:** It is the software that provides the functions and tools needed to store, record, analyse and interpret geographic information. These software are either developed on open-source domains that are available for free or through commercial software.
- **Data:** It is the most important component. The geographic data can be collected in-house through surveying or from a commercial data provider. The spatial data can be in the form of satellite imagery or aerial photography. These databases are then georeferenced. However, most GIS data are available in built database management systems.
- **Users:** They manage the system and develop plans to apply it. The GIS software often has a user-friendly interface that helps non-technical users to have easy access without knowing the detailed software commands.

**GIS database**

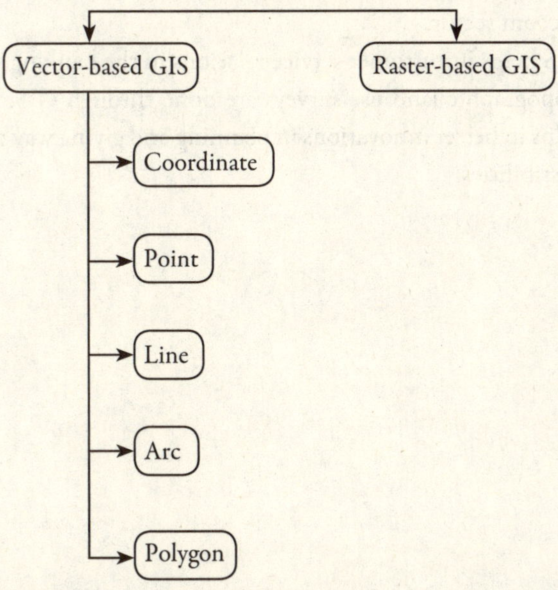

Vector is the data structure for spatial data. It comprises lines or arcs that meet at nodes defined by the beginning and end points. Raster is the method used for storing and processing the display of spatial data. The area is divided into rows and columns that form a matrix. Each matrix contains location coordinates and attributes values. The process of converting vector data, that is, a series of points, arcs or polygons, into raster data is comparatively easier than converting raster data into vector data.

***Applications of GIS:***

- GIS helps in mapping and helps people commute and communicate. For example, through Google and GPS.
- It can be used to monitor road safety measures, identify accident locations and minimize accident hazards.
- It helps in analysing, locating and monitoring urban growth.
- GIS is needed for the conservation of natural resources and protection of the environment.
- Better customer relations can be enhanced by using GIS in the telecom sector.
- GIS helps in customer service relations in the banking sector.
- Topographic land use surveys are done through GIS, which helps in better innovations in planning and giving way to new possibilities.

ACKNOWLEDGEMENTS

I would like to express my heartfelt gratitude to all those who have contributed to the completion of this book.

First and foremost, I extend my deepest thanks to my family for their unwavering support, encouragement and patience throughout this journey. Your belief in me has been my greatest source of motivation.

I also owe a debt of gratitude to my seniors, teachers and colleagues, whose insightful feedback and constructive inputs have greatly enriched the content of this book.

Lastly, to my dear ones and well-wishers, thank you for your constant encouragement and belief in my abilities.

With gratitude,

Paromita Roy
March 2025

# ACKNOWLEDGEMENTS

# IMAGE COPYRIGHT INFORMATION

Page 12: Latitudinal zones of the Earth: Inkoly/Shutterstock.com
Page 16 (top): Summer solstice: Peter Hermes Furian/Shutterstock.com
Page 16 (bottom): Winter solstice: Peter Hermes Furian/Shutterstock.com
Page 21: Structure of the Earth: Kolonko/Shutterstock.com
Page 23: Types of seismic waves: VectorMine/Shutterstock.com
Page 30: Rock cycle: Drp8/Shutterstock.com
Page 37: Plate boundaries: GraphicsRF.com/Shutterstock.com
Page 49: Weathered rock: Darren J. Bradley/Shutterstock.com
Page 57: Davisian cycle of erosion: Public domain
Page 69: Types of mountains: GraphicsRF.com/Shutterstock.com
Page 83: Meandering stream: VectorMine/Shutterstock.com
Page 96: Sand dunes: Chris Bucanac/Shutterstock.com
Page 105: Moraine: zombiu26/Shutterstock.com
Page 119: Volcanic eruption: VectorMine/Shutterstock.com
Page 125: Plutonic bodies: VectorMine/Shutterstock.com
Page 129: Earthquake magnitude scale: VectorMine/Shutterstock.com
Page 156: Pressure belts: Pooja Sitharthan/Shutterstock.com
Page 169: Water cycle: brgfx/Shutterstock.com

Page 173: Types of clouds: Fluke Cha/Shutterstock.com
Page 182: Cyclone and anticyclone: Designua/Shutterstock.com
Page 194: Oceanic landforms: stihii/Shutterstock.com
Page 214: Ocean currents: BlueRingMedia/Shutterstock.com
Page 233: Biogeochemical cycles: VectorMine/Shutterstock.com
Page 237 (top): Food chain: brgfx/Shutterstock.com
Page 237 (bottom): Food web: BlueRingMedia/Shutterstock.com
Page 252: Distribution of life on land: VectorMine/Shutterstock.com
Page 271: Age sex pyramids: W.Y. Sunshine/Shutterstock.com
Headers on chapter openers: LizHari/vectorstock.com
Section dividers (world map): Freepik.com. These pages have been designed using assets from freepik.com.
End page image: Vectorfair/Shutterstock.com

# NOTES